NATIONAL
GEOGRAPHIC
TRAVELER
NORWAY

TRAVELER

NORWAY

Valerio Griffa

National Geographic
Washington, D.C.

CONTENTS

pp. 2–3: The Lofoten Islands extend beyond the Arctic Circle.
Left: A wooden walkway along the coast of the island of Senja

TRAVELING WITH EYES OPEN

Alert travelers go with a purpose and leave with a benefit. If you travel responsibly, you can help support wildlife conservation, historic preservation, and cultural enrichment in the places you visit. You can enrich your own travel experience as well.

To be a geo-savvy traveler:

- Recognize that your presence has an impact on the places you visit.
- Spend your time and money in ways that sustain local character. (Besides, it's more interesting that way.)
- Value the destination's natural and cultural heritage.
- Respect the local customs and traditions.
- Express appreciation to local people about things you find interesting and unique to the place: its nature and scenery, music and food, historic villages and buildings.
- Vote with your wallet: Support the people who support the place, patronizing businesses that make an effort to celebrate and protect what's special there. Seek out shops, local restaurants, inns, and tour operators who love their home–who love taking care of it and showing it off. Avoid businesses that detract from the character of the place.
- Enrich yourself, taking home memories and stories to tell, knowing that you have contributed to the preservation and enhancement of the destination.

That is the type of travel now called geotourism, defined as "tourism that sustains or enhances the geographical character of a place–its environment, culture, aesthetics, heritage, and the well-being of its residents."

ABOUT THE AUTHOR

Journalist and photographer **Valerio Griffa** has worked as a correspondent for many Italian newspapers, edited three webzines, and participated in several collective photo exhibitions. In addition to his experiences as a reporter and photographer, he has interviewed numerous cultural figures including Ole Henrick Magga, a linguist and the first Sami president of the Norwegian Parliament. He has traveled to Norway some 50 times, from Oslo to the Arctic, and is the author of numerous books and guidebooks.

CHARTING YOUR TRIP

Norway offers a multitude of exhilarating experiences, having such a diverse range of environments, situations, and cultures within its 1,056-mile-long (1,700 km) territory that stretches from Oslo to the North Cape, squeezed between Sweden and the Atlantic coast with its fjords.

Land of Fjords & Mountains

Norway is not just fjords and the North Cape. The landscape ranges from the southern coast overlooking the Skagerrak Strait and Denmark to the great Oslofjord, from central-southern regions like Telemark or the great plateau of Hardangervidda to the North, with its magnificent patchwork of mountains, jagged coastlines, and endless fjords, from Bergen to Trondheim and Tromsø. The fjords and coast offer very diverse views. Orogenesis and glaciation have left behind different types of mountains and islands. Then there is the northern mainland and archipelago. The mainland, from Tromsø to Kirkenes, is a vast plateau that borders Finland and Russia, with bays and fjords, jagged coastline on the Arctic Sea, conifers, birches, and tundra. The northernmost islands, on the other hand, are a gateway to the North Pole, a final mountainous land before the great ice. And this is just Norway's geography and nature, which harbor two fascinating, beautiful phenomena: the midnight sun and the northern lights.

When planning a trip, two other things should be taken into consideration: experiences and people. This is where the true wealth of a country can be found. A boat or a kayak trip in a quiet fjord is a sure cure for today's anxieties. Anywhere you go in Norway, nature will offer relief for the soul. There are many outdoor activities to be enjoyed here: rock climbing, trekking in national parks, trips by cable car, bike rides along southern beaches or on the islands north of Trondheim, hopping from one island to another by ferry. Geology has created unique conditions in the land, and humans have figured out the best and most thorough way to use them.

NOT TO BE MISSED:

Rådhusbrygge marina in Oslo 72

North Sea Road, Nordsjøvegen 123

Urnes Stavkirke 160

The Jugendstil city of Ålesund 178–181

Vega Archipelago 214

The northern lights in Lofoten and Vesterålen 229–249

Sami Region 281–285

Over the centuries, Norwegians have worked to make their country's beauty enjoyable, and it won't leave you indifferent. Try and take the train down to Flåm, along the magnificent Sognefjord. Watch the musk oxen of Dovrefjell, wild reindeer in Hardangervidda, or salmon swimming upstream in a rushing river. Witness the terrifying force of the maelstrom whirlpools or a peak or glacier above a fjord. You are undoubtedly bound to be impressed.

Norwegian National Tourism Board

Visit Norway is the name of the Norwegian National Tourism Board. It has a website and app *(visitnorway.com)*.

There are also many cultural things to see. Three historic periods are worth exploring. The country's splendid past is seen in the Viking ships in Oslo and in the *stavkirke,* iconic wooden churches in the central region. More recent history is represented by the white wooden houses on the southern coast and in the Jugendstil buildings of Ålesund. Finally, the bright contemporary is especially present in Oslo—but not only there. Many cities and towns have invested recent wealth in architecture, dramatically improving the quality of life for their citizens.

Kayaking in the waters of a fjord

But design and architecture also know how to positively interact with nature, as evidenced by the magnificent Tverrfjellhytta—better known as Snøhetta viewpoint—in Dovrefjell National Park.

And we mustn't forget the museums, which have been transformed to become places of dialogue rather than exclusion, promoting a different awareness of heritage and how to preserve and display it. Then there's the food, a diverse cuisine that is the product of global influences and yet strongly rooted in Nordic tradition.

Lastly, one of the features that differs most from one area of Norway to another is the people. Norwegians are generally tied to where they come from and very proud of their various dialects that have equal linguistic and communicative dignity. There are different habits, sensibilities, and ways of doing things depending on where you are geographically. Living on the southern coast, which serves as a sort of riviera in the summer, is not like living on a fjord in a small town in the deep North, or in a big city like Oslo or Stavanger. Then there are the Sami, descendants of Finns and Russians, and recent immigrants. Norwegian people offer a range of encounters that are sure to be enriching, if approached openly.

How to Get Around

When planning your trip, don't just consider planes and rental cars. It is a little more difficult to organize and perhaps more physically strenuous, but a trip that takes advantage of the many other means of transportation available in Norway is definitely more satisfying. The two most highly recommended are the train and the mail ship. The former covers the south-central region, the latter the North. These are comfortable travel options that allow you to focus on the landscape. You can find more details in the Travelwise section.

If you are visiting Norway from May to September, another suitable means of travel is bicycle, especially an electric one. It is the best way to navigate Norway's jagged terrain, ideal on dirt roads, trails, and the various types of paths you will encounter. They can even be carried on trains, ferries, and boats, giving you the chance to enjoy a truly immersive journey experience.

Norwegian Currency

The currency in Norway is the Norwegian *krone* (plural *kroner*), divided into 100 *øre*. Its international code is NOK, and the current exchange rate is 1 krone to $0.095 USD. Unfortunately, you likely won't even see the orange 10-NOK notes with their beautiful Viking ship or the 10-øre coin, since electronic payment is prevalent. Visa and Mastercard are accepted everywhere, as are all payments with smartphones, PayPal, Apple Pay, and Google Pay.

Driving in Norway

You need a valid driver's license to drive in Norway. There are limits on speed, alcohol, and some medications. You must have insurance, and a yellow vest and red triangle must always be in the trunk. Severe penalties are enforced for driving while holding a phone or beverage. In addition, there are greater limits on speed. You must be at least 18 years old to drive, keep your seatbelt on at all times, including passengers, and fit winter tires at times of the year that require them. In addition, because of the high concentration of wildlife, special attention must be paid while driving through rural areas. To rent a car, some agencies require a minimum age of 21. In any case, drivers under the age of 25 are charged a higher daily rate.

Planning a Trip

A good starting point is looking at the magnificent pictures on the Norwegian National Tourism Board website *(visitnorway.com)*, to better understand what you want to do in this multifaceted land.

The most important thing is to not give in to performance anxiety. Like anywhere in the world, Norway should be enjoyed a little at a time. So choose a region and a couple of activities, and focus on those. If, on the other hand, you want to get a more general look first and then decide what is best for you, think of something doable based on the time you have. For example, with two weeks, you can consider a couple of days in Oslo, the Oslo-Bergen trip by train, a couple of days in Bergen, a couple on a fjord, two days in Lofoten, one in Tromsø, and a couple to get to the North Cape. You do not need to see everything, but you need enough time to see what you have selected.

The train connecting Oslo and Bergen

HISTORY & CULTURE

Houses on the seafront in Bergen

NORWAY TODAY

What does Norway of the 21st century look like? We could list a series of adjectives, summarizing the country's journey over the past 30 or 40 years: rich, independent, secure, deeply transformed, open, forward-thinking, perhaps a little afraid of losing the privilege it has. Are there only positives? Of course not. But the positives seem to largely outweigh the negatives.

Norway has benefited from a number of circumstantial factors, three of which are particularly significant. The first and most fundamental was having discovered and exploited North Sea oil and gas, which, like an unexpected inheritance, has further stimulated welfare expansion, social harmony, the arrival of foreign investment, and business development. The second factor, which also brought in profit, was not joining the European Union, but rather signing agreements with member states in a favorable position and activating an economic zone with the other Scandinavian countries. The third factor was knowing how to manage the first two and not squandering what was gained, building a new, more modern society, and moving away from the closed and proud, even somewhat resentful, Norway of the long post-war period.

Oil platform off the southern coast of Norway

A Norwegian salmon farm

Did you know that the Norwegian Sovereign Wealth Fund is the largest in the world? It surpasses that of Saudi Arabia and the United Arab Emirates, and offers a freedom of investment that a country with a base population of 5.5 million otherwise could not have.

This gives you a general picture. If you are visiting today, you might be surprised to find any stereotypical ideas you had of Scandinavia debunked by facts. Norwegian cities have absorbed influences from Western metropolises and from the southern European way of life, but they have managed to retain their character, which makes them livable places with excellent services, full of attention to nature and the environment, and a sense of respect for things. The two most obvious results of this attitude are the almost entirely digital payment system and electric cars, as well as an excellent rail system. Those who visited Oslo before the 2000s would find now a completely different city. One of the most changed places is the waterfront: harsh, contained, and somewhat boring before; bold, excessive, and interesting today.

And what about the negatives? Well, on the one hand, there's the contradiction of a country that funds green projects with fossil fuels; on the other, there's the eagerness of salmon farmers who seek to profit around the world. According to some, farmed fish can cause pollution, and the species *Salmo salar* is more accustomed to the freedom of swimming upstream, rather than being forced to live in a habitat where it doesn't belong.

Government & Administration

The majority of Norwegian citizens are happy with their country's political and administrative system and are convinced that the monarchy still has a purpose. This isn't surprising, considering the GDP per capita in 2023 was $100,000.

The constitution of 1814, one of the oldest in the world, unusually bestowed on a country that was not independent at the time, is still the foundation for the system of government, although it has been amended several times. Within the constitutional monarchy, parliament–the Storting or Stortinget–has legislative power, the crown and government have executive power, and the Supreme Court of Norway has judicial power. Executive power might fall to parliament, but the supreme court can reject parliamentary decisions if considered unconstitutional.

The unicameral parliament, which has 169 members, is elected for a four-year term and cannot be dissolved. Laws must be countersigned by the king to become executive, although this is only a formal intervention. General elections—for the national parliament and the 39-member Sami parliament—and administrative elections—for *fylke* (region) and *kommune* (municipality) councils—are held every four years alternatingly.

All citizens of at least 18 years, registered as residents, have the right to vote; men were granted this right in 1898 and women in 1913. The major political parties in parliament are the Labor Party, winner of the last election (2021) along with the center-left coalition, and the Conservative Party (*Høyre*). Then there is the Socialist Left Party and, on the right, the Progress Party. In the center are also the Christian Democratic Party, the Center Party, and the Liberal Party. The government includes the prime minister and several ministers, chosen from parliament or outside; in the former case they cease to be parliamentarians. The current king is Harald V, who ascended the throne in 1991.

National Day of Norway is May 17.

Administratively, Norway is divided into 11 fylkes, or regions, including the capital. An elected municipal council and a governor appointed by the executive regulate matters within each county. An ombudsman is instated to protect citizens' interests in certain matters. Trade unions and businessmen have established industry organizations to settle disputes and set costs and prices of services and goods.

Society

In Norway, it is difficult to find an industry or a profession—or a social, humanitarian, religious, cultural, sporting, or leisure activity—that does not have its voluntary organization or association.

The seat of parliament in Oslo

In this nation, interests and ideals take shape only through collective participation, always supported by a network of associations that fosters a shared sense of belonging, although social change has loosened these ties. This tradition goes back a century and a half to when idealist organizations took hold, starting with organizations in support of a national language, anti-alcoholic organizations, public high school organizations, and women's social organizations. Then came the labor, professional, and industrial associations. The foundations were laid, and alongside the democratization process, organizations grew, both in number and political clout. Social associations accompanied the process of welfare state building, intervening directly or influencing government choices. Special interest associations then built a dense network of economic relationships and counterbalanced powers. In general, associations participated in the preparation of laws and influenced legislative activity at various levels.

And they naturally have relationships with political parties. Norway has thus acquired a social model that is integrated with its power structure, in which political power is filtered through systems of consultation with these interest groups that are not only economic, but also social and idealist. The cooperation and influence of these organizations are recognized and accepted.

From a social perspective, the Norwegian model is well tested. There is a good welfare system, and the healthcare system is based on prevention, particularly for children in their early years, which allows for early diagnosis and intervention. Norway is third in the world in terms of per capita healthcare spending. Through general taxation, 85 percent of the cost of individual services is provided for each citizen, with the remaining 15 percent covered by co-payments, excluding hospitalization and exemptions.

Education is a complex and multifaceted system. The ten years of compulsory schooling, ages 6–16, include *barneskole* from 6–13 and *ungdomsskole* from 13–16. High school, or *videregående skole,* goes from 16–19. The latter, which is not compulsory, offers two possible paths: a specific vocational education and a generic one. At the end, an exam verifies the level reached and issues a certificate called *vitnemål.* English is studied from an early age. A bachelor's degree lasts three years, with an added two years for a master's degree. The schools are public and free, but there are also private institutions.

There are a total of 29 universities in Norway. Some of the highest ranked are Universitetet i Oslo, Trondheim University of Science and

The University of Oslo is the oldest in Norway.

Technology (NTNU), Universitetet i Bergen, and UiT Norges arktiske universitet, and Tromsø Arctic University.

More than 2 percent of the GDP is allocated to research and development. There are many projects that focus on the Arctic as their investigative area, particularly those involving meteorology, oceanography, marine biology, and the northern lights. Tromsø also hosts Eiscat, a European ionospheric radar station, whereas Antarctica is home to Troll, a permanent Norwegian research station.

Military service is mandatory for men and women from the age of 19. Basic training lasts 12 months, with subsequent periodic recalls or service for an additional seven months to be completed by age 44.

Norway cooperates as part of the UN and is a member of NATO. After World War II, this traditionally neutral country would have liked to have played a mediating role between major powers, but it was burned by the Nazi invasion, and events of those years convinced it to join the Atlantic Alliance in 1949. However, it did not agree to host foreign military bases within its borders or install nuclear warheads in peacetime. By the 1970s, everything was in place to welcome Norway into the European Community. A divisive internal debate and a referendum in September 1972 prevented its entry with 53.5 percent negative responses. This was confirmed by a second referendum in November 1994. However, the country is part of the European Economic Area.

Media

Norwegians like their media. Although they are mostly privately owned and supported by the state, national media outlets typically self-regulate. Freedom of expression, after all, is protected by the constitution of 1814. NRK is the national radio-TV station; it has four digital TV channels and many radio stations, both FM and digital. Then there are the commercial TV2 and TV3, and TVNorge-Discovery. Commercial, local, association, and web-based radio stations have also been established.

More than 60 percent of the population uses social media. Newspapers and magazines, both print and digital, are mostly regional, with local themes and distribution. Those with national circulation include *Aftenposten,* the most widely circulated, followed by the tabloid *Dagbladet; Dagens Næringsliv,* focused on business; *Dagsavisen,* a social-democratic outlet; and then the smaller ones, such as *Nationen,* agricultural; *Dagen,* conservative; *Klassekampen,* socialist; *VG (Verdens Gang),* a tabloid; and *Morgenbladet,* a weekly.

Norsk Presseforbund (NP), the Norwegian Press Association, groups together the union of journalists, the publishers association, and the media business association, and oversees the press code of ethics.

Taxes & Banks

Norwegian citizens pay indirect taxes, with a standard 25 percent VAT and 12 percent minimum, and direct taxes, concerning income, annuities, earnings, and interest, at a rate of 22 percent. Then there are local taxes and national healthcare contributions. In 2022, the income tax rate was 39.5 percent.

The country's major banks are DNB ASA, which is 34 percent state-owned, and then Nordea, Danske Bank, and the commercial Handelsbanken. The Oslo Børs, or Oslo Stock Exchange, was founded in 1818 and opened to business the following year. It also trades securities of international companies, mainly in the oil and shipping sectors. As of 2019, it is part of the Euronext group, Europe's largest financial market.

The Norwegian currency is called krone, plural kroner. It is represented by the NOK code, and its value compared to other currencies varies based on the international price of oil. ■

A Norwegian krone

Economy

We only need to look at one factor to understand the basis of Norway's economy and how it works: as of today, the sector with the largest number of businesses is undoubtedly the service industry, followed far behind by finance, insurance, and real estate, which draws a fairly accurate picture of what the population lives on.

Of course, Norway has a highly developed mixed economy, with state-owned properties in areas considered strategic. For example, the state has bought shares in companies operating in oil, hydropower, banking, and telecommunications. This has resulted in control of about 35 percent of the value of listed companies, even though the market is liberalized. We should also remember that Norway has a high standard of living, even when compared to the rest of Europe, and an enviable welfare system. At the same time, it is clear that all this development and welfare is supported largely by oil and natural gas extraction.

HISTORY OF NORWAY

The Vikings forged the first semblance of Norway, going so far as to unify it and expand territories to the west, from the Scottish islands to Iceland and Greenland. Then foreign rule began, formally Danish but German in trade with the Hanseatic League, and then British and Dutch. In the 19th century came unification with Sweden, followed by independence in 1905 and rather unorthodox development.

For thousands of years, ice covered Scandinavia. After the last ice age, the ice began to recede, freeing Fenno-Scandia. The oldest human traces found in Norway are those of the Komsa culture in Alta and the Fosna culture in Møre, dating from 9000–8000 B.C.: tools and food remains of hunters who most likely came from central Europe. Toward the end of the stone age, people lived in the fjords and along the coast, fishing and hunting. From 3000 B.C. onward, they made great progress by abandoning nomadism to cultivate grains and raise livestock. Artistic and historical evidence of this period include drawings, probably engraved for magical rites. In the bronze age, 2300–700 B.C., tools and weapons were perfected with bronze, which, however, had to be imported and was thus reserved for chieftains or wealthy men.

From the engravings we can understand the importance, even then, of navigation and reindeer. Iron was discovered later, around 500 B.C., a period that coincided with an unfavorable change in climate. Then, at the beginning of our era, the climate changed again, the population increased, and early Norwegians encountered the Romans. After A.D. 400, the invasion of Germanic tribes began, as it did across all of Europe. A few centuries later, the Viking period began.

A reconstruction of a Viking ship

The Vikings

For all of Scandinavia, the Viking period was one of expansion. The

Norwegians, in particular, settled in the Shetland and Orkney Islands. Viking expeditions were characterized by their warlike nature. They began with quick raids by small groups lured by riches. Then they became organized expeditions, perhaps caused by overpopulation on the coast, with fleets and armies conquering invaded countries. Vikings even reached Kiev and went as far as Byzantium, serving the emperor as mercenaries. One of them was the Norwegian Harald Sigurdsson–exiled following the death of St. Olav in 1030–who was appointed chief of the imperial guards for his military valor and later became king of Norway. In the west, Norwegians and Danes began attacking the English coast. They then also targeted Ireland, Scotland, and France, where they founded kingdoms in various regions. In 885, a large army composed of Danes and Normans (*nor mann* means "men of the north") besieged Paris. The situation repeated itself, so much so that Charles the Simple of France granted Rollo, one of the Viking leaders, the title of duke and associated land that would from then on be called Normandy. Later, there was the invasion of southern Italy and England and participation in the Crusades. When the push for invasions wore off, military routes became trade routes. Erik the Red, banished first from Norway, then from Iceland, gradually reached Greenland, followed by about 4,000 compatriots. His son, Leif Erikson, reached Newfoundland around the year 1000. The new land, called Vinland, had stable contact with Greenland until the 14th century.

The Lofotr Vikingmuseum in Vestvågøya

The ruins of the Tønsberg fortress

Apart from these explorations, the Vikings were notable for their successful administrative organization in invaded countries, where they taught the art of sailing. They, in turn, learned about different art, religion, and morals, the use of currency and trade, and the building of cities. In the ninth century, the first Norwegian city was founded: Tønsberg.

At home, the Vikings were self-sufficient farmers and lived along the fjords and in the valleys. They inhabited large houses, up to 100 feet (30.5 m) long, and developed craftsmanship. Scandinavian mythology, which reflected the Viking ideals of battle, courage, and valor, was established during this period. Religious culture developed, which saw the worship of different deities, including Odin, god of war and wisdom, and Thor, god of good crops and enemy of trolls and giants. However, the nomadic tribes gradually became sedentary, and the chieftains became kings. This set the preconditions for the transition to Christianity.

The First Norwegian Kings

Until the ninth century, Norway was divided into principalities of varying importance. The lords had the title of *konge* (king), *jarl* (count), or *herse* (baron). Unification occurred around 900 by Harald Harfågre, called Fairhair, king of Viken in the Oslo region. With an army, he set out to conquer the North and soon subjugated it.

Olav Haraldsson

The historical period from unity to 1319 is called Saga because it is recounted in the Norse chronicles or sagas, specifically in the one written by Icelandic author Snorri Sturlason. Harald's sons divided up the country, but the youngest of them, Haakon, reunited it by defending it against Danish advances. Haakon the Good, educated in the Christian religion in England, attempted to impose it on the nation but failed. However, he did organize the local courts into a regional system with legislative and judicial power and established the Leidang, a maritime fleet that included local vessels.

Another Haakon, count of Lade, seized power around 970 with the help of the Danes, later managing to rid himself of his guardians, whom he pushed back in battle. He was killed, however, during a revolt. Then, Olav Tryggvason, grandson of Harald Harfågre, appeared on the scene. Baptized in England, he reunited Norway and imposed the new religion by force, destroying pagan temples and building churches.

The revolt that followed overwhelmed him, dividing the country once again and bringing it under Danish control. In 1015, however, another descendant of Harald Harfågre arrived to set things right. His name was Olav Haraldsson, later known as St. Olav. He reunified Norway by relying on the great landowning families, who became his feudal lords. Then he finally imposed Christianity, founding a Norwegian Church, organizing it with English priests and appointing bishops. Hard-tempered, irascible, and individualist, he soon attracted the resentment of the clan chieftains who were still tied to the Lade family. Allied with the Swedes against the Danes, he was defeated. The king of Denmark then took control of Norway, entrusting the regency to a Lade. Olav tempted fate with an army that was defeated at Stiklestad, near Trondheim, and died on July 29, 1030. Olav was buried in secret near the river. From then on, partly as a reaction to Danish misrule, the legend of his sainthood began. Miracles were attributed to him, a large church was built and dedicated to him, pilgrimages began, and the cult was exported to England, throughout Europe, and as far as Rome. The church was then reorganized into bishoprics, with the archbishop in Trondheim.

Magnus the Good, son of Olav, claimed the Norwegian throne and even went so far as to inherit Denmark, but it was short-lived. His successor, the already mentioned Kiev- and Byzantium-enriched Harald Sigurdsson, even had sights set on England, but he ended up killed in battle. Before he died, however, he seems to have been able to initiate the founding of Oslo. Shortly after, Bergen was also founded, which quickly became a major trading center based on the export of Lofoten stockfish, a trade that made it the largest of all Scandinavian cities.

A period of conflict began in 1130 between various parties, backed by influential figures, who exploited the discontent of different social classes or regional animosity. The conflicts continued for more than a century, until the emergence of Haakon Haakonson, who firmly resumed control by ascending the throne as Haakon IV in the 13th century. The vast Norwegian kingdom intensified its ties with European states through trade agreements, like the one that brought the Hanseatic League to Norway. The country's administration was also changed, bringing all members of the government together at court, entrusting a chancellor with foreign relations, and forming a king's council. The ruler resided in Bergen at Haakonshallen. As part of the feudal reorganization of the state, his son Magnus the Legislator could claim credit for imposing a single legal

Akershus Festning in Oslo

system throughout the country, introducing the public trial, and considering crime an attack on society. His younger brother, who succeeded him as Haakon V, moved the capital to Oslo in 1299 and his residence to the Akershus Festning, the fortress overlooking the city's harbor.

Unifications

Haakon V had no sons, so upon his death in 1319 the crown passed to his grandson, who had also been elected king of Sweden. It was a single, short-lived reign, but it sparked an era of unification in Scandinavia, specifically, the reign of Erik of Pomerania from 1389 over Sweden, Denmark, and Norway. A period of decline began in the 14th century, and in 1536 the Norwegian territory was incorporated into the Kingdom of Denmark.

There were various causes of Norway's decline. First, a wave of Black Death in the mid-14th century halved the population, leaving entire territories depopulated and the country poor. Political and economic weakness led to the Hanseatic League taking over trade with a stable trade concession in Bergen, and a monopoly on trade in Oslo and Tønsberg. Thus, the Hanseatic League bound the kings to them as they depended on them economically and then succeeded in thwarting the council, which also wanted to liberalize trade for the English and Dutch. In addition, the decimated nobility were forced to marry off their daughters to Danish and Swedish nobles who, by right, sat on the Norwegian council, bringing it into an increasingly favorable position for the foreign king. Finally, in 1537, the archbishop of Trondheim fled after losing his battle to keep Norway Catholic and independent. Then Christian III, a staunch Lutheran who imposed the Reformation on the Norwegians, ascended the Danish throne. The council was then dissolved and the country was run directly by the king of Copenhagen.

Danish Rule

Despite these facts, Norway mustered the strength to limit the power of the Hanseatic League, first through the loss of their monopoly in East Norway, then in Bergen. New competition from merchants who came from Scotland, the Netherlands, and Denmark then revived local trade. These merchants, who later became Norwegians, formed a new bourgeoisie with solid capital. Sailors and laborers working in Holland learned the latest shipbuilding techniques and opened many shipyards along the country's southern coast. Cod and herring, however, were still being exported on foreign ships. To resolve this, Norway soon established a commercial fleet.

The invention of the water sawmill then enabled the exploitation of the country's large forests and the sale of timber to those countries experiencing major economic growth such as Holland and England, which needed wood to build ships, houses, and mines. Many Norwegian towns and villages sprang up around these sawmills, erected at river mouths. Mining also provided an economic boost. It was Christian IV who became particularly interested in Norway and its minerals, founding silver mines in Kongsberg, copper mines in Røros, and iron mines in the east and south. Furnaces proliferated along with the mines, producing ingots and various other objects. This business, like fish, wood, and shipping, was held by the Norwegian bourgeoisie. The king and this new middle class thus made a pact, cutting out the nobility.

The statue of Admiral Peter Wessel in Trondheim

In the 17th century a royal charter granted all towns the right to trade; shortly thereafter, artisans were grouped into guilds. Agriculture then experienced significant growth as a result of the sale of state farms, which wiped out the sharecropper class in a century and a half, and handed over land to new owners. The merchant fleet also grew. In this sense, the kingdom's neutrality in the wars of the 18th century enabled Norwegian shipowners to do big business and equip the fleet to sail every sea. Then came the Great Northern War (1700–1721), which pitted the Swedes against the Dano-Norwegians once again. Norway, however, did not fall, thanks in part to the legendary exploits of Admiral Peter Wessel, better known as Tordenskiold.

Trade with other European countries fostered cultural relations with English and French intellectual circles. A national spirit arose that led to two immediate demands: the establishment of a Norwegian bank and university. The latter didn't materialize until 1811; as for the bank, the idea continued to be rejected by the Danish royalty.

Dano-Norwegian neutrality, which had yielded great results in the past, was no longer possible with the Napoleonic Wars. The country was drawn into the continental blockade against England, causing a halt in maritime traffic. These were hard years, which ended only when unity with Denmark dissolved.

A stamp from Posten Norge

The Year 1814

Sweden emerged from the Napoleonic Wars strengthened and with a new international role. It had a liberal constitution and a new king, Napoleonic Marshal Jean-Baptiste Bernadotte, who in 1814 obtained Norway from Denmark. He then ascended the throne as Charles XIV John.

There were those who viewed the new union favorably, for example merchants, who hoped to use their connections with the Swedes to forge increasingly strong relationships with the English market. There were also those who saw that the time for independence was coming. Among them was the Danish prince Christian Frederick, sent from Copenhagen as governor and remaining in Norway as regent, who coveted the throne. In May 1814, at Eidsvoll, the newly elected assembly of Norwegians prepared and approved a democratic constitution and elected Christian Frederick king of the newly independent kingdom. That was on May 17, today a national holiday. The constitution established a division of powers between the king, a cabinet of ministers appointed by him, and the Storting or parliament, elected under a limited vote. In short, it was a hereditary monarchy with limited powers. Those in power, however, decided otherwise. Despite a mission to England and a brief war with Sweden, Norway eventually yielded, but it was granted a compromise: the constitution was preserved, but Christian Frederick had to abdicate, and the two countries were united under one king–the Swedish one of course.

Unification with Sweden

In 1816, Norges Bank, the Bank of Norway, was finally established and by the middle of the century public accounts were restored. The relationship between the Swedish king and the Norwegian government was based on the Eidsvoll constitution, which severely limited royal powers and included public participation in political life. When new liberal ideas took hold in Europe, Norway also adapted. The peasants, a large social base without representation, elected their own delegates to the Storting, thus promoting the decentralization of political decision-making and less taxation by cities. As throughout Europe, liberalism was accompanied by nationalism, supported by the great Romantic intellectuals of the 19th century such as Henrik Ibsen and Bjørnstjerne

Bjørnson. Culture was reborn, and with it a sense of belonging to the nation, from Munch's paintings to Vigeland's sculptures, Grieg's music to Hamsun's novels, Abel's mathematics to Hansen's medical research that discovered the bacterial cause of leprosy.

In the economy, great progress was made, laying the foundations for today's prosperity. Early industrialization began mid-century, in Oslo and Bergen. Textile industries were soon followed by paper, pulp, and canning industries. Agriculture and fishing also changed, the former by diversifying production, now able to rely on means of transportation that opened up the city market, and using better machines and methods; the latter by modernizing boats, methods, and materials. The new fishing boats opened up the North Sea to seal and whale hunting. At the same time, merchant shipping grew in quantity and quality. Beginning in the 1880s, sailing ships were replaced by steam-powered ships. It was during these years that Richard With had the great idea to connect coastal towns and villages every day of the year with the Hurtigruten ferry. Then railroads, telegraph, and telephone followed. These advancements corresponded with an increase in population and rapid urbanization. As early as the turn of the 20th century some Norwegians made their way to the New World, but it was only later that the phenomenon became unrelenting.

Between 1830 and 1920, 800,000 Norwegians emigrated, choosing the United States and Canada as their new homeland. In 1848, Marcus Thrane founded Norway's first workers' organization.

The old Bank of Norway building in Oslo

***Sverd i fjell* is a monument erected in 1983 near Stavanger.**

It was a movement that managed to mobilize agricultural laborers, forcing large and small landowners to side with opposing parties in the following decades: the former, along with officials and the bourgeoisie, founding the Conservative Party, Høyre (Right), and the latter, with the progressive intelligentsia, forming the Liberal Party, Venstre (Left).

Unification with Sweden was effectively a cage for a rising nation like Norway. The struggle of the two parties became intertwined with the question of independence. The Liberal Party, under the leadership of Johan Sverdrup, wanted to achieve universal suffrage and a parliamentary government, with an executive connected to the Storting, loosening ties with Sweden. The Conservatives, on the other hand, wanted to maintain the division of power, with a cabinet of ministers under the king, and intensify ties with the powerful guardian. The Liberal victory in the 1882 elections paved the way for parliamentarianism–officially introduced in 1884–and a series of major reforms.

Universal men's suffrage (1898) and women's suffrage (1913) favored the Labor Party, founded in 1887. The Union however was still a major problem. The pretext for declaring it defunct was the issue of consulates: since the constitution provided that Norwegian foreign policy was in the hands of the king, who was Swedish, parliament decided to open consulates. The king, however, vetoed it. This gave rise to a tug-of-war that on June 7, 1905, led the Storting to declare the Union dissolved. The decision was confirmed by a referendum two months later; however, a second referendum determined the monarchy to still be the institutional form. The Danish prince Carl, whose genealogical line goes back to the Fairhair lineage, namely Harald Hårfagre who united the Norwegian cantons for the first time in the ninth century, became the king of Norway under the name Haakon VII, and was crowned in Trondheim's cathedral.

Independent Norway

Electricity was the engine of Norwegian development after independence, a resource that was in danger of falling into foreign hands because of the many foreign investments made in those years. The government then found itself needing to pass restrictive laws, which limited and controlled interventions beyond the national border.

The 20th century saw the arrival of social, labor, insurance, and welfare laws, which were mainly thanks to the Labor Party. However, the new century also brought with it World War I, in which the country remained neutral. This did not prevent the blockade of the coast by the British and attacks by German submarines, which resulted in serious food shortages and skyrocketing inflation. Once the conflict was over, Norway claimed sovereignty over Svalbard, the Arctic islands of Bear and Jan Mayen, and the Antarctic islands Peter I and Bouvet, as well as a slice of Antarctica, Queen Maud's Land. These were requests justified by geography or the activity of whaling ships flying the Norwegian flag, and in all cases, found no opposition. The great explorations that nearly took Nansen to the North Pole and Amundsen to the South Pole were coming to an end, but they left behind a host of emulators.

After the war, leftist parties split up and clashed. The merger of Labor and Social Democrats was rewarded, and with it the new party's return to a progressive agenda. Social laws, pensions, paid vacations, and unemployment insurance came into focus again.

Fortifications of the Atlantic Wall built by the Nazis on the island of Kamøy

The Massacre at Utøya

On July 22, 2011, a massacre took place that is considered the biggest shock in recent Norwegian history. Anders Behring Breivik, then 30 years old, detonated a car bomb in the government quarter of Oslo, killing eight and injuring 209. Then, disguised as a policeman, he entered the Labor Party youth rally on the nearby island of Utøya and fired indiscriminately on the young people, killing 69 and seriously injuring 55. Arrested immediately, he declared himself Christian, anti-Laborist, and anti-immigrationist, later claiming that he killed those people because they had embraced multiculturalism. Judged to be of sound mind, he was tried in 2012 and sentenced to the maximum prison term under Norwegian law: 21 years.

In 1939, at the beginning of World War II, Norway again declared neutrality. But this time, it was not enough. Swedish iron left Narvik and was sold to Germany, and the British wanted to block it, whereas the possibility of controlling England from the Norwegian coast convinced Hitler to invade the country. In April 1940, German troops occupied all the major ports up to Narvik, then proceeded inland. King, government, and parliament left the capital, along with the gold from the National Bank. They embarked for England, followed by thousands of young men who went to form an army to support the Allies. Back home, far-right general Vidkun Quisling attempted to impose a German-backed dictatorship, but was unsuccessful. Instead, a resistance movement against the occupiers formed, with groups of saboteurs targeting German interests. The Nazis, defeated on the continent, surrendered in Norway, not before they had burned all bridges in the North.

Post-war Period

Post-war problems brought Norway to its knees after German occupation: bombed cities, destroyed factories, housing shortages, and a merchant fleet reduced to an all-time low. The desire to rebuild and recover, and the help of the Marshall Plan, reversed this situation in a few years, leading to a modernization of the production system as well as widespread employment. In the 1960s, the socialist and labor parties managed to gain a few more seats than the non-socialist, liberal, centrist, working-class, Christian, and conservative parties. In any case, the already long tradition of social policy was not abandoned; rather, it received new impetus from favorable economic conditions.

After 1965, a period of coalitions between the non-socialist parties began, with intermittent Labor periods. This was a fluid situation, due to a fluctuation of voters who no longer voted based on their social position, but on contingent considerations. New political formations appeared, such as the Progress Party, and the government was continuously seesawing between parties.

It was a Labor government that had to handle the matter of joining the European Economic Community in 1972. With the memorandum of understanding with the Community already signed, Norway became embittered and divided, later voting "No" in a national referendum. Among the reasons for rejection were a fear of losing the country's newly regained autonomy and a lack of understanding of Europe. In addition to this issue, the major political debates of those years concerned the democratization of working conditions, equal opportunity for men and women, the issues of the Sami minority, and environmental protection.

Beginning in the 1960s, the economy also experienced alternating phases. While the discovery and exploitation of oil and gas deposits enabled rapid growth that led to the financing of numerous social and environmental protection reforms, the maritime and fishing crises brought a lot of uncertainty.

An active member of the UN, Norway has worked on several fronts to promote cooperation with developing countries and to establish a more equitable approach in North-South relations. Despite the debates and uncertainties associated with the nuclear choices of the 1970s and early 1980s, Norway joined NATO, but left an open dialogue with the USSR. In the 1990s, the country came to international attention for its economic success, environmental protection, and quality of life it offers its citizens, as well as for its repeated "No" to the European Union, making it a non-EU but wealthy country.

In 1981, a woman, Gro Harlem Brundtland, was appointed prime minister. A Labor Party member, she remained in office for three terms, until 1996. Since then, the Norwegian Sovereign Wealth Fund has become the largest in the world. The last election, in 2021, was won by the Labor Party with leader Jonas Gahr Støre becoming prime minister. This term brought inequality, climate change, and regulation of oil use as issues of primary concern. ■

The current prime minister of Norway is Jonas Gahr Støre.

THE SAMI

The Sami were called Lapp or Lopar, a name possibly referring to running on snow with wood on their feet. The Norwegian Sami make up the largest part of the community, which also extends into Sweden, Finland, and Russia, covering an area called Sápmi, or Lapland.

Traditional Sami crafts

Although they have been called various names, Sami is what they call themselves in their language, a Finno-Ugric language of the Uralic family, although their physical features are different from those of Finns.

Originally, the Sami were exclusively hunters and led a semi-nomadic life. Each group had its own hunting area, and their favorite prey was wild reindeer. However, walrus, seal, and whale were also hunted.

The Sami live in the north of the three countries of the Scandinavian Peninsula. There are about 80,000 Sami in total, half of them in northern Norway.

They got around on skis, sleds, and boats. Bows and arrows, spears, and dogs were used for hunting, whereas hooks, nets, and harpoons were used for fishing. Different kinds of tools were made from materials such as bone, horn, and iron.

Colonization, first by the Norse and then other peoples, brought agriculture and animal husbandry, as well as wool, weaving, wooden boats, and the fur trade. The region's abundant fur-bearing animals attracted many merchants and their companies, who gradually developed a monopoly trade with the various Sami families. The wealth of this trade did not elude the Scandinavian and Russian crowns, which imposed direct tribute.

The Sami developed a social system suited to their living conditions based on hunting groups or *siida,* governed by an assembly in which each family was represented by one member. As for religion, popular belief was based on two things: ancestors and the forces of nature. Shamans, called *noaid,* were intermediaries between humans and supernatural entities. Their ability to free the mind from the body was enhanced by chanting and the prolonged rhythm of a ritual drum, the skin of which was painted with the figures of the thunder god, wind-man, and animals.

During the 17th century, several actions were made to convert the Sami people to Christianity, much of which was discriminatory: a prayer book was printed in the local language, after which tribal drums were collected and set on fire, and even some shamans were too. The influence of Christian belief grew due to the passionate work of Knud Leem, a missionary who learned the Sami language, made a grammar book and dictionary, and devoted himself to helping the people in various ways. Then there was the more rigid interference of Swedish pastor Laestadius in the 19th century, who fiercely preached to the Sami, framing them in a puritan morality and uprooting them from their traditions.

Official Norwegianization, loss of traditions, and differentiation of economic activities almost caused their disappearance. Then, a revival took hold. Since 1985, elementary and middle school classes in Sami communities, as well as at Karasjok High School and some universities, have been taught in the native language. In addition, following protests in the 1970s and 1980s over the construction of a dam on the Altaelva, a river in the town of Alta, the Sami parliament was formed in 1989. Elected every four years and established in Karasjok, it is an advisory body to the Norwegian parliament regarding language and culture, education and research, nature and the environment, land and water rights, and other institutional matters. Anyone who speaks Sami, or has parents or grandparents who were native speakers, can be entered into a national register and become a voter.

Other traditions that have been reinvigorated in recent decades include the *joik,* a traditional Sami song form with distinctive vocal characteristics used for various daily occasions. It was banned from schools in the 1950s for being considered sinful. Today, it is increasingly used by artists who mix it with other musical forms, creating a continuum between the past and the present. Special mention should also be made for *duodji,* Sami handicrafts, and *kofte,* the brightly colored traditional dress.

Despite the difficult interchanges that have taken place over the centuries to the detriment of the Sami people, it seems that today relations, at least with Norway, are more relaxed. It certainly helped that in 1999 the Norwegian government formally apologized for the abuses it had committed, including banning the Sami language in the 1900s and forcing the people to learn Norwegian.

Sami wearing their traditional *kofte*

IMPORTANT FIGURES

Like anywhere in the world, Norway has its own internationally known figures who have helped define a more precise idea of the country. These are mainly 19th- and 20th-century artists, such as Munch and Vigeland, and explorers, such as Nansen and Amundsen, and we can't forget Nobel, although Swedish, for the global relevance of the Peace Prize, awarded in Norway.

Edvard Munch

The Scream, which exists in four versions, the most famous painted in 1893 and the last in 1910, is something of a universal icon, so much so that it even inspired an emoji, as if it were a widely accepted image of anguish.

Munch (1863–1944) was a disruptive artist with an innovative language, a true painter of the soul. Painting states of mind—anxiety, anguish, jealousy, betrayal—in such a complete and radical way has changed the way we view the expressive arts. Among his most striking canvases, in terms of their use of color, composition, and themes, are *Melancholy* (1891), *Evening on Karl Johan* (1892), and *Death in the Sickroom* (1893).

Gustav Vigeland

If you pass through Oslo, be sure to visit the stone park that bears his name. It is his life's work, his dream, and legacy. Gustav Vigeland (1869–1943) must have had that sacred representation in his mind for some time. Perhaps it was the Renaissance statues he had seen in Florence or the art of Rodin he admired in Paris that gave him the idea.

When the city of Oslo agreed and built him a new studio, he moved there and spent 20 years working on his project in nearby Frogner Park. It is a collection of human characters and feelings—from joy to anger, from resentment to happiness—encased in stone, bronze, and iron, and shaped with skill. The series of 212 figures ends with a circular sculpture, the *Wheel of Life,* composed of adult and child figures intertwined to symbolize the cycle of existence.

Henrik Ibsen & Edvard Grieg

Henrik Ibsen (1828–1906) and Edvard Grieg (1843–1907), Norway's greatest playwright and foremost composer, were brought together by *Peer Gynt,* a dramatic poem in five acts written by Ibsen in 1867, to which Grieg set the music in 1875 for its staging the following year. The protagonist is a young man who would like to recover the money his father has squandered, but is lost in vague dreams, doing nothing. Involved in a fight, he begins his escape, real and

Fridtjof Nansen

Roald Amundsen

dreamlike, which will end only with his return to Solvejg, the young woman who has patiently waited for him throughout his wanderings.

Grieg created two suites for *Peer Gynt*, including "Solvejg's Song." "Morning Mood," however, is his best known piece, written to accompany the protagonist in the desert, yet it is also suited to the environment of the fjord and its morning air. After *Peer Gynt*, Ibsen strung together a series of masterpieces, from *A Doll's House* (1879) to *Ghosts* (1881) and *Hedda Gabler* (1890), giving voice to a theater of social criticism.

Alfred Nobel

His last name is known worldwide as synonymous with the awards given to people who have distinguished themselves in various scientific and non-scientific fields. Born in Sweden in 1833, Nobel went on to study chemistry and devised the formula for dynamite, becoming extremely wealthy. Criticized with the epithet "merchant of death" and having no children to inherit his fortune, he decided to establish a foundation that would annually honor the most outstanding individuals in the fields of medicine, chemistry, physics, and literature, dedicating one also to those who had contributed to world peace.

His name appears here alongside Norwegian figures because at the time Nobel decided that the decision of the Peace Prize–the most difficult and thorniest prize–should be entrusted to Oslo, which at the time was still united with Sweden. And so, every December 10, the committee appointed by the Norwegian parliament announces the winner for the year.

Fridtjof Nansen & Roald Amundsen

World exploration was a centuries-long European disease driven by the need to know every corner of the world. By their time, the late 19th–early 20th century, most of the world had been discovered. Only the poles remained.

What could have been more fascinating than seeing the most extreme points on Earth? Fridtjof Nansen (1861–1930), explorer, scientist, and politician, crossed Greenland on skis; then, with the ship *Fram,* he attempted to reach the North Pole, arriving at 86° N, just a step away from his goal. After World War I, he was elected high commissioner of the League of Nations and devised the Nansen Passport, an international document for refugees.

Roald Amundsen (1872–1928), on the other hand, was the first to reach the South Pole in 1911, five weeks ahead of a British party led by Robert Scott. Amundsen and his team returned safely to their base, while Scott and his companions died on their return journey. In 1926, Amundsen flew over the North Pole in the airship *Norge,* designed and led by Italian engineer Umberto Nobile.

Mari Boine

Mari Boine lived at a time of heightened concern for Indigenous peoples, but she was nonetheless a brave woman for having taken the *joik,* a traditional Sami song, and combined it with major international music genres in a political, social, and artistic move. She debuted in the early 1980s, but success came in 1989 with *Gula Gula*. She mixed joik with jazz, rock, and Andean music, thus reaching a much wider audience.

Contemporary Artists

Among Norway's most influential people today is Jon Fosse, who won the Nobel Prize in Literature in 2023. He is considered a living legend for his works of poetry, prose, and drama and is the most performed writer in Norwegian theaters. His works, with their minimalist and deeply introspective themes written in Nynorsk (Neo-Norwegian), have been translated into dozens of languages. Remaining in the literary field, international standouts include Jostein Gaarder, who in 1991 published the philosophical novel *Sophie's World,* and world-famous writer, musician, and journalist Jo Nesbø, who explores human ugliness in a raw way. And then there is "Lady of Crime" Anne Holt, a former minister of justice who, in the wake of Nordic noir, has probed Norwegian society with her female investigators.

In the musical sphere, in addition to the aforementioned Mari Boine, two true standouts should be noted: Mari Samuelsen, a violinist who masterfully interprets classical and contemporary pieces, moving with equal passion from Philip Glass to Antonio Vivaldi, and Tine Thing Helseth, an award-winning trumpeter and magnificent interpreter of pieces for trumpet and piano or for trumpet and orchestra. ■

ARTS & CULTURE

Although Norway has always been on the fringes of the major European currents of thought, it has a strong idea of its own culture, which is embodied in its literature—including popular literature—art, architecture, design, and film.

Literature

One of the richest and most distinct of the medieval Germanic literatures is undoubtedly Norse literature, whose center, however, was in Iceland. The reason is very simple: there, the spiritual heritage and cultural tradition of the Germanic peoples were preserved longer than on the continent because Christianity arrived later and came with less suffering. Christianity was the official religion, but everyone had to know the stories of the golden days. When at the end of the ninth century Harald Hårfagre conquered one by one the 30 cantons into which Norway was divided, many lords and their retinues emigrated to Iceland. It was thus on the island that Viking stories were orally passed down, until they were written down a few centuries later. The Vikings, in fact, used the runic alphabet only for short inscriptions on stone, metal, or wood.

Beginning in the ninth century, skaldic poetry became widespread in royal courts. This was a genre characterized by a strong stylistic sophistication, which could be found in poems with long stanzas in which a wide variety of themes were represented. Characteristics of this poetry are alliteration, that is the repetition of homophonic consonants or syllables, and kenning, a compound periphrasis used to allude to certain elements or images. For example, the expression "bloody snake" could be used for "sword," or "forest of swords" to say "army."

However, around the year 1000, under Irish influence, poetry mutated, and assonance and rhyme had to coexist with alliteration. With the introduction of Christianity and the use of scripture, the ideas of honor and disregard for death that had characterized the Viking age waned, and with them the skaldic poetry that had interpreted and narrated it.

Over the following centuries, however, some characteristic features of the skaldic genre were revived. An important literary find took place in the 17th century, when the Icelandic bishop Bryniólf Sveinsson discovered a manuscript dating back to the 13th century; this was later called *Poetic Edda,* or *Codex Regius*. The poems contained within are about gods and heroes and originated in the Viking age, though under the influence of already Christian civilizations, such as Irish, Anglo-Saxon, and French.

Particularly well known as a medieval source is the work of Snorri Sturluson, a powerful Icelandic lord and poet who around the mid-13th century wrote

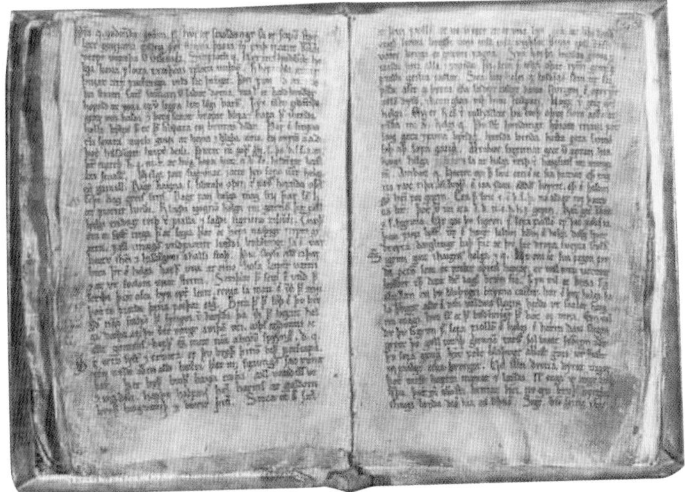

Pages from the *Poetic Edda*

the *Edda* in prose, a collection that until the 17th century remained the largest available document on Norse mythology. However, Sturluson's masterpiece is undoubtedly the *Heimskringla,* or the *Old Norse Kings' Saga*. It is a series of biographies that begins with the mythological account of the origins of the Yngling lineage. The work opens with the words *"Kringla heimsins,"* meaning "The orb of the Earth," which echoes the title and also the universal intention of this book. King Olav the Saint, who is called Rex Perpetuus Norvegiae in the book, often intervenes as a ghost at critical moments in the nation's history.

The narrative saga–chronicle or biography in prose–first oral and then recorded on parchment, was particularly significant for Norse literature. The custodians of this art were the *sagnamenn,* who repeated their stories at banquets, in a concise style and with realism, yet admitting the intervention of the supernatural.

Virtually nothing original was produced after the 13th century. Following the union with Denmark and the adoption of Danish as the language of culture, Norwegian literature was silenced. It was not until the early 19th century, with the advent of Romanticism and the national revival, that Norway again emerged as a literary subject.

The author who best epitomizes the revival of the era is undoubtedly Henrik Ibsen, who was initially inspired by the Norse sagas and then began to delineate what would come to be called "Ibsenian characters," who struggle with the "ghosts of the brain and the heart" because their worst enemies are inside. Disappointed with his compatriots and the Nordic Romanticism of the time, Ibsen left Norway for Italy, where in 1867 he wrote *Peer Gynt,* one of his best known works. Here the hero is a dreamer wandering uselessly, a lazy and immature seeker of the "fleeting moment." It was, however, *A Doll's House,* in 1879, that made Ibsen known throughout Europe. The character of Nora, who abandons her family to search for herself, is perhaps an early feminist depiction, although Ibsen never confirmed a direct link to the 20th-century women's emancipation movement.

From the same period, Bjørnstjerne Bjørnson (1832–1910) , who received the 1903 Nobel Prize in Literature, was a liberal and republican, supporter of the national cause, critic, storyteller, poet, and man of the theater. He wrote the text of the Norwegian anthem "Ja, vi elsker dette landet," set to music by Rikard Nordraak. After a number of historical dramas, such as *King Sverre* and the trilogy of *Sigurt the Violent,* he traveled around Europe and focused on themes related to positivism and science as progress. His most successful works include *Beyond Human Power* (1883), in which he recounts "the impossibility of the impossible," and *When the New Wine Blooms* (1909), a comedy in three acts of contradictory praise of the family.

Slightly later, Knut Hamsun (1859–1952) spent several years of his life doing a variety of jobs before turning to the novel. Among his earliest works is the autobiographical short story "Hunger" (1890), in which Hamsun rejects the realistic and positivistic portrayal of society, exalting instead the unconscious life of the soul. Then, in *Pan* (1894), another of his main themes emerges: a romantic return to the nature of the North. Hamsunian production is extensive and earned the author the Nobel Prize in Literature in 1920.

The 20th century, with Norway's independence and the drama of the two World Wars, the emergence of fleeting trends, foreign cultural influence, and the rise of mass media, saw Norwegian writers searching for their roots both in religious and political faith. We should mention *The People of Juvik* by Olav Duun (1876–1939), which recounts in Nynorsk the saga of a peasant family from the 18th century to the 1930s, and *The Last Viking* by Johan Bojer (1872–1959), in which the virtues of Norwegian peasants are extolled and the challenge of the "last Vikings" to nature is evoked.

Relevant to the religious discourse is Sigrid Undset (1882–1949). Already in her early novels and short stories there are all the signs of moral crisis. Her characters seek solutions to an unsatisfying life and do not find the "certainty of faith." With her novels *Kristin Lavransdatter* and *Olav Audunsson,* religious drama and the contrast between earthly love and divine love become universal themes. In 1928, she was awarded the Nobel Prize in Literature.

In the post-war years, the center of literary debate is the Nazi invasion, its failures and resistance. More recently, crime fiction authors Anne Holt and Karin Fossum have come to the fore, in addition to, of course, Jo Nesbø and Jon Fosse, 2023 Nobel laureate.

Folklore

Once upon a time there were two young students, Peter Christen Asbjørnsen and Jørgen Moe, who loved tales of peasants from their homeland and adored reading the fairy tales of the brothers Grimm. Peter and Jørgen thought that Norway, with its mythology, fantasy, and landscape, could also contribute to the universal storytelling of myths and legends. So they collected, transcribed, and published peasant stories. The first volume of *Norwegian Folktales* came out in 1842. At that time, the written language was similar to Danish, but the oral tales were expressed in different dialects. The two researchers, therefore, found a need to reinvent the language itself, so that they could transcribe words that had been expressed orally.

These folktales were an immediate and lasting success, partly because they were interpreted as "national stories," a redeeming part of the period of Danish rule. The audience of those stories were simple people who lived far from the cities and had no contact with the kings and princesses of the royal world. That is why, often, the ruler narrated in the tale seems to be the landowner, the rich merchant, or whoever offers work. The turreted castles of the central European tradition give way to manor houses built of wood.

The protagonists—mainly trolls—also belong to the Norwegian landscape. Inhabitants of large coniferous forests, hiding under moss, in mountains, among the trees, they are rulers of the night and losers during the day. A single ray of sunlight is enough to turn them to stone. Women, on the other hand, are depicted as princesses to be rescued, or as rough peasants. There is no shortage of exceptions, however, such as a young woman who frees a bewitched prince. The fjords, mountains, and forests of the real Norwegian landscape evoke a perfect fairy-tale setting to these stories.

Trolls at a stall in Bergen

Art

It would be easy to brush off the topic by simply citing Viking art and Edvard Munch's canvases, exploiting the universal popularity that they both have. But it should be said that there are

The pulpit of the Rosekyrkja, in Stordal, from 1789

many forms of Norwegian art, and they have existed since ancient times. Prehistoric art, such as cave paintings and engravings, depicts the values of the time: animals, hunting and fishing; and human and supernatural interactions. Alta's rock art is the most significant testimony of those ancestors, so much so that it has been included in the UNESCO World Heritage List.

Jumping forward in time we encounter the Vikings, who laid the foundations of a homogeneous civilization in Scandinavia. Their art can be found mainly in their decorations, jewelry, weapons, and ships, which are so elegant and functional that they might be the origin of that unique and world-famous Scandinavian design. And how can we not mention the runic stone decorations, found mainly in Sweden?

Another important Viking artifact from Norway, albeit indirectly, are the wooden pole-bearing churches built in abundance from the 12th century onward. Their forms and decoration, as well as style, are direct heirs of Viking art and craftsmanship. In the 18th and 19th centuries, a decorative style developed in rural areas such as Telemark for walls, furniture, and objects, called *rosemaling,* which literally means "rose painting." A flourish of lines and colors graced homes, not unlike rural decorations found throughout Europe.

And it was in the 19th-century climate that a national spirit was reborn and the Romantic current spread. It is worth mentioning Johan Christian Dahl (1788–1857), the father of Norwegian landscape painting, who transposed the panoramas of his land onto canvas. One of the figures who helped redefine "Norwegianism," Dahl was also a leading cultural figure, central to the founding of the National Museum and the restoration of Nidaros Cathedral.

After him there was Erik Werenskiold (1855–1938), an illustrator who drew rural life and portrayed famous people in the wake of newfound 19th-century patriotism. Of note was his work to illustrate the popular edition of Snorri Sturluson's *Heimskringla.*

Then came Edvard Munch, a unique expressionist, and the mood changed forever. Mental illness, death, melancholy, and anguish were his most prominent themes. Munch broke with conventions and brought painting into the 20th century. Few in the world have had the same disruptive force, which also accompanied the development of psychoanalysis.

Finally, there were the Vigeland brothers: the sculptor Gustav who gave life to Vigelandsparken in Oslo with its large granite and bronze sculptures, and the younger Emanuel (1875–1948), a decorative artist best known for the splendid stained glass windows he made for a number of churches, including the Oslo Domkirke, the capital's cathedral.

Architecture

Norway's building tradition is based on the use of wood. One need only recall the ancient nail-less carpentry schemes of the *tømmerhus* and the pole system of the *stavkirke*. Stone buildings, such as the cathedral in Trondheim or the fortified Akershus complex in Oslo, come later and are still limited. In the 18th century, wooden paneling began to be applied to buildings, concealing the load-bearing framework and offering more decorative possibilities. This is evident in towns along the coast, which show European influence. In terms of urban planning, however, these towns were modeled on the open farms of Telemark and Gudbrandsdal, which are composed of a main building

The Oslo Domkirke, or cathedral, towers over the roofs in the capital.

Iconic wooden houses in Lillehammer

surrounded by other smaller structures, with one courtyard for people and one for animals. This pattern, replicated in urban areas, leads to a non-canonical building composition suited to a society that already boasted a strong tradition of individual freedom.

The 19th-century nationalistic awakening also challenged architects and town planners with finding an authentic Norwegian style suited to the needs of the new industrial middle class. The first answers were borrowed from the continent. From the rigid classicism of the Royal Palace and the University of Oslo, we move on to the German-influenced Romanticism of Trinity Church in Oslo and art nouveau.

However, their search found its own way when workers' organizations caused the attention of architects to shift to social contents. While Oslo's working-class neighborhoods of the early 20th century are built on classicist principles—and even the early post-war period is steeped with them—the 1930s make rationalism their own—at first rigidly, then with lively floor plans and a return to wood. At the beginning of the decade, Norwegian society identified itself with a functional rationalism that seemed popular and progressive, then subsequent aesthetic focus responded to the psychological need of the new social subjects. An important signature of this latter phase was Wenche Elisabeth Selmer, who specialized in wooden structures.

Around the 1950s, Oslo, like the other Nordic capitals, approved a master plan that would change its layout, preparing it somewhat for contemporary challenges. The rest is recent history. As already pointed out, it is oil wealth that has profoundly transformed society and its needs, along with, of course, globalization, the digital revolution, and international tourism. To define itself, Oslo has built a new backdrop, in which no one style prevails except the personal style of freely competing architects.

Design

Scandinavian design emerged in the 1950s and developed around two basic concepts: minimalism and functionality. Prompted by the best known Swedish and Danish designers, the Norwegians gradually charted their own course, for example, with the Ekstrem chair designed in 1984 by Terje Ekstrøm.

Today, even in the wide variety of styles and offerings, designers focus on light, graceful lines, and inspiration from nature, channeling their ideas into lamps, furniture, and tableware. Also worth mentioning is the work in apparel design, where the focus has been on outdoor clothing as well as warm wool clothes. The hottest names currently include Andreas Engesvik in the industrial field, Kristine Five Melvær in textiles and graphic design, and Victoria Günzler in ceramics. Also of note is the work on lamps by Northern Lighting and the blown glass by Hadeland Glassverk.

Norwegian design also has some unique aspects, such as the fact that work is commissioned for state sectors, or that the design of banknotes has been entrusted to leading studios like Snøhetta and The Metric System. Design elements have even been applied to passports, as if elegance should also be expressed through a travel document. The Oslo School of Architecture and Design reflects on the role of design in reducing carbon emissions and building a sustainable society, optimizing a range of processes, like the work done with the University Hospital in Oslo aimed at reducing waiting times.

The Ekstrem chair by Terje Ekstrøm

Film

At the turn of the 20th century, the first movie theaters opened in Christiania. These were owned by foward-thinking private individuals who seized the opportunity to enrich themselves. With social democracy came an attempt to take film distribution away from private entrepreneurs: screening rooms became municipal, so mayor and councilors became distributors and programmers. The stated political and pedagogical purpose of the operation brought about folk or local themes, as well as film adaptations of national literary works.

In 1932, Norsk Film was founded, a national production company that built its studios in Oslo and remained operational for 70 years. Before the war, however, 90 percent of the films shown in Norway were American. During World War II and the German occupation, production stopped, apart from Nazi propaganda films.

The municipal system became less rigid after the war, permitting the production of films with an international scope, such as Titus Vite-Müller's *The Battle for the Atomic Bomb* and the films of Arne Skouen. A renaissance seemed to take place around this time, with the government re-establishing the private circuit and founding the Norsk Filminstitutt, the Norwegian Film Institute, in 1955. But in the 1960s, television arrived to shift the trend. In the following decade, the government dismantled the municipal system and financed 100 percent of productions approved by a committee of experts. A film movement was born that was committed to interpreting the issues of the time, like the feminist films of Anja Breien. In the 1980s, Norwegian cinematography reached maturity, with films such as Vibeke Lokkeberg's *Løperjenten (Betrayal)*, Erik Gustavson's *Blackout*, Oddvar Einarson's *X*, and even Ola Solum's thriller *Orions belte (Orion's Belt)*. Also of note was the first Sami film, Nils Gaup's *Veiviseren,* nominated for Best Foreign Language Film at the 1988 Oscars. International attention was then garnered by Gustavsson's *Telegraphist,* based on Hamsun's novel *Dreamers.* Lastly, there was the production of notable short films, such as *Taktikk* (1999) by Eva Dahr.

Runic inscription

Language

The earliest evidence of the Norse language can be traced back to runic inscriptions. These engravings, the oldest evidence of which dates back to the first centuries A.D., show a common language throughout the North, at least until the Viking period. A rune, from the Norse *runar*, is a written mark of the alphabet of the Nordic peoples, probably a distortion of the southern alphabets passed down through the Gothic or Celtic tribes. Whoever could carve runes held the power of writing, a religious and magical power. Runic inscriptions were made on tombs to keep grave robbers away, on utensils so that food would keep better, and on weapons to make the warrior who owned them invincible.

The portrait of Henrik Wergeland appears on the 100 krone bill.

Christianity introduced the Latin alphabet, and writing remained the preserve of the clergy. Danish rule imposed its language as the official and literary language, especially in cities and centers of power. Norse-Norwegian survived only in villages, which brought very little innovation. However, 19th-century nationalism didn't ignore the issue of language. Henrik Wergeland, an important 19th-century writer, fought for language reform, so that the words and sentence construction of Norwegian dialects would once again be used in speech in cities and then be reintegrated into the written language. Peter Christen Asbjørnsen and Jørgen Moe, who had collected folktales and legends, went even further, modifying the syntax to bring it closer to everyday speech.

The reformation of the language, which is still ongoing, already brought about major spelling and grammatical changes at the time. Philologist Ivar Aasen compiled a grammar book and dictionary of Nynorsk—or Neo-Norwegian—based on the rural dialects of the west and mountainous regions, and the adoption in the late 19th–early 20th century of Bokmål (literally, "book language") as the language of the kingdom.

The language is considered Dano-Norwegian, given the inevitable influences that Danish rule had in structuring an independent language, to which eastern Norwegian forms were added. The result of the clash is a near tie: although Bokmål is used by 90 percent of Norwegians, Nynorsk is alive and rooted. One could say that both are written forms of mixed languages, with different inflections. Of course, the official language of a country is never a monolith, but here they really love the diversity. This is also where the language of northern minorities and those of immigrants fit in today.

Sports

The national sport in Norway is cross-country skiing, which is extremely popular. It has ancient roots throughout Scandinavia: rudimentary skis first made of branches and bark and then animal skins were used for hunting and fighting as early as the Middle Ages; even kings were sent into exile by ski. The first documented sports competition dates to 1843, in Tromsø. Later, Fridtjof Nansen's crossing of Greenland on skis in 1888–1889 set the tone worldwide. Cross-country skiing has been part of the Winter Olympic Games since the first edition, held in Chamonix in 1924 (women were not admitted until 1952, in Oslo). Leading the Olympic medal table with 52 golds is Norway (quite a distance behind are Sweden, USSR/Russia, and Finland), and Norwegians also perform very well at World Championships (171 gold medals, far ahead of all other nations). Petter Northug (Framverran, 1986) received 13 gold medals between 2007 and 2015 in the relay, skiathlon, and sprint. In 2018, cross-country skier Marit Bjørgen (Trondheim, 1980), the sportswoman with the most medals (15) and gold medals (8) at the Winter Olympics, hung up her skis. A few years earlier, the scene was dominated by Bjørn Dæhlie (Elverum, 1967), who with 8 Olympic and 9 World Championship titles is the most victorious athlete in the history of cross-country skiing. There have also been numerous successes in alpine skiing, mostly at the men's level, since the 1990s, including Kjetil André Aamodt (Oslo, 1971), who is the most titled athlete in the history of the Winter Olympic Games with 8 medals, Lasse Kjus (Oslo, 1971), Aksel Lund Svindal (Lørenskog, 1982), Kjetil Jansrud (Stavanger, 1985), and, most recently, Aleksander Aamodt Kilde (Bærum, 1992).

Cross-country skier Petter Northug

Sprinter Karsten Warholm

Chess grandmaster Magnus Carlsen

Norway has also been making waves in track and field recently, especially with two young men who have emerged in the past few years. Jakob Ingebrigtsen (Sandnes, 2000) is the reigning Olympic champion in the 1,500 meters and world champion in the 5,000 meters (he finished second in Budapest in the 1,500 meters), and he holds the 2,000-meter and two-mile records (both records were set in 2023). Karsten Warholm (Ulsteinvik, 1996) became Olympic champion in the 400-meter hurdles in Tokyo 2020, and is the reigning world and European champion, as well as the world record holder in the specialty, the first to go under the 46-second mark.

But, thanks in part to the media hype of soccer, the most famous Norwegian sportsman of the moment is undoubtedly Erling Haaland (Leeds, 2000), a bulky forward standing 6 foot 3 (194 cm) and weighing 207 pounds (94 kg) for Manchester City, who won the 2022/2023 Champions League. He continues breaking record after record. To name just two: he scored five goals in a single game and is the only one to have managed to score a hat trick on his debut in the competition. With multimillion-dollar contracts from clubs and sponsors, Haaland is destined to win the Ballon d'Or soon (in 2023, he was beaten out by Lionel Messi, who had led Argentina to the 2022 world title).

Between 2013 and 2023, another Norwegian was world champion: chess player Magnus Carlsen (Tønsberg, 1990), considered one of the best players in history. He became a grandmaster at the age of 13 and during his career remained undefeated for 125 games. He achieved the highest score ever in the system used to evaluate chess players. After deciding not to defend his world title, he was succeeded in April 2023 in Astana by China's Ding Liren. ■

THE NATURAL LANDSCAPE

Norway is a long, narrow country located in the western part of the Scandinavian Peninsula. It stretches far to the north and east, with a very long and rugged coastline largely shaped by islands and fjords. It contains 47 national parks and more than 3,000 protected areas, which increasingly have to face the realities of global warming and the resulting melting of ice.

If we include the Svalbard Islands, Norway lies between 57° and 81° N latitude, and 4° and 31° E. The country borders Sweden, Finland, and the Russian Federation. The seas that touch its shores are the Barents Sea, the Norwegian Sea, the North Sea, and the waters of the Skagerrak Strait. An essential feature of the Norwegian landscape is the permafrost, which is rocky and sandy soil cemented by ice, found mostly on the highest mountains, in the Finnmark region, and on the Svalbard Islands. Other special features to mention are the Sognefjord, which with 126 miles (204 km) of shoreline is the longest fjord in the world, and Hornindalsvatnet Lake, which is the deepest in all of Europe. In short, the country is rich with unique natural features, all waiting to be discovered.

Mountains, Highlands, Fjords, Islands

Mountains form the backbone of a large part of the country, a 1,056-mile-long (1,700 km) spine stretching from southwestern Stavanger to northeastern Varanger Peninsula. The Scandinavian Alps, especially in the South, were formed by the Caledonian orogeny during the Paleozoic, which dates them to the same era as the mountains of Scotland, Ireland, the Svalbard Islands, and eastern Greenland. The highest peak is Galdhøppigen: it reaches 8,100 feet (2,469 m) and is located in the Jotunheimen massif, between Bergen and Ålesund. It should be mentioned that all the major peaks in the Scandinavian chain are Norwegian, and several exceed 7,200 feet (2,200 m). However, the landscape varies considerably: while the mountains on the west coast slope rapidly toward the North Sea and the Norwegian Sea, there are several areas of flat land in the southern part of the country.

Geologically, Norway predominantly contains Precambrian granite, but there is also no shortage of gneiss, slate, sandstone, and limestone rocks. The terrain has been shaped by erosion, especially during the glaciations 2–3 million years ago. Back then, Scandinavia resembled Antarctica today. Numerous glaciers descended directly into the sea, resulting in the deep furrows that, once flushed with water, formed the fjords of today. The mountains around such glaciers have rounded shapes, surrounded by undulating plateaus

The village of Reine in the Lofoten Islands

traversed by deep glacial valleys. The latter have rather steep outer edges, the result of erosion caused by rivers. The ancient ice cap has thus remained in a few places at higher elevations. Other glaciers, however, are of the alpine type, with a broad tongue descending into the valley.

Along the coast the landscape can be alpine, with steep mountains or gentler, rolling lands that meet the sea sheltered by a myriad of islands. There are about 50,000, one of the richest features of Norway's coastline, which stretches 2,112 miles (3,400 km).

As for rivers, they tend to be short along the coast, flowing in deep valleys and often interrupted by waterfalls. Moving to the south-central area, however, you run into longer and less rushing waterways. The most important, the 305-mile-long (604 km) Glomma, flows between Røros and Oslofjord. Another feature that characterizes Norway's geography is undoubtedly its numerous lakes.

The Climate & Flora

The coastal climate is essentially marine, with Atlantic winds bringing abundant rainfall and the Gulf Stream keeping temperatures relatively high. This causes averages to have small variations throughout the year, with cool summers and mild winters. The winter average is 19°F (-6.8°C),

The town of Ny-Ålesund in the Svalbard Islands

but it varies widely. In the interior, by contrast, the climate is continental, with colder winters and warmer summers. Often, especially in the Finnmark region, it drops to -4°F (-20°C); in 1999, a record frost of -60°F (-51°C) was recorded in Karasjok.

Summer temperatures also show similar variability to winter temperatures. In the interior, a maximum of 65°F (18°C) can be reached, whereas, on the coast there can be peaks of 77–86°F (25–30°C). We must, however, consider the influence of climate change. Between 2015 and 2023, maximums have seen sharp increases. In June 2023, the maximum in Oslo reached 89°F (31.8°C), and farther northwest, in Gulsvik, 93°F (33.9°C). On the Svalbard Islands, which basically have a polar climate with very cold winters and cold summers, temperatures exceeded 68°F (20°C) for four consecutive days in July 2020, reaching a record 71°F (21.7°C), the highest temperature ever recorded in the European Arctic.

The interior is blanketed by snow for many months, while the coast is the realm of rain. Total precipitation ranges from 59 to 118 inches (1,500–3,000 mm) per year. Given the latitudes, it is certainly one of the most favorable situations for forests that exists on Earth. For example, deciduous trees can survive up to 64° N, but they normally do not go beyond 54° N. The humidity and climate favor forests, particularly pine and fir, which cover 25 percent of the land. Depending on latitude, these trees reach an altitude of 1,640–3,280 feet (500–1,000 m). Farther north the conifers give way to birches, and then to grasslands that become true tundra, with a short, intense summer bloom. Below the Arctic Circle are broadleaf trees, particularly oaks, beeches, elms, and more birches. There are about 2,000 plant species, some unique to Norway.

Fauna

While the polar bear can only be found on the Svalbard Islands, far beyond the Norwegian mainland, other animals are common and protected by law. A few limited species can be hunted and fished only at certain times. Reindeer, moose, and salmon are part of the official iconography, and are linked to Norwegian forests and rivers. Reindeer are mostly domestic, but wild ones can be found in large numbers on the Hardangervidda Plateau. Moose can be found in the southeast of the country and along the Russian border, whereas salmon diligently ascend the rivers that have always been their home, especially in Finnmark and the fjord region. The brown bear has almost disappeared, and can be spotted basically only in Pasvikdalen, near Kirkenes. There are numerous other species of predators and prey, such as the arctic fox, lynx, otter, wolf, deer, lemming, arctic hare, and ptarmigan, as well as seals and whales of course. For the latter, hunting remains open. Although the

An arctic fox

international community has declared whale populations at risk of extinction and that hunting should not be practiced, Norwegian experts propose assessing the number of living specimens on a case-by-case basis and regulating accordingly since the practice has been a significant part of the country's customs and traditions for centuries.

National Parks

Norway has 47 national parks, including seven in the Svalbard Archipelago, and more than 3,000 differently protected areas. With the exception of Hardangervidda Nasjonalpark, which contains Europe's largest plateau, all areas are under county jurisdiction and administered by the Nature and Forestry Directorates. All animals living within the national parks are protected, as are their eggs, nests, and habitats. Some of the most important and spectacular national parks are Jotunheimen, which includes Norway's highest peak, Galdhøpiggen; Jostedalsbreen, famous for its glaciers, such as the magnificent Nigardsbreen; Dovrefjell-Sunndalsfjella, a must-see for wild reindeer and musk ox; Saltfjellet-Svartisen, where the Svartisen Glacier, the second largest in the country, is located; and Nordvest-Spitsbergen, in Svalbard, where you can see seabirds, Svalbard reindeer, and walruses.

Nigardsbreen, part of the Jostedalsbreen Glacier in Vestland

The Issue of Emissions

According to the Numbeo global database, Norway ranked third in the world among the least polluted countries in 2022, after Finland and Iceland. The ranking is based on eight criteria, including waste management and air quality.

The governmental agency Miljødirektoratet, reporting directly to the ministry of environment and climate, is responsible for reducing greenhouse gas emissions, preventing pollution, and protecting Norway's nature, including through an inspection and monitoring department. Klimaloven, a law enacted to reduce greenhouse gas emissions by 40 percent by 2030, was passed in 2017.

Several measures have been put in place to achieve this goal. For example, only modern clean-burning woodstoves are currently sold, and replacement of older models is being promoted through local incentives. Air quality, with respect to both PM 2.5 and PM 10, is considered good, with the major cities—such as Oslo, Bergen, Trondheim, and Tromsø—having decidedly reassuring values compared to European

A vehicle in the Oslo tram system

averages. According to the European Environment Agency, Norway is among the countries with the lowest risk of premature death from PM 2.5 pollution. However, it should be considered that particulate emissions are deposited on snow and ice, reducing the latter's ability to reflect sunlight. The result is that the Arctic is warming twice as fast as other parts of the world.

Although the oil industry is striving to reduce its impact on the environment by constantly improving extraction technologies, and the government is attempting to regulate the massive salmon farming industry and its pollution, it must be noted that Norway's geographical location does not facilitate the well-being of the ecosystem. The interplay of winds and sea currents means the country receives pollutants from abroad, particularly sulfur dioxide from Russia.

Despite the difficulties that have arisen, Norway has managed to achieve excellent results in its efforts to reduce harmful emissions because the political class has taken a strong stance on the matter. Even the then deputy mayor of Oslo, Vegar Andersen, mentioned this at COP25 in Madrid, making it clear that the impact of carbon dioxide must be treated as a governance issue. And these are not just words. Oslo is the only country in the world to have introduced the Climate Budget, in 2016, planning actions in energy, environment, transportation, and resources. The idea is to turn thinking on its head: you start with how many tons of CO_2 you can allow, and from there you structure actions that do not exceed that limit.

For example, the electrification of cars and transportation in the port will reduce emissions by 85 percent by 2030, aiming for zero impact by 2050. Similarly, through subsidies, rebates, and other types of incentives, the purchase of electric vehicles has been promoted so convincingly that almost the entire population will have transitioned to green vehicles in a few years. By 2022, 79.3 percent of new cars sold in Norway were electric. It is measures of this kind, along with the country's overall vision, that led to Oslo being awarded the European Green Capital Award, given annually by the European Commission to the city that has achieved important goals in environmental protection and sustainable economic development. Undoubtedly, the ministry of finance's involvement in environmental issues contributed to this achievement, which means giving climate change primarily economic significance.

As of 2015, the Norwegian Sovereign Wealth Fund, the world's largest, no longer invests in coal-fired mines and power plants. In addition an agreement with the European Union for a Green Deal on climate change, climate neutrality in 2050, and green industry development was established in 2023. ■

FOOD & DRINK

What image immediately conjures the essence of Norwegian cuisine? Salmon, perhaps smoked, is the first thing that comes to mind. Herring is too boring, reindeer meat too particular, and cloudberries too unknown. However there is one Norwegian product that is truly popular abroad, even if it is not always associated with its place of origin: cod. From here we can start on a journey through Norwegian cuisine.

Norwegian food has changed a great deal over the centuries. A prime example is the *koldtbord,* or cold buffet, a table of many dishes that once encapsulated the meaning of feasting and sharing. Today, such a meal no longer makes much sense for Norwegians, as the country's development has all but eliminated poverty and thus also a form of cooking that tended to group everything on the table together. Everyone knows where their next meal is coming from, but they still offer the cold buffet to visitors to acquaint them with the country's culinary history. In a koldtbord, you can find typical dishes such as herring, with sauces and brown bread; then there's shrimp and crab, followed by fish–salmon and trout, of course–but also mackerel, halibut, and eel. Poached, smoked, marinated, peppered, with sauces, or with cream. And then vegetables, especially tomatoes, cucumbers, and button mushrooms. And don't forget the meats, such as salted and dried leg of lamb, dried or marinated reindeer, roast beef, and ham. You also get cream cheeses and dark goat cheese,

Lefse **is a soft, traditional bread.**

EXPERIENCE: *Lefse*

That bread is essential in any Norwegian meal is a well-known fact. It is found in so many different versions, from the classic wheat loaf to the more sought-after brown bread enriched with various seeds. However, there is one product in particular that represents the Norwegian soul: *lefse*. Often underestimated, this flatbread is actually an ideal base to be stuffed to one's liking. It is a type of flatbread made from flour, potatoes, and milk. Try it with butter, cinnamon, and sugar, or use it as a pastry to accompany a savory dish!

and to close out the buffet, berries like blueberries, strawberries, raspberries, and blackberries, fresh or canned, accompanied by liquid or whipped cream.

The 21st century has also brought simultaneous revolutions in the culinary field that are seemingly divergent: on the one hand, you have the Nordic cuisine movement, with a certain degree of fusion, and on the other, the arrival of foreign foods, such as pizza, pasta, and tacos. Added to this is a strong focus in daily diets on healthy foods with proven properties that can contribute to the prevention of certain diseases, not to mention the variety of flavors that have gradually become available. The cuisine mirrors a way of life, which in turn is a direct heir to economic prosperity and social dynamics; that is why Norwegian dishes have evolved according to the needs and preferences of the historical period.

First and foremost, the Norwegian daily diet includes *frokost,* which is a sweet or savory cold breakfast accompanied by coffee. In each of the two versions, the key ingredient is bread *(brød),* which can be filled with butter and jam or with smoked salmon and scrambled eggs. This is followed by *lunsj,* which is a quick, cold meal in the middle of the day, and *middag,* the much needed hot dinner.

Fish *(Fisk)*

As already mentioned, cod *(torsk)* is king when it comes to fish dishes. It can be served dried or salted–stockfish and salt cod respectively–or poached with potatoes and melted butter, which is arguably the best. During the Christmas season, however, cod is processed in a special way to create the traditional

An iconic Norwegian buffet always features herring, salmon, and brown bread.

***Lutefisk* is one of the longest-living traditional dishes in Norway.**

lutefisk. With its jelly-like appearance and texture, it certainly does not appeal to everyone. Its peculiarity lies in the fact that the fish is cured for two or three days in lye, then thoroughly rinsed and cooked. It is one of the longest-living traditional dishes, consumed as early as the 1500s!

Other fish specialties include *spekesild,* salted herring served with potatoes and beet, and *sursild,* or pickled herring. There is also *stekt fisk,* smaller filleted fish dipped in flour and braised in butter; *rakfisk,* trout or char salted and fermented for two to three months; *røkt laks,* smoked salmon served thinly sliced, with scrambled eggs or creamed spinach; and *gravlaks,* salmon marinated with salt, sugar, and dill. Also worth mentioning are *fiskesuppe,* a soup made with various kinds of fish, carrots, onions, potatoes, and milk, and *kongekrabbe,* the king crab that has invaded the north coast.

Meat *(Kjøtt)*

Although bordered by the sea, Norway also has a rich tradition of meat dishes. Some of the most common are *kjøttboller,* minced meatballs first fried and then boiled in a sauce, and the typical Christmas *juleskinke,* a ham marinated for three weeks and then boiled.

Then there is *svinekoteletter* and *svinestek,* pork prepared as a braised stew or roasted; *spekemat,* smoked meat and sausages accompanied by scrambled eggs, margarine, sour cream, and flatbread; and *ryper,* ptarmigan braised in milk, with sour cream, goat cheese, and cranberry jam. Visiting Norway, however, one cannot miss the chance to try *dyrestek,* roast reindeer, which has the same preparation and seasoning as ptarmigan, or *reinkjøtt og buljong,* boiled

Kjøttboller **are minced meatballs.**

reindeer and consommé. It is the quintessential Sami dish, to be enjoyed in a tent or around a fire. Lastly, there's game meat, such as elk, deer, and grouse, served both fresh and cured.

Cheese *(Ost)*

The most famous, the brownish *brunost* is actually composed of caramelized goat's milk lactose. It is often used sweet, spread on slices of brown bread or on typical Norwegian pancakes, called *lappers*. Other types of dairy products include *gamalost,* an overripe sour cow's milk cheese, found almost only in Vik; *pultost,* with sour milk and caraway seeds; and *nøkkelost,* with caraway and cloves. Finally, a special mention should be made for *kraftkar,* an aromatic cheese that won the World Cheese Award in 2016–a first for Norway.

Fruit & Desserts

Norwegians like to end their meal on a high note. After finishing the main course, they refresh their palates with fruit, such as strawberries, cranberries, blueberries, apples, and, in

Bread and *gamalost*

some regions, the rare cloudberry *(multe),* before ending with a tasty dessert. On the dessert front, there's *tilslørte bondepiker,* stewed and breaded apples topped with whipped cream; *riskrem,* rice pudding accompanied with fruit sauce; and *trollkrem,* egg whites beaten with sugar and marsh blueberries. For special occasions, people enjoy some *kransekake,* a dessert consisting of almond cake disks of different sizes stacked on top of each other to form a cone. Other must-try desserts include *bløtkake,* a soft layer cake filled with cream; *krumkake,* a delicious sweet wafer rolled and filled with cream; and *rabarbrapai,* the traditional rhubarb cake.

A traditional *kransekake*

Must-try Dishes

There are several ways to taste the many local specialties. One highly recommended experience is a visit to a mountain farm. There are about 700 total, and they are open to visitors from June to early September. Also not to be missed are the fruit and cider villages, in the great Hardangerfjord and Sognefjord. In 2016, *kraftkar,* an aged blue cheese, was the first Norwegian cheese to win the World Cheese Award, giving relevance to a land with many dairy products that are little known abroad. All of these are products that symbolize the new vision of Norwegian cuisine, which embraces a high-quality local supply chain and imported, innovative techniques. Although pasta, pizza, tacos, and tapas are now widely available, don't miss the upscale local dishes and the traditional street food.

Drinks *(Drikke)*

Strange as it may sound, Norwegians are among the top in the world in per capita coffee consumption. The most traditional and widespread way to drink it is by dissolving soluble powder in boiling water. There are other methods as well, and coffee shops serve a variety of options. The quintessential mineral water is Farris, which has a long history in the Norwegian springs near Larvik. As for alcoholic beverages, the most popular beers are the Danish Carlsberg, Hansa, and the local Mack. Each region has its own, however, and the evolution of microbreweries has brought several innovative options. Other alcohols consumed are *aquavit,* which is a potato distillate flavored with caraway seeds, especially *linje aquavit,* matured on ships that travel to the equator; *mjød* or mead; and *sider,* cider, in local and limited production. Note that in Norway, all spirits with an alcohol content above 4.75 percent are available only at Vinmonopolet or other licensed stores. ■

An apple orchard in Hardangerfjord

A gateway to the rest of the country, the capital city, where tradition and modernity coexist, is surrounded by forests and lakes to the north and the fjord bordering Sweden to the southeast

OSLO & AROUND

Contemporary buildings overlook the waters of Oslofjord.

OSLO

This innovative, eco-friendly city is proof that a balance between lush nature and orderly urban development is possible. Sea, lakes, and forests coexist here with a vibrant metropolis, which has no shortage of museums and parks, a bit of the Middle Ages, 19th-century architecture, and a strong presence of 20th-century traits.

Oslo is a happy city. Not so much because of the various ratings published periodically, but because it is a balanced city: not too big; well organized, orderly, and planned; and rich enough to carry out projects—architectural, urban, social—and complete them in reasonable amounts of time. It is thus an exception. Two-thirds of its territory consists of protected areas, rich in lakes, forests, and hills. It was named the European Green Capital of 2019. Then again, a metropolitan city with a population of 1.5 million but covering an area the size of London shows how the Norwegian idea of a city endures. It also boasts the highest number of fully electric cars per inhabitant.

Oslo has one of the highest GDP per capita in Europe, is among the most expensive cities on the continent, and produces a quarter of Norway's gross domestic product. It has become an ambitious city, which can be seen in its new icons, so different from those of yesteryear. Its citizens have realized that what was thought to be local and minor is instead a treasure to be proud of. Oslo has thus focused on the Munch Museum and the renovation of the Viking Ship Museum, which will open in 2026 as the Viking Age Museum. Can you see the shift in thinking?

The new Oslo is a flourish of spectacular buildings and trendy areas. The 21st century has arrived, and it is jaw-dropping: affordable luxury is combined with sustainability and a mix of genres and approaches. Art, whatever the term means today, has been blended and made accessible for all. The concept of museum has been networked, spread on social media, liquefied. Out of this thinking came a new space, which is conservative only in name: the National Museum.

NOT TO BE MISSED:

Nasjonalmuseet 72
Operahuset 79
Munchmuseet 79–80
Trips in the fjord 82
Vigelandsparken 85–86
Holmenkollen 86–87
Norsk Folkemuseum 92
Kistefos Museum and its sculpture park 94
Marka 95

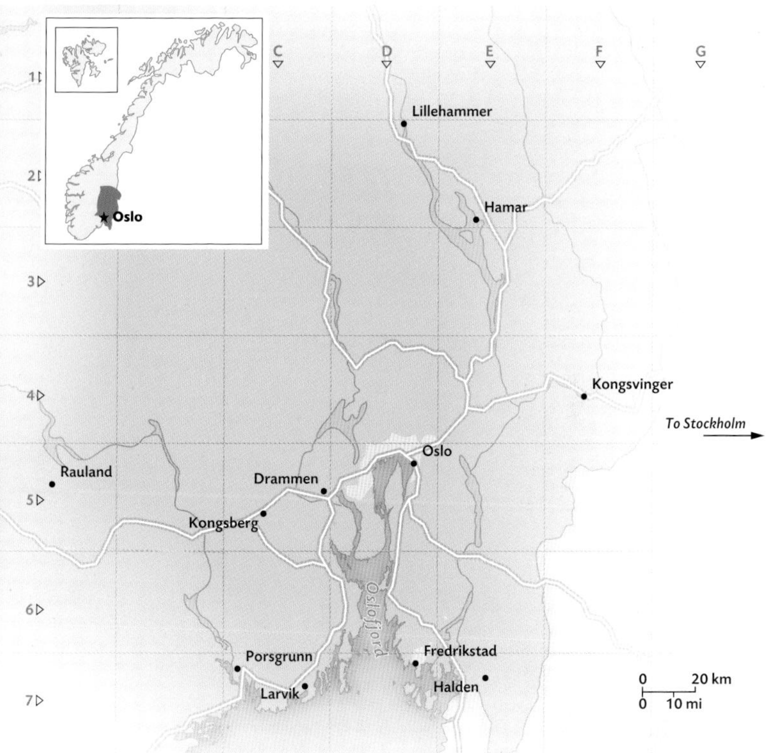

Otherwise, it is a mix of Shanghai, Toronto, and Seoul, a showcase that has little that is national. From the height of their model country, Norwegians can afford to play with their brand, knowing that Norwegianism is not in question. For now.

Oslo is growing rapidly, with 700,000 inhabitants in the city and as many in the metropolitan area. The city lies at the end of Oslofjord, in the Skagerrak Basin. The highest point is 2,066 feet (630 m), and around it lie 40 islands, 343 lakes, and the Akerselva River. The average temperature in January is 23°F (-4.5°C), and in July 62°F (17°C), but in summer it can reach peaks of 86°F (30°C). About half the days of the year are rainy, totaling more than 29 inches (750 mm) of precipitation.

According to Snorri's *Saga*, it was founded in the 11th century, fortified in the 14th century, and decimated by the plague that same century. It became Danish in the mid-16th century, as did the whole country. The Protestant Reformation and religious strife followed. In the 17th century, the city, built of wood, was destroyed

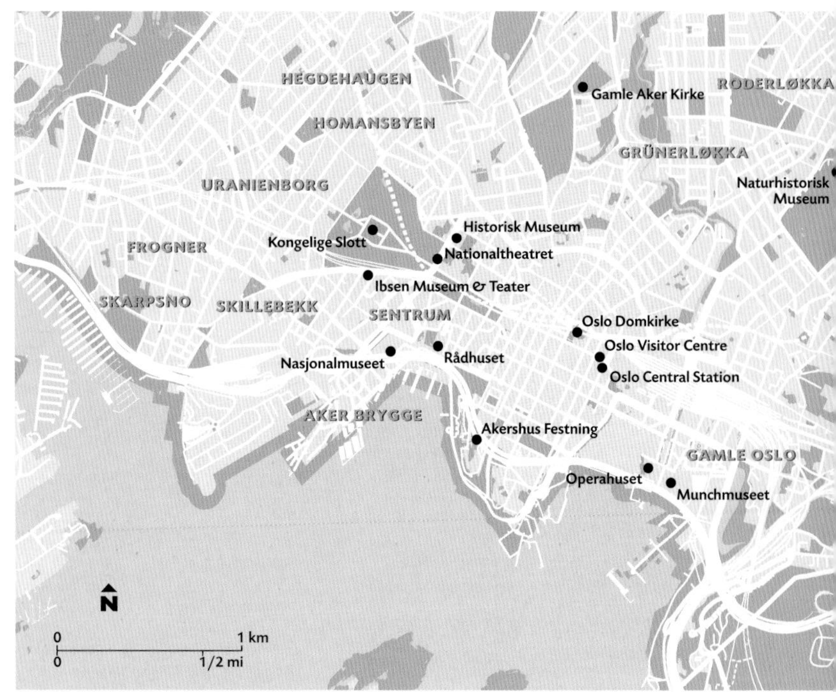

by fire and then rebuilt and renamed Christiania, in honor of Denmark's King Christian IV. In the 19th century it became the capital, but within the Kingdom of Sweden and Norway, whose center was in Stockholm. In the middle of the century, industrialization began, which brought the railway, horse-drawn streetcars, and then electric ones. In 1905, it was restored as the capital of an independent Norway, and in 1925 it regained its former name, Oslo. In 1948, it absorbed the metropolitan area, and in 1966, the first subway line opened.

Information, maps, free Wi-Fi, tips, tickets for events, transportation, and tours can be found in the **Oslo Visitor Centre.**

Downtown Oslo

The center of Oslo roughly stretches between the Aker Brygge district to the west, the Royal Palace to the north, and the Central Station to the east. The icon of 20th-century Oslo

Oslo Visitor Centre ✉ Jernbanetorget 1 ☎ 231 06 200 🕒 June–Aug., Mon.–Sat. 8:30 a.m.–6 p.m., Sun. 9 a.m.–5 p.m.; Sept.–May, Mon.–Sat. 9 a.m.–6 p.m., Sun. 9 a.m.–4 p.m. **visitoslo.com/en**

is undoubtedly the **Rådhuset,** or City Hall, a strong mark of the city's architecture and its link to the centers of power. It was Mayor Heyerdahl who wanted it there, instead of in the "vice" district of Pipervika. Arnstein and Poulsson were put in charge of the project in 1920, which was built in the 1930s and 1940s. The Rådhuset opened in 1950, on the 900th anniversary of the founding of the city. It is an excellent representation of Norwegian architecture and decorative arts of the time for the essential lines of the central building and towers, the 28-foot (8.5 m) clock on the right tower, and the decorations in the courtyards and halls, which were part of a competition between artists and craftsmen from all over Norway. It tells the story of the city from a political, folk, and labor perspective, with city symbols like the Young Man of Oslo, the Swan Fountain, and the Court of Honor. The decoration expresses the restlessness of existence, which is marvelously conveyed in Munch's painting *Life* in Munch Hall. Also worth seeing are the Astronomical Clock and the wooden bas-reliefs telling the saga of the *Edda* (made by sculptor Werenskiold and located in the Court of Honor), the Hall of Festivities (where the Nobel Peace Prize is awarded each year on December 10) with a large canvas by Sørensen and frescoes in the galleries, and the Banquet Hall. In the eastern tower is

Rådhuset ✉ Rådhusplassen 1 ☎ 218 02 180 🕒 9 a.m.–4 p.m., guided tours in English **oslo.kommune.no**

The Rådhuset, or Oslo City Hall

a carillon with bells that play music every hour, from 7 a.m. to midnight. On summer Sundays at 3 p.m., a real concert is put on.

In front of Rådhusplassen is the Rådhusbrygge marina, enclosed by the Rådhuset towers, the fortress, and Aker Brygge. Ferries to Bygdøy and boats that tour the fjord depart from its four piers. The sailing ship *Christian Radich,* a magnificent three-masted vessel from the 1930s that has been a training ship for decades, is moored at the Akershus pier and is available for a cruise of the fjord. The port offers various rental options, from boats to electric catamarans. In summer, this area is decked out in bright colors, flowers, tents, and umbrellas, and becomes a waterfront promenade full of gastronomic delights.

Nearby stands the new **Nasjonalmuseet,** the National Museum, which displays not only its beautiful architecture but also a new concept: bringing different aspects of Norwegian culture, such as art, design, and architecture, together in one place. In short, it is speaking to the world, saying, "We are here too; this is our cultural heritage."

The museum, designed by architect Schuwerk, opened in 2022 and offers a smarter way of looking at things, mixing styles, trends, currents, so it is easier to follow the flow of culture, including material culture. The second floor is dedicated to visual arts, from the 15th century to the present. Comparing the Flemish landscapes of the Golden Age with Dahl's early 19th-century Norwegian landscapes is eye-opening. So is putting sculptures, paintings, installations, and other objects in the same space. To have artistic styles and fashions from other times interact with each other, and to have international works in dialogue with a very large collection of more than 6,500 pieces of art, architecture, and design, spanning a period of 3,000 years, is an endeavor that achieves two things: to present Norwegian culture in an original way, which is necessary in the global arena, and, as mentioned above, to consolidate a local sense of identity. Across just two floors, there are about 80 exhibition rooms. Design and crafts are on the first floor, from antiquity to the present, while art is located on the second floor, along with two rooms for architecture. Among the masterpieces on display are a version of Van Gogh's *Self-Portrait,* works by El Greco, Renoir, Monet, Cézanne, Degas, Gauguin, Picasso, Braque, and Matisse. Other collections not to miss include the largest non-Italian collection of Artemisia Gentileschi, the Norwegian tapestry of Baldishol, one of the oldest in Europe (dated between 1040 and 1190), the dress collections of Queens Maud and Sonja, and a history of Norwegian fashion. In addition to this extensive exhibition,

Nasjonalmuseet ✉ Brynjulf Bulls plass 3 ☎ 219 82 000 🕒 Tues.–Wed. 10 a.m.–8 p.m., Thurs.–Sun. 10 a.m.–5 p.m. **nasjonalmuseet.no**

The new Nasjonalmuseet opened in 2022.

Norwegian painting is also on display, from the classics to the proto-romantics and the romantics, such as Johan Christian Dahl, touching also on realism and impressionism with the works of Werenskiold and Krohg. Finally, an entire room is dedicated to Munch: Eighteen of his works are on display there, including the 1893 version of *The Scream,* a version of *Madonna,* the beautiful *Dance of Life, Girls on the Pier, The Sick Maiden,* and *Ashes.*

In front of the National Museum is the old **Nobels Fredssenter** building, the Nobel Peace Center, which tells the story of Alfred Nobel, the Prize he established, and those who have won it over the years. Nearby is **The Viking Planet,** a digital museum for learning and fun. If you like immersion experiences, virtual reality, gaming, holograms, reconstruction of objects–in short, a movie full of sailors and warriors–this is for you.

A short distance away is the **Konserthus,** the Concert Palace, an arena that hosts cultural events of different musical genres, equipped with two halls and a large organ. It is the main stage of the Oslo Filharmonien.

To the west is Aker Brygge, a major project that has transformed old wharves, warehouses, and shipyards into housing, commercial, and office

Nobels Fredssenter ✉ Brynjulf Bulls plass 1 🕒 Tues.–Sun. 11 a.m.–5 p.m. **nobelpeacecenter.org • The Viking Planet** ✉ Fridtjof Nansens plass 4 ☎ 469 42 495 🕒 Mon.–Fri. 10 a.m.–5 p.m., Sat.–Sun. 10 a.m.–6 p.m. **thevikingplanet.com • Konserthus** ✉ Munkedamsveien 14 ☎ 231 13 111 **oslokonserthus.no**

spaces. Recovering the 19th-century redbrick structures, the designers added the glass, wood, and steel of recent Scandinavian architecture. In place of the docks today are movie theaters, restaurants, stores, a theater, bars with busy patios, and a beautiful waterfront. Take the bridge to reach the Tjuvholmen District, where you can find art galleries, restaurants, and nightclubs. The neighborhood is also home to The Sneak Peak, a tower with a glass elevator that rises to 177 feet (54 m), allowing you to see Oslo from above. Nearby is the unique exhibition **The Salmon.** Its information center has a live stream from the North, showing what's happening in salmon farming and aquaculture. It shows visitors the history of salmon, and you can even try some at their restaurant.

Not far away is the magnificent **Astrup Fearnley Museet,** a museum of modern and contemporary art opened in 1993, which has been located in a new building designed by Renzo Piano since 2012. Here, you will find artists like Hirst, Neshat, and Cai Guo Qiang, as well as great temporary exhibitions. It is a museum as it should be, taking into consideration light, space, and display, and not forgetting the location.

The Salmon ✉ Strandpromenaden 11 🕒 Sun.–Tues. 11:30 a.m.–6 p.m., Wed.–Sat. 11:30 a.m.–10 p.m. **thesalmon.no • Astrup Fearnley Museet** ✉ Strandpromenaden 2 ☎ 229 36 060 🕒 Tues., Wed., Fri. noon–5 p.m., Thurs. noon–7 p.m., Sat.–Sun. 11 a.m.–5 p.m., guided tours in English **afmuseet.no**

Aker Brygge is a vibrant, redeveloped neighborhood.

The facade of the Kongelige Slott, the Royal Palace

Farther north, beyond Rådhuset, is the **Kongelige Slott,** the Royal Palace. Built starting in 1824 and completed in 1848, it is surrounded by a public park with no fences, emphasizing the "familiarity" Norwegians have with the monarchy. A palace with simple lines, it was commissioned by Charles XIV John, then king of Sweden and Norway, and still serves as a royal residence from September to May. On May 17, a national holiday, the king greets children from the balcony. Only the park, Slottsparken, known for its statues, can be visited. You can also watch the changing of the guard every day at 1:30 p.m.

On the north side of the park is **Kunstnernes Hus,** the Artists' Palace, dating from 1930 and considered a masterpiece of functionalist architecture. It is an independent institution that hosts exhibitions on Norwegian and international art and cinema; it also has a nice café-restaurant. To the west stands the Norwegian Nobel Institute, home to the committee that awards the Nobel Peace Prize each year (all other Nobels are awarded in Stockholm). At the entrance are two busts of Alfred Nobel, one of them the work of Gustav Vigeland.

Right next to the entrance to Slottsparken is the **Historisk Museum,** the Historical Museum, in a Jugendstil building containing valuable collections of gold and silver jewelry from prehistoric times to the Viking

Kongelige Slott ✉ Slottsplassen 1 **kongehuset.no • Kunstnernes Hus** ✉ Wergelandsveien 17 ☎ 228 53 410 🕒 Tues.–Sun. 11 a.m.–5 p.m., Thurs. until 7 p.m. **kunstnerneshus.no • Historisk Museum** ✉ Frederiksgate 2 ☎ 228 519 00 🕒 May–Sept., Tues.–Sun. 10 a.m.–5 p.m., Thurs. until 6 p.m.; Oct.–Apr., Tues.–Sun. 11 a.m.–4 p.m., Thurs. until 8 p.m. **historiskmuseum.no**

The Nationaltheatret at sunset

age (Treasure Room), sacred art from medieval churches (12th and 13th centuries, beautiful paintings from the Ål Church), an ethnographic section telling the story of the Inuit people through objects collected by Amundsen, and a collection of coins, seals, and medals from around the world.

Not far stands the **Nationaltheatret,** the National Theater, built in 1899 by architect Henrik Bull. The theater is considered a shrine to Henrik Ibsen, not only because the writer himself invested money in it, or because his plays still hold sway there today, but mainly because Norwegian theater began with Ibsen and has been profoundly influenced by him ever since. Twenty-one of his plays have been performed there, *Peer Gynt* 700 times, and *A Doll's House* just as many. Since 1990, it has been home to the International Ibsenian Festival, which is held every two years. The rococo auditorium offers a magnificent view, beautiful staircase, and ceiling with a five-part cycle by Eivind Nielsen. Also worth seeing are portraits of artists and, at the entrance, statues of the two rivals, Ibsen and Bjørnstjerne Bjørnson. Also not far away is the **Ibsen Museum & Teater,** the Oslo apartment where Ibsen lived from 1895 until his death in 1906. The studio still features the original furniture.

Nationaltheatret ✉ Johanne Dybwads plass 1 ☎ 220 01 400 **nationaltheatret.no • Ibsen Museum & Teater** ✉ Henrik Ibsens Gate 26 🕒 July–Sept. 11 a.m.–6 p.m.; Oct.–Dec. Mon.–Thurs. & Sat.–Sun. 11 a.m.–4 p.m. **ibsenmt.no**

Continuing on a tour of the Old Town, you will encounter Karl Johans gate, the city's main street, which connects from east to west the Central Station with the parliament, the university, the National Theater, and the Royal Palace. This is the bourgeois heart of Oslo. Half of the street is pedestrianized and full of boutiques; it is also the realm of buskers and street artists. Stop at the Grand Hotel, no. 31, a historic building where artists, businessmen, and politicians once gathered, and the site of the Nobel Peace Prize banquet on December 10. No. 47 is the university, built in the mid-19th century. The Great Hall was frescoed by Munch between 1910 and 1916, with 11 scenes, including *The Sun*. Here, you can attend readings and concerts and enjoy guided tours. In front is the tree-lined Studenterlunden, the Student Garden, with flower beds, fountains, and statues.

Ibsen Walk

The city pays tribute to Norway's greatest internationally renowned playwright by inviting people to take a walk with Ibsen from his house museum, to the Grand Café where artists met, the National Theater he inaugurated, and the Æreslunden cemetery, where he rests. Along the daily route he took between his home and the Grand Café, there are 69 quotes from his work placed on the city's sidewalks.

The Stortinget, also built in the mid-19th century and embellished inside with works by Norwegian artists, is the seat of parliament and hosts its sessions. It can be visited on request in summer. On the west side of the building is a garden, the Eidsvolls plass and, farther down, the Spikersuppa, a fountain that turns into a skating rink in winter.

Then, passing by the parliament and toward the station, you will encounter the Stortorvet (Great Square), a square that houses a flower market and a statue of Christian IV, and then the **Oslo Domkirke,** the cathedral, erected in the late 17th century but rebuilt in the mid-19th century and redecorated inside in the 20th century. Do check out the bronze doors by Dagfin Werenskiold that narrate the Sermon on the Mount, the baroque furnishings, the stained glass windows by Emanuel Vigeland (1910), and a 17th-century Dutch altarpiece. The church is dedicated to Our Savior. To the rear of the cathedral stands the Basarhallene, a lodge built between 1841 and 1858 that houses antique and craft stores.

East Oslo

East of the harbor is where the 17th-century part of the city begins, what is still called Kvadraturen, literally "square city," a checkerboard-shaped

Oslo Domkirke ✉ Stortorvet 1 ☎ 236 29 010 🕒 Mon.–Sun. 10 a.m.–4 p.m., Fri. 4 p.m.–11:30 p.m.

Nobel Prize Walk

This route takes you to all the places associated with the Nobel Peace Prize, chosen and awarded at the Oslo City Hall. It starts at the City Hall (Rådhuset), whose Hall of Festivities hosts the award ceremony each year in the presence of the royal family. You then visit the Great Hall of the University with works by Munch, where the awards were once presented, and then the Grand Hotel, where the winner of the year has a suite. You can also make a stop at the Nobel Institute, home of the committee that decrees the winner.

neighborhood built by Danish King Christian IV after the great fire of 1624. The area lies roughly between the Akershus Festning and Central Station. On the Rådhusgata is Christiania Torv, a square where a giant metal hand sculpture points to the ground to emphasize the king's desire to build from there.

This part of the city has many 17th-century buildings to admire, including the Engebret Café, the oldest in Oslo, and the first City Hall. And then there's Gamle Logen, a beautiful concert hall at Grev Wedels plass 2. The nearby Bankplassen (or Bank Square) is considered one of the most beautiful for its neo-Gothic and neoclassical buildings. In addition to the Engebret Café, the Nasjonalmuseet-Arkitektur (Museum of Architecture), which is part of the National Museum, is located here, housed in the former Norges Bank building, built in 1830 and then supplemented by a new building in 2008 to house collections of drawings, models, objects, plans, and photos from the 19th century to the present.

Moving toward the waterfront, one is fascinated by the **Akershus Festning** (Akershus Fortress), which dominates the harbor. Built in 1299 as a royal residence, it was later destroyed and rebuilt under King Christian IV. Today it is used as a government reception venue and houses models of Christiania from the 17th to mid-19th century, with maps, charts, and views of the city. The halls of the fortress are home to two other museums. The first, Norges Hjemmefrontmuseum, chronicles the Nazi occupation of the country during World War II and the subsequent Norwegian response. The second, Forsvarmuseet, illustrates military history from the Vikings to the last war. The centerpiece of the fortress is the *slott* (Castle), with its church, dining and reception rooms, and the Royal Mausoleum. In addition to enjoying a beautiful view of the harbor and Aker Brygge, you can watch the changing of the guard at 1:30 p.m.

Continuing eastward, in the bay area called Bjørvika, we find the two main icons of the waterfront skyline.

Akershus Festning ✉ Rådhusgata 32 ☎ 230 93 917 🕒 6 a.m.–9 p.m.
visitnorway.com/listings/akershus-fortress/432

The Operahuset overlooks the sea.

Both fill a gap and highlight a new characteristic of Oslo, which is less and less just Norwegian and more international, in moderation. Both are meant to impress as architectural marvels. They play with geometric shapes, emphasized by the light of the stained glass windows, projected toward the fjord and beyond.

The first is the **Operahuset** (Opera House), designed by studio Snøhetta and opened in 2008–it won the European Union Architecture Prize the following year. Constructed of white granite, aluminum, and Carrara marble, it has a glass facade overlooking a wide plaza, which in turn leads out to the sea, and wings leading to the roof, where you can catch an incredible view. The interior is made of oak, and each seat has a screen to follow the plays in Norwegian and English. The curtain looks three-dimensional and was made by scanning pieces of crumpled aluminum foil and reproducing them on a larger scale. It is the home of the Norwegian Opera & Ballet and offers performances, concerts, and events, including ones outdoors. It's as if the commissioners asked the designers to create a symbol for the new Oslo, a building that unites high and low, socioculturally speaking.

The second iconic structure in the area is the **Munchmuseet,** dedicated entirely to Norway's greatest painter. A collection of 1,100 paintings, 4,500

Operahuset ✉ Kirsten Flagstads plass 1 ☎ 214 22 121 🕒 Foyer Mon.-Sat. 11 a.m.–10 p.m., Sun. noon–9 p.m. **operaen.no • Munchmuseet** ✉ Edvard Munchs plass 1 ☎ 234 93 500 🕒 Sun.–Tues. 10 a.m.–6 p.m., Wed.–Sat. 10 a.m.–9 p.m. **munchmuseet.no**

The Scream by Edvard Munch (1893)

drawings and 18,000 prints, sculptures, letters, and books are displayed on a rotating basis. Munch, who believed one had to paint "people who live, breathe, feel, suffer, love," is the pioneer of expressionism, the only Norwegian painter to have influenced European art. Some of his masterpieces on display include *Melancholy* (1891), *Madonna* (1894), *Anxiety* (1894), *Separation* (1896), *Jealousy* (1907), *Starry Night* (1922), and *Girls on the Bridge* (1927). There is also *The Scream (Skriket)* from 1893; eight versions are held in the museum (one oil tempera, one drawing, and six lithographs). One version is displayed, in rotation, on the fourth floor to preserve them from deterioration. Admission is limited, so it is necessary to book your visit in advance.

In front of the museum is Opera Beach, where you can swim or enjoy one of the picnic baskets prepared at the museum café. Or stop by Munch Brygge, a shopping center with innovative architecture. But what is not innovative in the birthplace of functionalism?

Another evolving project near the Munchmuseet is Oslobukta, a kind of district grouping neighborhood stores, galleries, bars, restaurants, and sports centers that replaces an actual mall. Moving onto Langkaia, you find SALT, a nomadic art project consisting of a series of wooden buildings by architect Rintala that bring together art, food, music, and architecture.

Then, behind the Opera, at Anne-Cath Vetslys plass 1, stands the new Deichman Bjørvika, the main branch of the public library. A remarkable building that hosts readings, art, and cultural events, it has a terrace to enjoy yet another city vista. But it is the nearby Barcode, on Dronning Eufemias gate, that attracts the most attention. Designed not surprisingly by MVRDV of Rotterdam, the set of 12 skyscrapers, varying in height and width, gives the impression of a barcode, as the name implies. The buildings are different in so many details, each original by nature.

Across the bay, the transformation of Sørenga's old docks has resulted in a pleasant neighborhood full of buildings with interesting details, canals, gardens, bars, and restaurants, and, at the far end, the Sørenga Sjøbad, an outdoor saltwater pool with beaches in summer and saunas in winter.

In the center of the bay stands Monica Bonvicini's 39-foot-high (12 m) installation *She Lies,* resting on a moving platform that sways to the rhythm of the tide and winds, changing the perception it conveys due to the light passing through the glass. In this sense, it lies, as the title says, because it is never the same.

Farther east, **Ekebergparken** is a beautiful forested park that contains an incredible sculpture collection, including works by Hirst, Graham, Lucas, Bourgeois, and Cragg, to name a few. But also, if we go classical, Rodin, Renoir, Vigeland, Dalí, and Botero. And, most significantly, the perceptual installations of James Turrell, master of land art, who has outdone himself here by creating *Skyspace,* a container that makes natural light interact with artificial light, and which at dawn and dusk offers special perceptual experiences, as well as *Ganzfeld: Double Vision,* a unique play of light and color.

Ekebergparken ✉ Kongsveien 23 ☎ 214 21 919 🕒 Ganzfeld, free guided tour, Sun. 10 a.m.–4 p.m. **ekebergparken.com**

The Munchmuseet is dedicated to the foremost Norwegian painter.

Oslofjord offers a lot in terms of outdoor activities.

The fjord is also home to several islands that can be reached from Rådhusbrygge and visited by an organized tour. The closest are Hovedøya, with forests, beaches, and the ruins of the Cistercian monastery built in 1147 by monks who came from Kirkstead, England, and then burned in 1532; Bleikøya, part nature reserve; and Lindøya, a place of summer residences that also boasts a 1949 Olympic swimming pool.

Moving northeastward into Gamle Oslo, one of the city's 15 districts, we find Ruinparken, a part of medieval Oslo in which you can

EXPERIENCE: Exploring Oslofjord

From the docks, you can book many activities in the nearby fjord. You can rent a Viking rowboat, take Jet Skis or kayaks, hop on a ferry to visit the islands for a hike, or rent a sailboat or electric yacht. There is no shortage of fast boat rides for groups, or the chance to go fishing on a guided boat tour, pedal along the coast to a beach, or have dinner, brunch, or appetizers on an electric boat. Last, take a break in a sauna overlooking the fjord or on a floating platform.

find the remains of the St. Hallvard Cathedral (11th century), dedicated to the city's patron saint; the St. Olav Monastery (13th century); and a cruciform church (14th century). Next to the park stands the Oslo Ladegård (Bishop's Palace) erected in the 13th century but rebuilt in the 16th century as the seat of the burgomaster. The present building dates from 1725 and displays plastic models and finds from medieval Oslo. The reception hall has been restored and displays antique furniture and paintings.

Northeast Oslo

In the northeastern part of the city, we encounter the Vaterland District, which encompasses the Sentralstasjon (Oslo S) area (Central Station), from which trains depart for the rest of the country, Sweden, and Europe; Storgata Street, and down to the Akerselva River. Also in the same area are the Oslo Bussterminal (bus terminal); the Oslo City, Byporten, and the Galleri Oslo shopping centers; the Spektrum concert hall, which also houses the Nobel concert hall; the Radisson Blu Plaza Hotel; and the Posthuset building.

Connecting the harbor with the northeastern districts is Akersgata, the street where you can find Garborg square; Trefoldighetskirken, or the 19th-century Trinity Church; the Civic Library, founded in the late 18th century; and the Swedish Margareta Church. Another important thoroughfare is Akersveien, which connects Akershus Fortress with Oslo's oldest church, **Gamle Aker Kirke.** Built in 1080 in the Romanesque style, it has a three-aisled interior and is still used today as a parish and concert venue. Also on Akersveien are the Catholic cathedral of St. Olav and the wooden houses of Bergfjerdingen, an old artisan and working-class district. These are houses from the 18th and early 19th centuries, which is why as many as 53 buildings are protected as historical monuments.

Along the Akerselva, on the other hand, is the new Vulkan District, designed by Snøhetta. It is an area designed primarily for pedestrians and cyclists, and is meant to limit environmental impact in every way. The neighborhood includes a local power plant to harness geothermal energy—reaching 984 feet (300 m) below ground—solar panels, hotels, schools, offices, cultural spaces, restaurants, stores, and apartments. In short, a place where everything is available on foot in just 15 minutes.

Farther east is Grünerløkka, a neighborhood that has changed appearance, becoming one of the trendiest, with hip bars, street art, designer boutiques, and stylish secondhand shops. An influencer's paradise. There are also beautiful pedestrian paths and small parks along the Akerselva and, needless to say, chic industrial concert venues.

In the same area, on Sars' gate, stand the university museums, grouped under the **Naturhistorisk Museum** (Museum of Natural History), which includes zoological collections from various parts of the world, with a section dedicated to Norwegian fauna. There are also geological collections, with a model of Oslo's soil, and paleontology collections. Also part of the complex is the Botanisk Hage (Botanical Garden), known for its waterfalls, forest, more than 1,000 local plants, and exotic greenhouse. Since it is a university museum, it is closely linked to both outreach and research.

Also in the northeast, but considerably farther away, is the interesting **Norsk Teknisk Museum** (Museum of Science and Technology), with an extensive collection of objects, models, and illustrations that tell the story of the development of technologies. Devoted to communications and telecommunications from the Vikings to the present, the Teknoteket section has 100 interactive installations, including one to test your reaction time. Others explain how blood flows through the body and demonstrate 3D printing. The **National Museum of Medicine** covers the history of public health in Norway since 1850.

Gamle Aker Kirke ✉ Akersbakken 26 🕒 Thurs. 4–6 p.m. **visitoslo.com/en/product/?tlp=2978293** • **Naturhistorisk Museum** ✉ Sars'gate 1 ☎ 228 51 630 🕒 Museum 10 a.m.–5 p.m., botanical garden 7 a.m.–5 p.m. **nhm.uio.no** • **Norsk Teknisk Museum** ✉ Kjelsåsveien 143 ☎ 227 96 000 🕒 Tues.–Fri. 9 a.m.–4 p.m., Sat.–Sun. 10 a.m.–5 p.m. **tekniskmuseum.no**

Vigelandsparken features sculptures by Gustav Vigeland.

Northwest Oslo

Just behind the Royal Palace, toward the northwest, lies the Uranienborg District, the name of which is taken from none other than the Danish astronomical observatory on the island of Ven, now Swedish, or Tycho Brahe's laboratory. The neighborhood shares its name with the local park and church. The latter also has stained glass windows made by Emanuel Vigeland.

Farther out, in Frogner, stretches the large **Vigelandsparken,** which displays more than 200 granite, bronze, and wrought iron sculptures containing 671 characters that depict the story of life. They were built in the 1920s based on models developed by Gustav Vigeland. The sculptor's workshop-home, **Vigeland Museet,** with his drawings and engravings, is a must-see.

Also in the park, the **Bymuseet** (City Museum), in an 18th-century manor house, tells the story of Oslo-Christiania through models, paintings, and objects. The collection privileges the city of the 19th and 20th centuries, its houses, streets, transportation, trade, and civil and religious life. One corner is devoted to Ibsen,

Vigelandsparken ✉ Frognerparken **vigeland.museum.no/vigelandsparken**
Vigeland Museet ✉ Nobels gate 32 ☎ 234 93 700 🕒 Sept.–Apr., Tues.–Sun. noon–6 p.m.; May–Aug. 10 a.m.–5 p.m.
Bymuseet ✉ Frognerveien 67 ☎ 232 84 170 🕒 Tues.–Sun. 11 a.m.–6 p.m., Thurs. until 7 p.m. **oslomuseum.no**

with the table, armchair, and glasses reserved for him at the Grand Café. The Bymuseet also includes the Teatermuseet (Theater Museum), which displays costumes, sets, paintings, photos, and caricatures illustrating the history of theater from the beginning of the 19th century.

Finally, in the northeast part of the park is the **Skøytemuseet** (Ice Skating Museum), which tells the story of skating and Norwegian skaters.

In the northeast is the **Internasjonale Barnekunstmuseet** (International Museum of Children's Art), an original exhibition of drawings, paintings, ceramics, sculptures, textiles, and general crafts made by children from 180 different countries. It's a picture of the world from the eyes of its youngest inhabitants.

On the way to Holmenkollen is the **Emanuel Vigeland Museum,** dedicated to the sculptor's brother, famous mostly for his stained glass windows. If you love the genre, it is worth a visit. There is a large vaulted room with a painted cycle of life depicting man from cradle to deathbed, with the interlude of procreation, plus drawings, portraits, sketches, and bronze statues that reinforce the mystery of life.

Continuing northwest we come to the hill that is perhaps the city's greatest icon: Holmenkollen, a center for many things but most importantly national identity, with a place in the hearts of its citizens. At the center is the Holmenkollen Nasjonalanlegg ski arena, where competitive ski jumping was born in 1892. The *Morgenbladet* newspaper of those days reported that there were 20,000 spectators and that the King's Cup was won by Svein Sollid of Morgedal. Since then, the jump has been rebuilt several

Skøytemuseet ✉ Middelthunsgate 26 🕒 Tues. 10 a.m.–2 p.m., Sun. noon–3 p.m. **skoytemuseet.no • Internasjonale Barnekunstmuseet** ✉ Lille Frøens vei 4 ☎ 226 91 777 🕒 Tues.–Thurs. 9:30 a.m.–2 p.m., Sat.–Sun. 11 a.m.–4 p.m. **barnekunst.no • Emanuel Vigeland Museum** ✉ Grimelundsveien 8 🕒 Sun. 11 a.m.–4 p.m., reservations: **emanuelvigeland.museum.no**

The ski jump in Holmenkollen was built in 2011.

times, always improving technique and comfort. The current tower, built in 2011 by Danish architects JDS, is 196 feet (60 m) high and ends in a stadium surrounded by stands that can accommodate 30,000 spectators. Athletes walk up the long staircase and plunge headlong down the 338-foot (100 m) runway before taking off. The record flight distance is 472 feet (144 m), set in 2019 by a Norwegian athlete, Robert Johansson. The women's record is only 32 feet (10 m) shorter, held by Sara Takanashi of Japan.

The competition, Holmenkollen Ski Festival, takes place in March and is an unforgettable spectacle in terms of competitiveness and audience participation. However, cross-country skiing, biathlon, and Nordic combined are also practiced in Holmenkollen. It is the Norwegian way of doing skiing. The facility hosts many international competitions, and when there are no competitions, one can climb the tower to admire the view. Those who feel up to it can also zip-line or abseil down the tower.

King Olav V also participated in the ski jumping competitions in 1922, and since the beginning, the royal family has watched the competitions from their private box.

(continued on p. 89)

HUMANITY ACCORDING TO GUSTAV VIGELAND

Vigelandsparken is a place of psychology and poetry, where the saga of humankind is told through a 55-foot (17 m) monolith surrounded by 36 granite groups, half a mile (850 m) of promenade, and 212 sculptures in bronze, granite, and iron.

One of the 212 sculptures in the park

What artist has had as much freedom as Gustav Vigeland? Young Norway and its capital, Christiania at the time, after half a millennium of foreign domination, needed a grand artistic project that would reaffirm the nation's presence in world culture. So Vigeland was given money and, above all, time to realize his work: a "cycle of life" that slowly grew larger, expanding into an endless discourse, like life itself. Certainly his fiercely pietistic father—and all that comes with that—or his religious crises drowned in alcohol did not help him.

It did help him artistically, however, to frequent Rodin in Paris. Vigelandsparken grew out of Vigeland's concept of humankind, realistic and intimate, and this is what he portrayed in his sculptures: not gods, not heroes, but humans. Better yet, humans caught in certain moments of life. His work is a review of universal moods: love, hate, loneliness, solidarity, joy, play, tenderness. There is also no shortage of relationships, motherhood, fatherhood, the cycle of birth, the restlessness of the teenage years, the anxieties of old age, the disagreement between men and women, the dreams of man, anger, and despair. Included among the park's panoply are six men of different ages holding together a vessel filled with water. The attitude in bearing the "burden of life" is different, but the water continues to inexorably flow downward, toward the roots, from which another cycle develops, from birth to death.

The heart of the park, however, is the monolith and its 121 figures, which raise a tangle of suffering humanity to the sky, on the top of which are placed children, a symbol of hope for the future.

Be sure to check out the bronze statue of King Olav V skiing alongside his dog; the beautiful houses in the neighborhood below the hill; the Holmenkollen Park Hotel's wooden neo-Gothic building; Skiforeningen (Oslo's ski club), the most prestigious in the country; the simulator at the base of the jump that lets you experience the thrill of the incredible jump; and the Frognerseteren restaurant and the chapel, both made of wood. And of course, there is a great view of the fjord and the Marka forests.

Near the facility is the **Skimuseet** (Ski Museum), which just turned 100 years old. Opened in December 1923, it is the oldest in the world and tells the story of 4,000 years of skiing, from prehistoric drawings and Viking skis to the present day. It also displays equipment from the polar expeditions of Nansen and Amundsen.

Farther out, near Frognerseteren Metro Station 1, is **Rosenslottet** (Rose Castle), an art installation that chronicles the dark periods of the 20th century, anti-Semitism, the Nazi occupation, the resistance, and Liberation. The area houses 200 paintings by artist Vebjørn Sand and sculptures by his brother Eimund.

Skimuseet ✉ Kongeveien 5 ☎ 916 71 947 🕒 10 a.m.–4 p.m. (summer 10 a.m.–5 p.m.), Thurs. until 8 p.m. **skiforeningen.no** • **Rosenslottet** ✉ located in forest near Frognerseteren Station ☎ 901 13 205 🕒 winter 11 a.m.–5 p.m.; summer 10 a.m.–6 p.m., Thurs. until 8 p.m. **roseslottet.no**

Oscarshall is the royal family's summer residence.

To the west, on Bogstad Lake, stands Bogstad Gård, the vast, 18th-century home of the then prime minister in which furniture, paintings, and, porcelain are displayed. It was one of the centers of Norwegian politics for an entire century, as well as being the first English-style romantic park conceived in Norway.

West Oslo, Bygdøy

The Bygdøy Peninsula is one of the city's most exclusive areas. Accessible by boat from Rådhusbrygge, it is home to the Royal Farm and stables, noble palaces, villas, embassies, beaches, marinas, and museums.

Sights include **Oscarshall,** the summer residence of the royal family, built in the English Gothic style in 1847–1852 at the behest of King Oscar I. Inside are 19th-century furniture and a collection of paintings from Norway's Romantic period. You can also visit the park. Several gems have since found a home on Bygdøy, outside the city, perhaps because at the time there was not much belief in their tourist potential. The largest, however, is temporarily closed for renovations that will create a new semicircular building with triple the space: the Vikingskipshuset (Museum of Viking Ships). The new space, to open in 2026, will be called Vikingstidsmuseet (Viking Age Museum); in addition to three ships and numerous objects, it will offer a multimedia tour to showcase the country's heritage. It is sure to be spectacular, especially the three ships–*Gokstad, Oseberg,* and *Tune*–which date back to the ninth century and have provided answers to the many questions about the Vikings and their construction techniques. Discovered in the fjord region of the capital between 1867 and 1904, the oak vessels were grave goods of influential figures of the early Viking period, perhaps even royal entou-

Oscarshall ✉ Oscarshallveien 15, Bygdøy ☎ 220 48 700 🕒 summer, Tues.–Sun. 11 a.m.–4 p.m., guided tours in English **royalcourt.no**

Five Spectacular Views

Where is the best place to take in all the views of the capital?

1. The fjord, possibly from an electric catamaran. From here, you get the full impact of the city: the skyline is more Singaporean than Scandinavian.
2. Holmenkollen, more specifically the ski jump. It's like peeking backstage, seeing the city from behind, with low houses in the foreground and the fjord beyond.
3. Along the Aker River, where it connects Grünerløkka with the Vulkan neighborhood and its wooden working-class houses.
4. One of the new terraces: the Opera, the Munchmuseet, or the Deichman Library in Bjõrvika.
5. Summit Bar at the Radisson Blu or Eight Rooftop Bar at the Grand Hotel.

Fram Museet is dedicated to the ship of Nansen and Amundsen.

rage. Interred in burial mounds, they endured for a thousand years underground. Sometimes visited by thieves before their discovery, the ships were buried with artistic and everyday objects like sleds and a decorated carriage. Once found, the ships were meticulously reconstructed.

Another attraction on the peninsula is the **Fram Museet,** which tells the story of the 1892 ship of the same name that united Nansen and Amundsen, two exceptional men who ventured to the far extremes of the northern and southern latitudes by sea. It was a special destiny considering that the ship was built by the legendary Colin Archer and had also sailed the seas of Greenland. The *Fram* was carefully restored to its sturdy original state as a polar ship. The story of Norway's Arctic and Antarctic explorations is told in the area around the ship.

Next door, the **Kon-Tiki Museet** showcases the other face of exploration: the legend of Thor Heyerdahl, an ethnologist and anthropologist who carried out expeditions across three oceans in as many boats built with the ancient materials and techniques of which he was a passionate scholar. He challenged the sea and official theories, which held that contact between ancient civilizations

Fram Museet ✉ Bygdøynesveien 39 ☎ 232 82 950 🕒 summer, Mon.–Sun. 9:30 a.m.–6 p.m.; rest of year, Mon.–Sun. 10 a.m.–5 p.m. **frammuseum.no**
Kon-Tiki Museet ✉ Bygdøynesveien 36 ☎ 230 86 767 🕒 May 10 a.m.–6 p.m.; June–Aug. 9:30 a.m.–6 p.m.; Sept.–Apr. 10 a.m.–5 p.m. **kon-tiki.no**

Gol Church

separated by oceans was impossible. The *Kon-Tiki* (1947), a balsa raft, sailed across the Pacific from Peru to Polynesia; the *Ra II* (1970), made of papyrus, sailed from Morocco to the Caribbean; and the *Tigris,* made of reed, from the eponymous Iraqi river to Djibouti, passing through Oman and Pakistan. Only the first two vessels are preserved in the museum, along with a photographic history, some artifacts, and an explanation of the fascinating theory that hypothesizes a connection between the peoples at the beginning of history, well before the age of wooden ships.

The third place to visit is the nearby **Norsk Maritimt Museum** (Norwegian Maritime Museum). Given that Norway is a nation of the sea, this museum offers a good portrait of that identity. The complex relationship between humans and the sea is explored through ships, ports, lighthouses, navigational instruments, life on board, rescues and shipwrecks, passenger transport, maritime archaeology, and the evolution of materials and techniques. Also on display is the *Gjøa,* the polar vessel with which Amundsen tackled the famous Northwest Passage.

Another must-see is the **Norsk Folkemuseum** (Norwegian Folk Museum), an excellent picture of Norway, its rural and city architecture, crafts, and life in the past. In summer, the museum is brought to life by hundreds of performers playing music, dancing, cooking, and working as they once did. The complex consists of 140 buildings that represent the building techniques and styles of different Norwegian regions from the Middle Ages to the 21st century. On the hill is the reconstructed 12th-century Gol Church. Another section of the museum portrays 18th- and 19th-century Christiania, with a bourgeois house, pharmacy, and store. Inside are objects of rural and urban culture and a large fresco of everyday life. ■

Norsk Maritimt Museum ✉ Bygdøynesveien 37 ☎ 241 14 150 🕒 Apr.–Sept., daily 10 a.m.–5 p.m.; Oct.–Mar., Tues.–Sun. 11 a.m.–4 p.m. **marmuseum.no • Norsk Folkemuseum** ✉ Museumsveien 10 ☎ 221 23 700 🕒 May–Sept., daily 10 a.m.–5 p.m; Oct.–Apr., Tues.–Sun. 11 a.m.–4 p.m. **norskfolkemuseum.no**

GREATER OSLO

Oslo has a fairly large municipal territory. To the north lies the Marka, a belt of forests and lakes, a kind of green ring hugging the capital. To the west and southwest, on the other hand, are notable industrial features, some converted into art centers. Finally, to the southeast, you can follow the fjord, which extends toward the Swedish border.

Kistefos Museum, on the Randselva Riker

In the western part of Greater Oslo, more specifically on the Høvikodden Peninsula, along the fjord but a few kilometers from the city center, stands the **Henie-Onstad Kunstsenter** (Art Center), which has a large collection of international modern art. Figure skater and actress Sonja Henie, alongside her husband, conceived of an all-encompassing art center that holds concerts, performances, meetings, discussions, and exhibitions. The painting collection includes great modern and contemporary names, from Braque and Picasso to Miró, Klee, and Weidemann,

Henie-Onstad Kunstsenter ✉ Sonja Henies vei 31, Høvikodden
☎ 678 04 880 🕒 Tues.–Sun. 11 a.m.–5 p.m., Thurs. until 9 p.m. **hok.no**

who is considered by many the greatest contemporary Norwegian painter. Henie's collection of trophies completes the exhibition.

Continuing along the fjord, you come to Drammen some 24 miles (40 km) from Oslo, a town that uses the harbor on Drammensfjorden, parallel to that of the capital, for importing goods. Nearby, in Åmot, is **Blaafarveværket,** the Royal Factory. The factory was founded in 1776 to process cobalt mined nearby into a blue pigment to use in glass decorations, textiles, paper, and paints. By 1830, the factory produced 80 percent of the world's cobalt pigment. Ten years later a synthetic substance was made to replace cobalt; thus began the decline of the factory, which was saved from planned demolition in 1971. Today, it is possible to visit the factory, workshops, housing, and store selling glassware, ceramics, and gifts, as well as the nearby Haugfossen waterfall and cobalt mines that Danish King Christian VII had purchased for none other than Royal Copenhagen porcelain.

Farther northwest is **Bærums Verk,** a foundry dating from 1610 that processed iron, producing mainly stoves, which were exported for more than two centuries. The factory and workers' houses have been restored and now house a cast-iron stove museum and glassblowing workshops. There are also many stores and artisan shops. It is worth visiting for its pleasant atmosphere, old houses, streets, and a park that displays sculptures by Norwegian artists.

Continuing north, you come to Lake Randsfjorden, measuring 47 miles long (77 km). At its southern end is Jevnaker, which has a pleasant, well-preserved town center, and where you can find two gems: the **Kistefos Museum** and the Hadeland Glassverk. The former, on the Randselva River, is a museum with a very unusual structure and a bridge in the middle, connecting architecture, art, and industry. You can visit both the industrial museum in a late 19th-century paper mill, and a grand sculpture park, which contains works by Botero, Oldenburg, and Cragg, among others. The Hadeland Glassverk is an old glassworks dating from 1762 that is still in operation today. You can visit the workshops, see the glassblowers and molders at work, experience glassblowing, admire the collection of glassware from the 17th century to the present, visit the stores, and have lunch and a rest in the large garden. Children can also ride ponies.

Blaafarveværket ✉ Koboltveien 11, Åmot ☎ 327 78 800 🕒 May 11–Sept. 22 Tues.–Sun. 11 a.m.–5 p.m.; June 22–August 18 every day, **blaa.no**
Bærums Verk ✉ Verksgata 15 ☎ 671 30 018 🕒 Mon.–Fri 10 a.m.–8 p.m., Sat. 10 a.m.–6 p.m. **baerumsverk.no** • **Kistefos Museum** ✉ Samsmoveien 41, Jevnaker ☎ 613 10 383 🕒 late Apr.–mid Oct., Tues.–Fri. 11 a.m.–5 p.m., Sat.–Sun. 10 a.m.–5 p.m. **kistefosmuseum.com**
Hadeland Glassverk ✉ Glassverksveien 9, Jevnaker ☎ 613 16 400 🕒 Hours may vary **hadeland.com**

The King's Run

The Birkebeinerrennet *(birke beiner.no)* has taken place every year in March since World War II. The 34-mile (54 km) cross-country ski race from Rena to Lillehammer (see pp. 97–99) is reminiscent of the more famous Vasaloppet, but the event from which it is inspired happened well before that which gave rise to the Swedish race. In the 13th century, a civil war between supporters of the Baglers, the bishops' party that challenged the ruling family, and those of the Birkebeiner party loyal to the king forced the young heir to the throne to flee. He was taken by two Birkebeiner-skiers to safety in Rena. The child, Haakon Haakonsson, took the throne a few years later, restoring peace and unity to the country. The modern race, which tests the skills of more than 5,000 participants, comes from the future king's adventurous escape.

On the opposite shore of the lake, to the north, is the Dokka River delta, a protected wetland area for birds. The lake is rich with trout, providing an excellent opportunity for fishing. Also to the north but closer to the capital lies the Marka woodlands, which surround Oslo and other small towns with its lush green expanse. A protected municipal territory of 650 square miles (1,700 sq m), it is rich in forests and lakes, a great reserve of biodiversity. In winter, there are 280 miles (450 km) of cross-country ski trails, marked in red, some illuminated. In summer, these are trails, marked in blue, for walking or cycling, and the lakes are open for swimming. The Norwegian Trekking Association *(dnt.no/english)* also operates cabins open to the public for a rest, a meal, or a bed. For bike, e-bike, and mountain bike tours, you can contact Rouleurs of Oslo *(rouleur oslo.no)* and Offroad E-bike Adventure *(offroadebike.no)*.

Moving to the south side of the capital, an interesting place to visit is the **Roald Amundsens Hjem,** the home of the winner of the South Pole race, now a museum that chronicles the owner's passions and style. Farther out, toward the southern part of the fjord, is Drøbak, whose biggest attraction is Tregaardens Julehus (Santa's House), with a real Santa Claus, a post office where thousands of letters arrive from children from all over the world, and stores where you can find all things Christmas. You must then check out the village, its streets, and its wooden houses, which have been the refuge of many Norwegian artists, and the nearby beaches. Opposite Drøbak is a small island, on which you can visit Oscarsborg Festning, a fortress built in 1845 that provided the first resistance to the Nazi invasion in 1940.

Roald Amundsens Hjem ✉ Roald Amundsens vei 192, Svartskog
☎ 66 93 66 36 🕒 Aug.–Sept. Sat.–Sun. **mia.no/roaldamundsen**

About 24 miles (40 km) south of Drøbak lies Moss. Attractions here include the Konvensjonsgården, where the Moss Convention that united the Norwegian and Swedish crowns was signed in 1814, and the volcanic island of Jeløy, with its distinct vegetation. But the highlight of the area is Fredrikstad and its old town (Gamlebyen), which preserves fortifications and walls from the 17th century, with ramparts, moats, barracks, arsenal, and a church with a baroque interior. The 18th-century Slave Prison houses the city museum. The cobblestone streets are pedestrian-friendly and offer cafés, artisan stores, pottery, textiles, sculptures, theaters, galleries, concerts, and museums. ■

Five Themed Walks

These five themed walks offer unique perspectives on the city.

1. Middle Ages: Medieval Oslo is located in the eastern part of the modern city. Sites are found in Minneparken, entering from Bispegata. A park contains ruins of the Viking-Christian era, including St. Hallvard Cathedral, the bishop's residence, St. Mary's Church, Kongsgården, the Ladegård with models of the 13th-century city, St. Olav's Monastery, and excavations of the medieval city. Along the Akerselva, you can find Gamle Aker Kirke, a stone church from 1100, and the university's collection of antiquities.

2. 17th- and 18th-century Christiania: From the Akershus Fortress and the castle of the same name, you can reach the city designed by Christian IV after a great fire. Points of interest include the old City Hall, the old customs district (Tollboden), the Central Bank, the Stock Exchange, and the whole district, designed as a grid in Renaissance style.

3. Upscale Oslo: From the Royal Palace west is the most elegant part of the city, that of the 19th-century upper class. There are lots of mansions in different styles, parks, and "doll houses" to admire. The rich quadrangle stretches from Parkveien to Bygdøy Allé, Kirkeveien to Uranienborgveien. There are boutiques, upscale stores, embassies, and, in Frogner Park, the Bymuseet, the Oslo City Museum.

4. Working-class Oslo: The Oslo of the working class was more secluded, near the Akerselva. Little evidence of mid-19th-century industrialization remains, but what's left can be seen on Damstredet and Telthusbakken, in the wooden houses near the cemetery and the river.

5. Museums of adventure: The Bygdøy Peninsula contains all the museums that tell the story of Norwegian adventure, from the Vikingskipshuset and Norsk Maritimt Museum to the Fram Museet with Nansen's polar ship and the Kon-Tiki Museet with Heyerdahl's boat.

ITINERARY: THE 1994 WINTER OLYMPICS

The Winter Olympic Games, held in Lillehammer in 1994, left behind some incredible structures that have given an identity to these lands. The proposed itinerary uses multiple means of transportation: a train from Oslo to Hamar; a boat on Norway's largest lake, Mjøsa; and finally a bicycle along the Mjøstråkk loop.

The starting point of our journey is **Oslo Central Station** ❶. A comfortable train takes you to Hamar in just over two hours, about 80 miles (130 km) away from the capital. Trains leave every hour with Norwegian Railways (*vy.no*) and every four hours with SJ Nord (*sj.no*). During the journey, you can admire the landscapes of rural Norway, its well-maintained forests, and its lush meadows.

Hamar ❷ has been an episcopal seat since the 12th century, but it declined with the Reformation and was reborn with trade. It is home to the Domkirkeodden, a museum of regional history and culture, with the ruins of the 12th-century cathedral encased in a glass roof structure, and the Bishop's Farm, an open-air museum with 60 old buildings and an herb garden. Also worth seeing are the 19th-century Vang Church, with its medieval tower, and the Åkersvika Nature Reserve, ideal for bird-watching. The town's gem, however, is Vikingskipet, the skating arena built for the 1994 Winter Olympics and still used today for competitions, concerts, and meetings. Made of laminated wood, it conveys a lightness on the inside and solidity on the outside; with its inverted Viking ship shape, it looks as if it has been left on the lakeside for the winter. A true architectural marvel, it seats as many as 20,000 people.

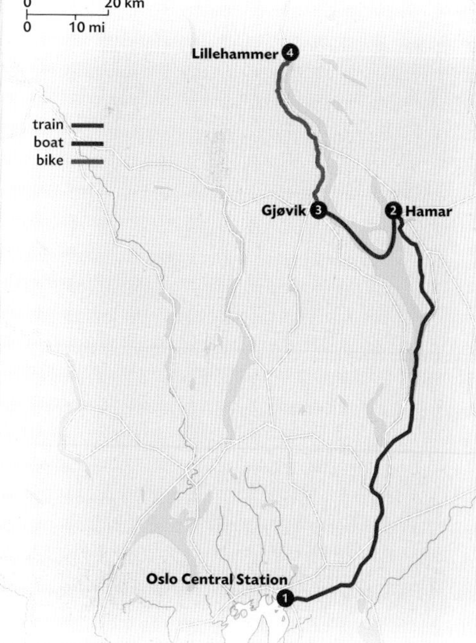

Storgata is the main road in Lillehammer.

Hamar is one of the possible starting points of the Mjøstråkk, the 155-mile (250 km) bike circuit around the lake (map at *visitnorway.com*). The less strenuous parts are between Hamar and Lillehammer (37 miles [61 km]), and Hamar and Minnesund (32 miles [53 km]), whereas between Minnesund and Totenåsen the circuit is more difficult, with more challenging climbs and descents. Hotels of various categories and rural accommodations can be found here, as well as restaurants and cafés. The important thing is to book in advance. Bikes can be rented at the various locations, but we suggest saving the bike ride for the last leg of this itinerary, so you can enjoy a boat crossing of the Mjøsa.

From Hamar, take a boat to **Gjøvik** ❸. You may want to opt for the *Skibladner (skibladner.no)*, an 1856 steamboat, the world's oldest in operation, that circles the lake as if it were its eternal sentence. The boat stops at several ports, so you can visit multiple places and combine means of transportation. It is worth trying at least one leg on the vessel for the Swiss atmosphere it suggests and out of curiosity for the sheer age of the machine and elegance of a bygone era. The Mjøsa landscape is rich with fields, forests, and wooden farmhouses. The reason to stop in Gjøvik is the Olympiske Fjellhall (Olympic Arena) carved into the mountain. It is a true masterpiece, putting Norwegian technology on the world stage. The stadium measures 298x200x78 feet (91x61x24 m), can seat 5,800 spectators, and is used as an arena for hockey and ice skating.

Finally, from Gjøvik, you can ride 29 miles (48 km) by bike along the Mjøstråkk Trail around the lake to reach **Lillehammer** ❹, the end point of our trip. The town has a particularly curious coat of arms: it is the only one in the world with a skier (a *birkebeiner*, to be precise). The ski, dignified by the royal escape (see sidebar p. 95), but still a tool for getting around, is elevated to the same rank as animals, real or symbolic, or weapons, scepters, crowns, and crosses that adorn the insignia of other towns. This coat of arms experienced its glory days in 1994, with the 17th Winter Olympics, which transmitted to the world an image of a snow-covered Norway, with its wonderful winter lights, cold weather of yore, impeccable technical organization, and also an unsuspected human warmth.

Lillehammer also has other cards up its sleeves. Its geographic location, for example, at the mouth of the Lågen River in Lake Mjøsa and at the gateway to the Gudbrand Valley has made it a natural gateway to the North since the time of the Viking sagas. Here, where the magnificent vistas of rural Norway contrast with those of modern fisheries, farmland and woodlands dot the landscape, as do farms raising livestock and processing milk. The idyllic landscapes and small Mesna River have inspired droves of painters and no less than two winners of the Nobel Prize in Literature, Bjørnson and Undset. Also not to be missed is the Maihaugen, a large open-air museum with farms, houses, and churches; 120 buildings, furnished with period furniture; and an exhibition of some 40,000 objects. Alongside 12th- and 13th-century buildings, like Garmo Church, are the blacksmith's, tailor's, glassmaker's, and potter's workshops: 30 ateliers offering a snapshot of Norwegian craftsmanship. Then stroll along Storgata, the main street bordered by two-story wooden houses from the 18th and 19th centuries, which won the national prize for its preservation.

Be sure to visit the Lillehammer Kunstmuseum (Art Museum). The 1992 Snøhetta-designed building highlights one of the best collections of Norwegian painting: some 1,500 works from the 19th century to the present, including Munch, Dahl, and Gude. Kunst Løype, a project that has brought paintings and photos of the city from the 19th and 20th centuries to the downtown streets, is a kind of branch of the museum, inviting visitors to stroll around to discover the places that most inspired local painters (download map from museum website; *lillehammerkunstmuseum.no*).

The last stop before leaving is Olimpiaparken, the track of the 1994 Winter Olympics. On the city's hill, it has 120- and 90-meter ski jumps, a 38,000-seat arena, ice arena, bobsled and luge track, and cross-country skiing stadium. Like everywhere else, there is a struggle to keep the facilities alive, despite good intentions. When you have finished visiting Lillehammer, you can choose to take a train back to Oslo, take another trip on the boat, cycle back to Hamar, or, for a multiday stay, take a trip to the tomb of St. Olav in Trondheim's Nidaros Cathedral, following the Pilegrimsleden paths *(pilegrimsleden.no)*.

The southern, less crowded part of the country is known for its beaches and coves, as well as important cities like Stavanger and Kristiansand

THE SOUTH

The statue of the first Norwegian king, Harald Hårfagre, in Haugesund

THE SOUTH

The southern coast, from Oslo to Haugesund, is the least known part of Norway. Not because it doesn't have anything to showcase, but more likely because international tourism tends to focus on two legendary areas of the country: the North Cape and the fjords. The South, however, has its own draws that go beyond the coast with its coves, islands, islets, and long beaches. Here, there is a different, more traditional feel that reflects neighboring Denmark, for geographical and historical reasons. From Stavanger, you can reach Preikestolen, the most famous and spectacular viewpoint in Scandinavia.

The first highlight of the region is Stavanger, hub of the Norwegian oil industry, one of the primary drivers of the country's prosperity. If you don't find oil interesting, know you won't be seeing drills and wells—that's done on offshore platforms—but there is a very compelling museum in the city, which once lived on sardines until that industry was pushed aside in favor of oil. The town and its surroundings have a lot to offer, but do not stop there. Explore the magnificent Jæren coastline, full of dunes and beaches, and Preikestolen, literally "the pulpit," a geological terrace

Lindesnes Lighthouse sits at the southernmost point of Norway.

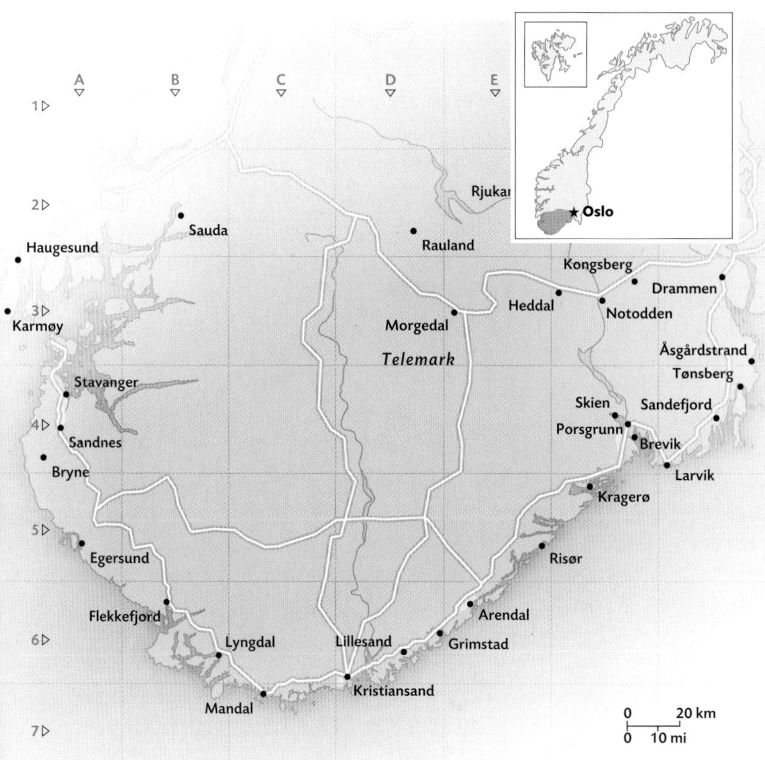

NOT TO BE MISSED:

overlooking the fjord that naturally invites contemplation. Don't miss the towns of Sørlandet (the southern region), a marvel of wooden houses that seem to follow their own unique style of architecture and urban planning. You can't help but long to ride a kayak, boat, or bicycle from islet to islet. Last, there is Telemark, one of the most emblematic regions of the country, although it does not lie on the coast. Here you can explore the canal of the same name, described in the itinerary, and a part of the inland region. ■

ALONG THE FJORD

Following the fjord from Oslo to the southwest, you enter the Vestfold area. It is a collection of historic towns that run along the coastline up to Larvik, where the coast turns inward to the Porsgrunn inlet and beyond, to Skien, the capital of Telemark.

The *vippefyret* is a lantern system that helps ships navigating the coast.

Åsgårdstrand

The main reason to stop here is the chance to visit **Munchs Hus** (Munch's House), purchased in 1898, where the famous painter lived for long periods. It was one of his favorite places: just look at the painting *The Garden of Åsgårdstrand* (1904–1905) to see why. He himself once wrote, "Walking here is like walking through my paintings."

Tønsberg

Moving a little farther to the south is Tønsberg. The city is mentioned in Snorri's *Saga* as existing before A.D. 872, and thus it is inferred to have been founded as early as A.D. 871, now believed to be its official founding year. If so, Tønsberg would be the oldest city in Norway. Allegedly, at the time, the king–who descended from the powerful local Ynglinge clan–

Munchs Hus Edvard Munchs gate 25, Åsgårdstrand 900 71 450
Open only in summer 11:30 a.m.–4:30 p.m. **vestfoldmuseene.no**

resided in the court of Sem and at the estate of Haugar, where the Haugating, the legislative assembly, was based. An early important event was the fortification ordered by King Haakon IV, who in the 13th century created the Castrum Tunsbergis, a large defensive system.

In the following centuries, Tønsberg became a seafaring town, so much so that it owned the world's largest shipping company, the Wilhelmsen, which dominated hunting in the polar regions. Today, Tønsberg is a beautiful seaside town where you can see the ruins of the fortification, the old town, and the patrician houses of Gunnarsbøparken.

From the center, cross a bridge to the islands of Nøtterøy and Tjøme. On the southern tip of the latter is Færder Nasjonalpark, a beautiful coastal area with islands, islets, and reefs that also serves as a nesting area for several bird species. Here, you can hike, swim, kayak or canoe, and camp. A local highlight is Verdens Ende, literally "the end of the world," a rocky point where you can see the *vippefyret,* an ancient lantern system used to help ships navigate.

Sandefjord

Continue southwestward until you reach Sandefjord, a town that sits on either side of the fjord of the same name, surrounded by 124 islands. Its coat of arms, featuring a Viking ship and whale, is linked to local history: here, in fact, a splendid Viking ship named *Gokstad* was found in 1880. It is now displayed in Oslo, but Sandefjord is left with the pride of having helped rediscover the roots of the nation. The whale refers to the fact that the town, at the turn of the 20th

The monument dedicated to whale hunting in Sandefjord

century, became a center for whale hunting. That Sandefjord owes a lot to these marine creatures can be seen in the large, forceful monument dedicated to them. Staying with the theme, the **Hvalfangstmuseet** (Whaling Museum), where the life-size statue of a large blue whale hangs from the ceiling, is a must-see. The museum, currently undergoing an extensive renovation, testifies to how life was in the golden age of whaling.

The city also boasts several art nouveau houses and buildings, as well as a beautiful sculpture park, featuring works by Knut Steen, at Midtåsen. Be sure to check out the "Walk of Fame," a sidewalk embedded with stars like that in Hollywood, dedicated to local entrepreneurs from the 19th century to the present, who have given and continue to give prestige to the town.

Larvik

When you think of Larvik, just think of its mineral water, a glass bottle with a silver-colored label and a simple name, Farris. Until a couple of decades ago, this town was the only source of mineral water in Norway. Yet another name comes to mind when mentioning Larvik: Colin Archer, the legendary boat designer and builder. The *Fram,* used by Nansen, was designed by him. The city was reborn in 1988 when a decree united five towns into one to become Larvik. Before, its history was that of the entire coast, i.e., lumber, maritime trade, shipyards. Today, apart from Farris, its mainstays are the timber industry and droves of tourists attracted by its magnificent beaches.

The **Sjøfartsmuseet** (Maritime Museum) in the old customshouse

Hvalfangstmuseet ✉ Museumsgaten 39, Sandefjord ☎ 947 93 341
🕒 Tues.–Sun. 11 a.m.–4 p.m., Thurs. until 7 p.m. **vestfoldmuseene.no**

Farris

Sometimes a mineral water can become the symbol of an entire country. That's what happened with Farris in Norway. The brand was born in the 20th century, but its story began earlier. In 1843, Karen Linaae opened a spa where guests could bathe in cold sulfur water and drink from the spring; the treatment became famous, and its effectiveness was proven. Knowing the value of the spring, Dr. I.C. Holm decided in 1880 to expand the Linaae establishment. Given the success, he began bottling the water through the local brewery in 1907. You can see the 1912 plant, which looks like a palace, that then expanded over time. For the first few years, until 1915, the bottled water was called Salus and, thanks to an agreement with the royal family, slogans included the use of King Haakon VII's name. To this day, the agreement stipulates that, should the king ask for it, free water will be delivered to him.

The town of Larvik is known for Farris mineral water.

displays models of ships, sailboats, and steamers, and preserves the memory of voyages across the oceans, particularly those of local sailors, such as Thor Heyerdahl.

The **Larvik Museum** is a city museum that also includes the 17th-century Danish governor's residence. It chronicles the period from the 16th to the 19th century, when Larvik was one of the two royal Danish counties in Norway. Lastly, check out the town church and the Farris spring near Bøkeskogen, that of the miraculous mineral water.

Porsgrunn

Follow the fjord to the inlet of Porsgrunn, a center of porcelain production since 1887. Today you can visit the town factory on a guided tour to see how porcelain is made and decorated. There is also a museum, **Porselensmuseet.**

Also notable is **Gea Norvegica,** a UNESCO Global Geopark whose visitor center is here in Porsgrunn. The park includes several sites in the Skien, Larvik, and Kragerø area. Take some time to inspect the rocks, to find out how they were formed and

Sjøfartsmuseet ✉ Kirkestredet 5, Larvik ☎ 481 066 00 🕒 Open only in summer Tues.–Sun. 11 a.m.–4 p.m. **vestfoldmuseene.no** • **Larvik Museum** ✉ Herregårdsletta, Larvik ☎ 481 06 600 🕒 June 22–Aug. 18 Mon.–Sun. 11 a.m.–4 p.m.; Aug. 19–Oct. 6 Sat.–Sun. 11 a.m.–4 p.m **vestfoldmuseene.no**
Porselensmuseet ✉ Porselensvegen 6b, Porsgrunn ☎ 355 44 500 🕒 Thurs.–Sun. 11 a.m.–4 p.m. **telemarkmuseum.no** • **Gea Norvegica** ✉ Porseleinsveien 6a, Porsgrunn ☎ 913 88 445 **geoparken.no**

The ruins of the medieval church of Kapitelberget, in Skien

what they look like. For example, at Bamble, the bedrock of smooth gneiss rocks covered by limestone cliffs and fossils testifies to the presence of an ancient sea. At Siljan, on the other hand, you will find volcanic rocks. When you have finished sightseeing, take Route 32 from Porsgrunn and you will almost immediately find the turnoff to Skien, the capital of Telemark.

Skien

Skien is Ibsen's town–or rather, one of Ibsen's towns. This is where the playwright was born and spent his childhood and adolescence. Skien boasts ancient origins, as far back as the beginning of the Viking age, and a strategic location at the mouth of the sea, on the waters that divide Hardanger and Telemark. Thanks to this, the town has always been a place of exchange with both the interior and the coastal cities.

Part of the territory protected by the Gea Norvegica park is located here. Discover some historical sites related to the geology of the region, such as the first documented iron mine in Norway–dating back to 1543–and Kapitelberget, the remains of a medieval church built on a 430-million-year-old coral reef. Fossils found in these rocks include the remains of sea lilies, honeycomb corals, goblet corals, chain corals, and an extinct type of sponge.

In the town center is the **Telemark Museum,** housed in the 18th-century Brekkeparken manor house, situated on an elevated terrace and surrounded by a beautiful English-style park. The house preserves its original furniture, ranging from the Renaissance to the Victorian age—and allegedly also a ghost, the Gray Lady. A bookstore, a pharmacy, and a barbershop show 19th-century life, along with houses from all over rural Telemark, all with the iconic "rose painting" decoration. The museum's collections are mainly focused on local handicrafts, such as woodcarving, but there are also four rooms dedicated to Ibsen. Nearby is the well-preserved Venstøp Farm, property of the Ibsen family, where the playwright spent his adolescence.

Also worth seeing in Skien are the 12th-century Romanesque church of Gjerpen and the Telemark Canal harbor at Hjellebrygga. The latter is a highlight of Norwegian pride, as well as a major tourist attraction, for its scenery and for a fascination with 19th-century aesthetic. From here, hop on a boat to the Løveid Canal, which connects Skien with Lake Norsjø, or go as far as Dalen.

Be sure to explore more by traveling farther north in Øvre Telemark (Upper Telemark), a land of hills, mountains, and valleys. ■

Telemark Museum ✉ Øvregate 32a, Skien ☎ 355 44 500
🕒 Tues.–Sun. 11 a.m.–4 p.m. **telemarkmuseum.no**

The Ibsen boat on the Telemark Canal

ØVRE TELEMARK

A region of rural traditions, named so because it was the administrative territory (march) of the Thelir, a Germanic tribe that settled here before the Viking era. Here the language most closely resembles Old Norse, and people are still tied to their traditional clothes, the *bunad*. *Rosemaling*, the "rose painting" used to decorate furniture, walls, and objects, was born here. Upper Telemark, it is worth noting, has a different feel from the Telemark of Skien and Kragerø.

Local handicrafts are decorated with *rosemaling*.

You can get there by cutting across the region on the E134, which travels from Drammen to Haugesund, right through Upper Telemark. You can get there from Bergen and Hardangerfjord via Route 13 to Skare. But you can also get there from Skien, of course, by following Route 36 to the northwest.

Kongsberg

The town's history begins with the discovery of silver in 1624. Kongsberg, literally "king's mountain," owes its birth and development to its silver core, even though the king in question was a Dane, Christian IV. Silver equals State Mint, an institution which is still based here today. In the 19th century, Kongsberg became Norway's second largest city. Its mines, however, ran dry in 1957, forcing development in other fields. The city is now home to a leading international high-tech company for the marine, defense, and aerospace sectors, as well as offshore oil, gas, and renewables.

The entrance to the Sølvgruvene silver mine, in Saggrenda

A must-see in town is the **Norsk Bergverksmuseum** (Foundry Museum), housed in the old town factory. It chronicles the discovery, exploitation, and processing of silver, displays large nuggets, and has a rich collection of coins and medals minted here, along with those from the Norges Bank Mint. There is also an interactive Geolab. One section of the building is devoted to the Skiing Museum, which celebrates the city's athletes who dominated the ski jumping scene from 1925 to 1950.

The next stop is Sølvgruvene, the silver mine in Saggrenda that is more than 3,280 feet (1,000 m) deep: hop on the underground train that runs through it for 1.2 miles (2 km).

Another local draw is the **Lågdalsmuseet,** which illustrates the other soul of Kongsberg, that of its rural life. Do not miss a visit to Kongsberg Kirke, an 18th-century church with a stunning baroque interior in which the altar, organ, and pulpit come together in a single design.

Lastly, do not forget to check out the so-called Kronene i Håvet (Royal Seals) on the rock of Håvet: from Christian IV, the founder of Kongsberg, to the current monarch,

Norsk Bergverksmuseum ✉ Hyttegata 3, Kongsberg ☎ 919 13 200 🕒 May–Aug. daily 11 a.m.–5 p.m.; rest of the year, Tues.–Sun. noon–4 p.m. **norskbergverksmuseum.no • Lågdalsmuseet** ✉ Tillischbakken 8–10, Kongsberg ☎ 327 33 468 🕒 Tues.–Fri. 11 a.m.–3 p.m. **buskerudmuseet.com**

Harald V, every King of Norway has left his seal here, testifying to the importance of this "royal mountain."

From Kongsberg, Route 40 climbs up the Numedal, a valley leading to the Hardangervidda Plateau and national park. Along this valley, Norway's medieval architecture is abundant: see the beautiful *stavkirker* of Flesberg, Rollag, Nore, and Uvdal, as well as 40 other historic wooden buildings, all set in a landscape of mountains, rivers, and moorland. The valley is also home to the Numedal Route, a bike trail that runs from Larvik to Dagalifjellet with a 3,280-foot (1,000 m) elevation gain.

Rose Painting

In the 18th and 19th centuries, an iconic style called *rosemaling* (usually translated as "rose painting") was developed in the rural areas of southern Norway and central Sweden. Actually, the word *rose* is a verb meaning to decorate or embellish. An original response to the baroque and rococo styles, rosemaling was first used to decorate domestic objects like bowls, plates, and boxes before extending to furniture, walls, and ceilings, all embellished with stylized flowers, geometric motifs, and bright colors. Check out the incredible walls of farmhouses in Telemark: they are made of overlapping logs and painted following the curves of the wood.

Notodden

About 18 miles (30 km) west of Kongsberg lies Notodden, a town that developed thanks to its hydroelectric power plant, which attracted industrial settlements. The impact that Notodden had throughout the 20th century, especially as a producer of nitrogen fertilizer, caused the town to be included, along with neighboring Rjukan, on the list of Industrial Heritage Sites under UNESCO protection. The history of the place is recounted today through the factory that sits near the waterfall.

The area boasts another highlight: the 12th-century Heddal Stavkirke, the largest of its kind in Norway. It is shaped like a basilica, with four portals and as many as 18 columns. The walls are decorated with sacred themes and the vivid ornamental motifs of rosemaling. The original bishop's chair still stands in the chancel.

From Notodden take Route 37, heading north, skirting Lake Tinnsjå, then veering west toward Rjukan.

Rjukan

On the edge of the Hardangervidda Plateau and sitting at the foot of the 6,177-foot (1,883 m) Gaustatoppen peak, Rjukan rises out of a deep valley. In the early 20th century, the only reason to settle here, in a place with no sun in winter, was the ingenious intuition of Norsk Hydro to use the local waterfalls and resulting hydroelectric power to produce nitrogen fertilizer. Vemork, built in 1911, was at the time the largest hydroelectric power plant in the world. Like

Notodden, this is also a UNESCO World Heritage site. To make up for the absence of light, a mirror system was installed to bring sunshine into the city even when it should not be there. Also worth seeing are the views by cable car to Gvepseborg and Krokan–a mid-19th-century mountain cabin, the first to be managed by the Norwegian Trekking Association (DNT). It has been the base for the crews of multiple movies, from *The Heroes of Telemark* with Kirk Douglas to Nils Gaup's *North Star,* starring James Caan and Christopher Lambert.

Continuing west along Route 37, head to Skinnarbu, which offers downhill slopes in winter, walks on frozen Lake Møsvatn, ice fishing, and snowmobile rides. Skinnarbu is also the starting point for many backcountry hikes, like those that venture into Hardangervidda and follow the routes of the resistance commandos that attacked Vemork.

If you head south from Skinnarbu, you reach Seljord, a village that hosts a festival of folk theater, music, and dance in July, and is home to the 12th-century St. Olav Church. The 1,256-pound (570 kg) boulder that stands outside the church is said to have been lifted by Nils Langedal, a giant from the 18th century. Seljord is no stranger to legends: apparently a monster called Selma lives in its lake.

Telemark Canal

The Telemark region is known for its special canal, which connects Skien and Dalen, taking advantage of lakes and traversing the height differences with 18 locks. The first section was built in 1861, from Skien to Norsjø, as the three Løveid locks. The second part, between Norsjø and Lake Bandak, was built in 1892, a grand undertaking for the time, requested by local factories to regulate the flow of water for the transport of timber sent to the water-powered sawmills in Skien and then exported to the Netherlands and England through ports on the south coast. In total, the canal is 65 miles (105 km) long and rises over 236 feet (72 m) in elevation. Its boats *Ibsen* and *Victoria* have been on the route since it opened, so they have a lot of stories to share. In 2017, the second section of the canal became part of the National Cultural Heritage. Note the Vrangfoss lock, the most impressive: 75 feet (23 m) in height difference with eight basins.

Today, the canal can be traveled by boat, canoe, or kayak. The Skien-Dalen trip by historic boat takes 8 hours and 40 minutes. You can combine a boat tour to an intermediate location with a return trip by bus. Or you can break up the trip by stopping to sleep at some point and resume the trip the next day. You can also take a bicycle on the boat, so you can ride sections as well.

The impressive Vrangfoss lock

Morgedal

A couple miles west of Seljord, Morgedal is known as the cradle of modern skiing, specifically that of Sondre Norheim, who modified the design of skis and built a binding that allowed them to bend effectively. You can visit his little house in Øverbø, with the slopes, woods, and roofs from which he used to jump while training. Then be sure to stop at the **Norsk Skieventyr,** where you will be treated to a multimedia journey of 4,000 years of skiing, discovering the story of Sondre, the Hemmestveit brothers–the first to open a ski school in Oslo in 1881–and the Telemark technique. The museum features an old ski workshop and a ski wax workshop, as well as memorabilia of 1850s Morgedal, Amundsen's race to the South Pole, and Olav Bjaaland, a local skier who participated in the expedition. The Olympic torch was lit in Morgedal for the Oslo Olympics in 1952, and it was also the starting point for the relay race at the Squaw Valley Games in 1960 and Lillehammer in 1994.

Farther northwest, on Lake Totak, lies Rauland, which can be reached from Rjukan by following Route 37. The interior of the local church, Rauland Kyrkje, is decorated with Norwegian motifs and two 13th-century Flemish fixed crosses. The town is a sports and vacation center, one of Norway's largest, with as many as 93 miles (150 km) of cross-country skiing and 46 alpine ski slopes. In summer, the resort is perfect for canoeing, fishing, and exploring the area's many hiking trails. If interested, you can visit the Raulandsakademiet (Folklore Academy), a school for studying folk music and crafts and preserving Telemark traditions. ■

Norsk Skieventyr ✉ Morgedalvegen 159, Morgedal ☎ 350 69 080
🕒 Open only in summer, Mon.–Sun. 10 a.m.–5 p.m. **visittelemark.no**

THE GERMANS' WATER

It was the year 1939, and scientist Otto Hahn had just discovered the technique for fissioning uranium at the Kaiser Wilhelm Institute in Berlin. It was the first step toward the atomic age, but the development of the bomb, what German strategists thought of as the ultimate weapon, was still far off, and it would involve Norway.

Scientists in Berlin needed uranium, which was easy to find in Germany, but they also needed a moderator for the reaction transition from uranium to plutonium, which they did not have. The moderator par excellence was heavy water (D_2O, the isotope deuterium instead of hydrogen in the water molecule), and the only known and accessible place in the world where it could be obtained in useful quantities was the Vemork power plant in Rjukan.

The Vemork power plant

In 1940, Germany invaded Norway, thus securing the raw material it lacked. But it was not until 1943, when it became clear that conventional weapons might not be enough, that the bomb project accelerated. The Germans in Vemork had increased their monthly production by 30 times in order to accumulate sufficient D_2O and were working at a frantic pace. Some Norwegians left early that winter from England, where the king and the Norwegian army command had sought refuge, and parachuted by the Royal Air Force onto the Hardanger Plateau. These resistance commandos moved on skis, stocked up on food in the isolated farms of the plateau, hid by digging shelters in the snow, and constantly changed bases and collaborators.

On February 28, the commandos attacked the Vemork plant, damaging the facilities and destroying the accumulated stock. The German command then decided to move machinery and production to Austria so that it could work safely. About a year later, in the winter of 1944, it secretly loaded a train with containers of heavy water, then transferred them to a ferry to cross nearby Lake Tinnsjå. The resistance intervened by blowing up the ferry, which sank with the accumulated supplies, along with Nazi hopes of getting to the atomic bomb before the Allies did.

THE COAST: ISLANDS & BEACHES

The so-called Norwegian Riviera is the part of the country that most appeals to the idea of a summer vacation, with picturesque towns with historic wooden houses, islands and cliffs, long beaches, and trips on land and at sea. This stretch includes iconic places such as Risør and Mandal, Norway's southernmost town, and medium-size settlements such as Kristiansand and Stavanger.

Artist Edvard Munch lived in Kragerø from 1909 to 1915.

Brevik

Brevik is one of Norway's best preserved 18th- and 19th-century towns, with wooden houses, the old customhouse, and town hall illustrating local architecture. The latter, a harmonious 18th-century building, houses the Brevik Bymuseum, a town museum dedicated to ships, trade, and the German occupation, with photos and memorabilia. The museum includes an emporium and pharmacy dating back to the 19th century. Boats depart from Brevik for the many islands in the Langesund Archipelago. The place is perfect for long walks and bike rides, as well as for kayak trips and swimming.

Kragerø

Following the coast to the west, you come across Kragerø. It is somewhat of a Norwegian hot spot for nostalgic tourism, celebrated and inhabited by artists. Its landscape and atmosphere are as you would expect: well-kept old houses, islands, islets, a harbor, and boats. Do not expect the glamour and scandal of the Mediterranean, which in any case wouldn't suit Norwegians, but Kragerø certainly has its charm. Munch, who painted his famous cycle for the University of Oslo here, clearly felt so. Even today's tourists have taken note, despite not always having the sensibility of yesterday's painters. Around the church, the artists' quarter is full of ateliers and galleries. Nearby is the Kittelsenhuset, the home of Theodor Kittelsen, Norway's greatest painter of elves and trolls. It is part of the **Berg-Kragerø Museum,** whose headquarters is in an Empire-style mansion owned by the powerful Homann family. It displays evidence of the town's maritime economy, based on timber and ice export.

Munch moved here in 1909, after returning from Copenhagen, where he had treated his nervous breakdown, and stayed until 1915, painting a lot. That's why the town is home to the Munch Walk, which chronicles his walks, views, and visual insights with ten panels featuring his works. But what you will want to seek out in Kragerø is the atmosphere of the cafés, somewhat upscale shopping, and art galleries.

Finally, on the coastal side stands Gunnarsholmen, the old fort that protects the harbor, with the batteries that drove out British ships in the 1810 war. Nearby, have a look at the 19th-century Støle Church and the lighthouses of Strømtangen and Jomfruland.

Risør

About 30 miles (50 km) from Kragerø lies Risør. The town makes you feel at home. The iconic white wooden houses are clustered along the shores, as if they all wanted their share. The beautiful, elegant sailboats circle the shoreline like moths attracted to the light. There is something both intimate and exclusive about this small town. Along Strandgata the atmosphere is familial, whereas a stroll through the back alleys makes you feel like

The Southern Archipelago

A treasure of the South, this archipelago consisting of thousands of islands, islets, and reefs stretches from the island of Jomfruland, off Kragerø, to the lighthouse at Ryvingen, south of Kristiansand. It is perfect for kayaking and canoeing. If you enjoy wilder and less organized environments, this place is for you. You can hop from island to island by ferry, boat, or taxi boat to sunbathe on a smooth, round rock, visit small villages, or take a dip in the sea. It is a special place that challenges the stereotypical idea one might have of Norway.

Berg-Kragerø Museum
✉ Lovisenbergveien 45, Kragerø
☎ 359 81 453 ⏲ Open only in summer **telemarkmuseum.no**

Sailboats bob gently in Risør's marina.

the windows hide the city's secrets. Take a tour with the *vaktmann,* the town watchman, with his uniform and lantern, who will reveal some of Risør's mysteries. The Risør Kirke is a beautiful 17th-century baroque church dedicated to the Holy Spirit. Other local draws are the central **Risør Kunstpark**—a gallery featuring resident artists and temporary exhibitions—and the **Kystkultursenter** in Moen, dedicated to the history of the coast and its shipyards. Make sure you do not miss a tour on the old 1950s ferry to Øysang and do some kayaking in the archipelago.

On the first weekend of August, ever since 1983, the town has hosted the Risør Trebåtfestival, a sailing festival that fills the harbor with boats of different eras and styles, from Viking ships to modern yachts.

To enjoy some relaxation before getting back on the road and exploring the coast, stop in nearby Lyngør, reached by ferry from Gjeving. The beautiful village is built on four islands arranged at the junction of two sea channels. Its natural harbor was of major importance in the era of sailing ships, which sought shelter from storms along the rocky, dangerous

Risør Kunstpark ✉ Prestegata 15, Risør ☎ 976 78 477 🕒 summer, Tues.–Sun. noon–4 p.m.; rest of the year, Sat.–Sun. noon–4 p.m. **kunstparken.no • Kystkultursenter** ✉ Moensveien 38, Risør ☎ 371 50 266 **visitnorway.com/places-to-go/southern-norway/risor/listings-risor/risør-kystkultursenter**

southern coast. The village has preserved its buildings and relaxed atmosphere, becoming an exclusive and peaceful vacation spot.

Arendal

The sea, the harbor, the wooden houses: this is what almost every town on the southern coast has to offer. But Arendal has something special. It was built on islands and islets, which makes it even more picturesque. It became a trade center in the 17th century and grew rich by selling lumber to the Netherlands. Visit the Empire-style Rådhus, the town hall, built in 1815 and today one of the largest wooden buildings in the country. Then head to the Trefoldighetskirken, the Trinity Church, an imposing neo-Gothic brick building with a 285-foot (87 m) steeple.

Tyholmen is the old town, situated on a southeastern peninsula. It is divided into two parts: the upper part, where sailors and craftsmen lived, and the lower part, inhabited by merchants and shipowners. It is a pleasant spot for a stroll with its relaxed atmosphere, cafés, narrow alleys, and beautiful houses. The place where people tend to gather most is Pollen Marina.

To learn more about the city, visit **Kuben,** a museum dedicated to local history and folklore that features an open-air area with period houses. On the island of Merdø, the Merdøgaard Museum, which occupies an 18th-century house, displays the collections

Kuben Parkveien 16a, Arendal 370 17 900 Tues.–Fri. 9 a.m.–3 p.m., Sat.–Sun. noon–4 p.m. **kubenarendal.no**

Trefoldighetskirken, or Trinity Church, in Arendal

of a captain who had traveled the world. Then head to Tromøy Kirke, the medieval church rebuilt in the 18th century on the island of the same name, opposite Arendal. Inside, you will find sculpted busts in the chancel and a ceiling painted like the open sky. If you have time, Raet Nasjonalpark, a marine park created in 2016 along the coast from Lyngør to Grimstad, is also worth a visit.

For a tour on the sea, the old sailing boat *Ekstrand* offers day trips from the harbor, as do other ships and boats offering island or coastal tours. A hydrofoil connects Arendal to Oslo in six hours in the summer.

If you continue along the coast on Route E18, you come to Grimstad, which flourished in the 20th century thanks to maritime trade. A young Ibsen lived here for a few years, working as a clerk in a pharmacy. The latter has now been turned into a museum dedicated to the town and the playwright, with memorabilia and old photographs. The town, its surroundings, and the coastline offer plenty of bike paths. Many hotels are cyclist-friendly, and the tourist office, at Jernbanebrygga 1, also serves as a bike and e-bike rental shop. There are also QR-code panels in town to help visitors get around. Farther south, in Lillesand, you can admire beautiful patrician houses from the 19th century. The nearby Blindleia Archipelago is rich with lush islands, reefs, and picturesque villages.

Kristiansand Domkirke

Kristiansand & Around

Sørlandet, the southern part of Norway, is called "Norway's sunshine coast." Kristiansand is its capital, also known as "the white capital" because of the traditional color of its wooden houses, and "the grid capital" for its checkerboard layout, designed long ago. People here may feel somewhat different from other Norwegians; they have another dialect, another temperament, perhaps even another climate. But their compatriots love this region, and have made it a major destination for domestic tourism, while foreigners tend to opt for the colder parts of Norway.

From here, it takes more than 1,553 miles (2,500 km) to reach the other extreme of continental Norway, while Denmark is just a hop across the Skagerrak Strait. The coastline around the city is rugged, made up of islands, rocks, and small fjords.

Despite this, Kristiansand was an industrial city known for its port, shipbuilding, and fishing industries. Then it entered the era of the oil boom. Many call it Norway's Florida, due to its climate attracting retirees, but the data say otherwise. For some years now, the city, alongside the University of Agder and its keen information technology skills, has adopted a policy to bring in young people, with new businesses and the promotion of start-ups. It is shifting its image from sleepy town to dynamic hub.

Kristiansand expanded east across the Otra River and west, leaving the central peninsula to its original Renaissance style. It was Christian IV of Denmark who wanted it that way, in 1641. Since then, despite fires that have decimated buildings, it has managed to maintain its character, a loyalty evidenced in its name too.

Before starting to explore, it is worth stopping by the **tourist office,** then heading straight away to the old town. Kvadraturen, the district King Christian IV ordered built, is the heart of the city and has a checkerboard of wooden and stone houses.

Here stands the **Kristiansand Domkirke,** an 1885 cathedral. Its two previous iterations, erected on the same site, were destroyed by fires. The park surrounding it contains statues by Gustav Vigeland. The old town has recently been graced with street art, seen on the Thon Hotel Norge and the Galleri Bi-Z.

Posebyen, on the west bank of the river, is a neighborhood of small white wooden houses that survived the last fire in 1892. One of the best preserved is Bentsens Hus, erected in 1855 at Kronprinsens gate 59. Needless to say, this is the city's spot for cafés, galleries, stores, and walks down Markens gate, the main pedestrian street. The area called Posebyhaven, on the other hand, is home to some buildings with gardens where you can have a snack or listen to music.

Also worth seeing is Oddernes Kirke, in the Lund District, east of downtown, a church from 1040 rebuilt in the 17th century with baroque furnishings. Its atrium preserves a runestone. Not far away, at Gimleveien 23, is Gimle Gård, a 19th-century manor house converted into a museum, with original furnishings and a picture gallery, as well as collections of furniture, silverware, porcelain, and glassware.

Christiansholm Festning is a 1674 fortress with thick walls and cannons. Planned under the Danish King Christian IV, it was to be part of a coastal defense system, but the only fighting it saw was against the British navy during the Napoleonic Wars. Evidence of more recent times

Kristiansand Tourist Office ✉ Rådhusgaten 18, Kristiansand ☎ 380 750 00 **visitsorlandet.com** • **Kristiansand Domkirke** ✉ Gyldenløves gate 9, Kristiansand ☎ 381 969 00 🕒 summer, Mon.–Fri. 10 a.m.–5 p.m.; rest of the year, Mon.–Fri. 11 a.m.–4 p.m. **kristiansanddomkirke.no**

Fiskebrygga is a colorful fishing quay in Kristiansand.

lies in the Kanonmuseum (Cannon Museum) in Møvik, in the fort built by the Germans in 1941. A twin fort was erected across the strait in Denmark to prevent the British fleet from entering the Baltic Sea. Inside, see the last existing 380-mm Krupp and other war machinery.

Heading back toward the city center and into the neighborhoods farther east, do not miss the **Kristiansand Museum,** which, like the Kanonmuseum and Gimle Gård, is part of the Vest-Agder-museet network, which groups together 11 museums in the region. The open-air area of the Kristiansand Museum consists of 30 old buildings from the city and the Setesdal region. It houses original furniture and objects as well as a collection of carpets and religious art, toys, traditional clothing, and cars. By contrast, representing this century is Kildenteater og Konserthus, at Sjølystveien 2, on the canal opposite Kvadraturen. This performing arts center houses the Agder Theater and the Kristiansand Symphony Orchestra. It was designed by local and Finnish architectural firms. From behind, it looks like a raised platform reaching out to sea, but from the front, a giant wave undulates over a massive glass facade. In short, the building is sure to impress, including its large concert hall that seats more than a thousand.

Kristiansand also offers several meeting areas, such as Bystranda, the town beach; the Strandpromenaden waterside walkway; Fiskebrygga fishing quay; and the marina. All areas

Kristiansand Museum ✉ Vigeveien 22b, Kristiansand ☎ 381 02 680 🕒 summer, daily 11 a.m.–4 p.m.; rest of the year for events only **vestagdermuseet.no**

have cafés, restaurants, and pleasant little squares. To the north, not far from the center, is the 19th-century Ravnedalen Park, which hosts concerts, theater performances, and festivals in summer.

Still farther north, in Vennesla on the Otra River, about 9 miles (15 km) from Kristiansand, architecture enthusiasts will be awestruck at the sight of the **Vennesla Bibliotek og Kulturhus.** It will make you wonder if the Norwegians have gone mad (in a good way), for having built such a masterpiece in a town of just 15,000 inhabitants. Opened in 2011, this stunning, award-winning building was listed by *The Huffington Post* as one of the five most beautiful libraries in the world. It feels like you are entering the belly of a whale, with the 27 ribs defining the space from ceiling to floor, and lights that emphasize this feeling with a soft red, a symbol of protection but also of connection and learning.

Nearby, in Grovane, the small Setesdal steam railway departs, running

Vennesla Bibliotek og Kulturhus ✉ Venneslamoen 19, Vennesla ☎ 909 65 456 🕒 Mon.–Fri. 10 a.m.–4 p.m., Thurs. until 6 p.m., Sat. 11 a.m.–3 p.m. **venneslakulturhus.no**

EXPERIENCE: The North Sea Road by Bike

Seen from a car window or from a train of the Sørland lines, this land is undeniably beautiful. But experiencing it from a bike, or e-bike, is something else entirely. Fjords, mountains, rolling moors, white sand or pebble beaches, islands, and cliffs will be part of the landscape you admire from the saddle. Indeed, Nordsjøvegen offers fascinating scenery, as many painters who came to capture the bright summer light knew well. From Egersund, pedal along the abandoned highway to Ogna, then follow the coast to Brusand, Vigrestad, and Hå. From there on you will see a succession of sandy beaches. From Sola, move to Sandnes and Stavanger, then take the speedboat to Nedstrand and then Haugesund. You can also hop from island to island by ferry in Rogaland County, for example to Finnøy and Kvitsøy.

5 miles (8 km) up the valley to Røyknes. This is all that remains of the 48-mile-long (78 km) Setesdal Railway, which was decommissioned in 1962 because it had a different gauge. It is a living museum, with steam locomotives and wooden carriages.

From the harbor of Kristiansand, many boats offer tours along the coast to Grimstad or nearby islands like Bragdøya and beaches.

The route from Kristiansand to Haugesund, following small coastal roads, is called Nordsjøvegen, or North Sea Road. It is a scenic route of long sandy beaches, fjords, islands, and reefs, vibrant with wind, light, and ever-changing skies. It is rich in evidence of the past, from rock art to Viking remains, from the Christian Middle Ages to Protestant churches, to the Norway of the sea, lighthouses, and sailing ships.

Mandal & the Nearby Villages

About 24 miles (40 km) west of Kristiansand lies Mandal, Norway's southernmost town. It was the birthplace of sculptor Gustav Vigeland and was one of the capitals of the salmon and timber trade. The town has a charming feel for its bright white wooden houses, narrow streets, islets, and long Sjøsanden Beach. The town is divided by the Mandalselva River, once one

A quiet alleyway in Mandal, the southernmost town in Norway

of Norway's richest in salmon, which reaches out to the sea. The town's coat of arms testifies to its connection with the fish, featuring three salmon.

The magnificent islets with their protected areas, Furulunden Park with its pine forests, and the many patrician houses proving the area's prosperity are all worth a visit. Then there's the **Mandal Museum,** in Andorsen Palace, dedicated to the history of maritime trade and fishing on the southern coast: it displays paintings by local artists and includes a visit to Vigeland Hus, the house where the Vigeland brothers spent their childhood. Also worth seeing are the large Empire-style Mandal Kirke, the houses and docks of the old Kleven Harbor, and the Mandalitten monument, dedicated to times of plenty, visually representing the old saying: "loaves of bread in your hat, salmon in your pocket, eggs in your shoes."

On a small peninsula west of Mandal, which you can reach on Route 460, lies the beautiful village of Lindesnes. Its lighthouse marks the southernmost point in Norway, which has earned it the moniker of "South Cape." From here to Stavanger is a succession of charming villages. Stop in Lyngdal to visit the Klokkergården Bygdetun open-air museum with its old local houses. Around the town, you will find several pretty farms that belonged to emigrants to North America in the last century.

Follow Route 43 westward to Farsund, a little gem built in the Jugendstil and pseudo-Swiss styles. Pass by it to reach Lista Fyr, the lighthouse on the peninsula of the same name, surrounded by rocks that boast 9,000-year-old carvings. A string of sand dunes runs along the sea, in an area rich in plant and animal life. Visit the Lista Museum, which includes all the significant sites in the area, from the Nordberg Fort built by the Germans in the 1940s to the Listaskøyta Kystkultursenter, a coastal culture center, and the open-air museum of Vanse.

Kvinesdal sits a little farther inland on the Fedafjorden. It has an interesting little museum called Lister Utvandrermuseum, which uses photos and objects to tell the story of emigrants to North America. A little farther west is Flekkefjord, with the beautiful "Dutchmen's" (Hollanderbyen) quarter that recalls the days of trade with the Dutch in the 16th century. Three centuries later, the great herring fishery sparked changes in the buildings. Today, the cityscape has changed again with street art. You can visit the Flekkefjord Museum, which illustrates the history of the town, and the Flekkefjordbanen, a 10.5-mile (17 km) railway line decommissioned in 1990. It has been now transformed into a spectacular rail bike lane: you can ride one of the rail bikes through no fewer than 17 tunnels.

Mandal Museum ✉ Store Elvegate 5, Mandal ☎ 951 55 592 🕒 Open only in summer or by reservation **vestagdermuseet.no**

Magma UNESCO Global Geopark

Egersund

From Flekkefjord, continuing along the coast on Route 44 and then on Sokndalsveien, you reach Egersund, home to some major companies in the fields of marine and oil rig technology. It has much to offer, starting with its spectacular nature—mountains, rushing rivers, fjords, islands, and beaches are all within a few miles—and is also part of the Magma UNESCO Global Geopark. A must-see is the **Fayancemuseum,** a museum of ceramics produced in the town from the mid-19th century to the 1980s, which is part of the Dalane Folkemuseum, a group of sites that illustrate ancient life here.

Stavanger & Around

Ekofisk, the oil and gas field in the Norwegian North Sea, and Equinor, the state-owned company that operates there, gave the city its modern identity. But Stavanger was here well before the arrival of the industry giants, having been supposedly founded in A.D. 1125, the year its cathedral was completed. More importantly, it has had periods of major development in fishing, shipyards, and trade.

(continued on p. 128)

Fayancemuseum Fabrikkgaten 2, Egersund 514 61 410 Open daily in summer 11 a.m.–5 p.m.; rest of the year, Wed.–Fri. 11 a.m.–3 p.m., Sat.–Sun. 11 a.m.–5 p.m. **dalanefolkemuseum.no**

JÆREN, A WONDERLAND

Norway offers endless remarkable landscapes, but the Jæren coast is truly special: 15.5 miles (25 km) of white beaches, dunes, and sand dune vegetation—a land of silence and the sea.

One of the beaches in Jæren District

The coastal area from Egersund to Stavanger makes up Jæren District, which means "edge" in Norwegian. The district is famous for its 15.5 miles (25 km) of white sand beaches. The wide-open sky and peculiar light make it a landscape painter's paradise. Two of the area's wonders are Orrestranden Beach, the longest in Norway, and Borestranden Beach, considered the most beautiful. The interior is mostly made up of farms, while toward the sea the land is wild and protected. The beaches range from Sirevåg in the south to Tungenes in the north, and can be sandy, pebbly, or have a moraine shoreline. None has rocky cliffs.

There are three ways to visit the region: by car, foot, or bicycle. By car, follow the Nasjonalturistveg, Jæren's scenic road, which is part of the Nordsjøvegen. It stretches from Flekkefjord to Bore, for a total of 80 miles (130 km). The 4.5-mile-long (7 km) section from Hellvik to Ogna is an unpaved road and was built in the late 18th century. The road on foot involves walking on historic trails, such as the 17th-century Kongevegen (the King's Way), sections of which can still be seen, enjoying the beaches along the way. The route is: Hå–Obrestad Port–Grødalandstunet–Varhaug parish. In addition to the landscapes, with green hills on the right and ocher dunes on the left, you also pass a rectory, a lighthouse, a mill, and a cemetery. The route is also categorized as a Kystpilegrimsleia (Coastal Pilgrims' Trail). The stage from Egersund to Stavanger is about 62 miles (100 km). Lastly, there is the 86-mile-long (140 km) Jærruta bike path, a 4-day tour from Egersund to Sola via Hå, Time, and Klepp.

But if there is one boom to remember, it is that of sardines, which were caught, smoked and canned here from the late 19th century to the 1950s. The unbridled growth of the industry fed sailors, the army, and the general population. And it was exported all over the world. The discovery of oil in 1969 offset the end of that industrial cycle.

Ekofisk is in Stavanger, inevitably making Stavanger the "oil capital of Norway," but this little Abu Dhabi has a more solid foundation than its Arab counterparts. In the last decades, the city has taken off, so much so that the latest available report speaks of a negligible unemployment rate of 1.6 percent! It is now a hub for engineering and has a strong university and stable international relations, with many foreign residents and visitors. This brings with it a remarkable expansion of services, and Stavanger also has much to share in the gastronomic space, with many institutions, centers, producers, and experts making advancements in the field and making a name as Norway's hub for the food sector.

It was King Sigurd I the Crusader who decided to build a cathedral here and put the English bishop Reinald of Winchester in charge of the diocese. With the bishop, the place was also made a city. Stavanger, now the capital of Rogaland, retains its old town, a substantial number of houses from the 17th and 18th centuries, becoming the foundation upon which the modern and international oil city has grown into a somewhat anonymous business center. Its soul has been sold to black gold, brokered by the big Norwegian and foreign companies, which have their offices here. The large platforms, riddled with lights, metal architecture, and men in helmets, are assembled here, where advanced geology is also researched. It is inevitable since oil is Norway's primary resource.

After passing through the **tourist office,** the first thing to see is definitely the **Norsk Oljemuseum** (Oil Museum), which recounts how the oil and gas fields were formed, how they were exploited, as well as all the issues related to the environment

The First Commercial

In the late 19th century, Christian Bjelland started the production of canned sardines in Stavanger and, before long, became a leader in the industry. So, in 1902, he proposed to King Oskar II of Sweden-Norway to use his name on a line of sardines and obtained the royal seal. The fact that three years later the Kingdom of Sweden-Norway dissolved, and Oskar was no longer king of Norway, was overlooked. The name in English, King Oscar, became the brand sold all over the world. Bjelland understood how things can unfold, so to give his product another boost, he ran the first filmed commercial in Norwegian history, called *Sardine fishing,* a full ten minutes long, to go with the slogan, "Out, to conquer the world!"

The Norsk Oljemuseum is dedicated to the history of the local oil industry.

and extraction technologies. For a taste of the contrast, be sure to plan a visit to Gamle Stavanger, the old town consisting of 150 wooden houses built in the late 17th and early 18th centuries, and the **Domkirke,** the cathedral erected in 1125 by English craftsmen under the orders of Bishop Reinald of Winchester. The style is Anglo-Norman Romanesque, and the patron saint is St. Swithun. The chancel, damaged by fire, was redone in the Gothic style. The facade is linear and three aisles precede the apse, which is illuminated by a large ornate polifora. The baroque pulpit is by Anders Smith (1658), and the modern chandeliers are by Emanuel Vigeland. Behind it towers the Kongsgård, the royal palace, for the bishop and governor, which has been a school for the past 150 years.

Stavanger Tourist Office ✉ Strandkaien 61, Stavanger ☎ 518 59 200 🕒 summer, Mon.–Fri. 8 a.m.–6 p.m., Sat.–Sun. 9 a.m.–2 p.m.; rest of the year, Mon.–Fri. 9 a.m.–4 p.m. **fjordnorway.com • Norsk Oljemuseum** ✉ Kjeringholmen 1a, Stavanger ☎ 519 39 300 🕒 summer, daily 10 a.m.–7 p.m.; rest of the year, Mon.–Sat. 10 a.m.–4 p.m., Sun. 10 a.m.–6 p.m **norskolje.museum.no • Domkirke** ✉ Haakon VIIs gate 2, Stavanger ☎ 518 40 400

Øvre Holmegate is the most colorful street in Stavanger.

While you're there, it's also worth passing by Sjøhusrekken, the harbor's wooden warehouses: these 60 buildings built in the late 19th century stored salt, lumber, and other goods and now serves as offices, restaurants, and stores. Afterwards, take a stroll along Øvre Holmegate—or, Fargegaten, as the locals call it—the most colorful street in the entire city. Here the wooden buildings bring to life a true palette of colors, enhanced by little flags and soft lights, making it a magical place to experience.

A little farther south, the **Stavanger Museum (MuST)** is a network of museums that portrays the region from different points of view. The network includes the Naturhistoriske Museum, which illustrates Rogaland's wildlife and biodiversity, the region's cultural history, and local crafts; the Children's Museum, dedicated to the history and culture of childhood; the IDDIS Museum, which in turn includes the Canning Museum and

Stavanger Museum ✉ Muségata 16, Stavanger ☏ 518 42 700
🕒 Tues.–Fri. 11 a.m.–3 p.m., Thurs. until 7 p.m., Sat.–Sun. 11 a.m.–4 p.m.
stavangermuseum.no

Gladmat Culinary Festival

The whole Norwegian food supply chain resides in Stavanger, which is saying a lot. This means the city has control over the quality, authenticity and sustainability of ingredients, and, when paired with a gastronomic culture honed over the years and a market that upholds certain prices, it leads to culinary wisdom. Free-range pigs, sheep, goats and cattle, and fish from the fjords are integrated with organic produce. Stavanger's pantry sounds very appetizing, and culinary writers are paying more and more attention to it. If you're doubtful, check out the festival Gladmat, held in June every year.

the Printing Museum; the Stavanger Maritime Museum, dedicated to ships, shipyards, and ports through the ages; the Stavanger Kunstmuseum, an art museum boasting a beautiful collection of Norwegian artists from the 19th century to the present, including works by Frida Hansen, Lars Hertervig, and Kitty Kielland; Breidablikk, the Berentsen family manor house, built in the Swiss style in 1881 and enhanced by an English garden; and Ledaal, owned by the Kielland family, and therefore featured in the novels of 19th-century writer Alexander Kielland, which was built in 1799 in Nordic baroque style.

Another surprise about walking around Stavanger is the street art. It all started with the Nuart festival, which brought in artists from all over the world and stimulated the local scene. Now you can see art in various places around the city, particularly in industrial buildings.

Do not miss the innovative **Viking House,** which allows visitors to immerse themselves in the Viking world through virtual reality and ride on a fast *drakkar,* with explanations in English and Spanish. Another must is the Stavanger Konserthus, a concert hall at Sandvigå 1, which opened in 2012. It is indicative of new times, with two separate halls and a large outdoor space, and is home to the Stavanger Symphony Orchestra.

Viking House ✉ Strandkaien 44, Stavanger ☎ 412 46 716 ⌚ Open when the cruise ships are in Stavanger **vikinghouse.no**

The Arkeologisk Museum, at Peder Klows gate 30a, narrates 15,000 years of natural and cultural history, focusing on the Viking period, while the Jernaldergården, the Iron Age Farm, is a reproduction of a settlement from that era, with dwellings, tools, and demonstrations.

As is immediately apparent, Stavanger is a vibrant, rich, dynamic city. Although it remains relatively small, it offers amenities worthy of a metropolis: a technological city that dabbles in old white wooden houses. To put it another way, it is a city with a high standard of living and hospitality. Take your time to browse the streets and the harbor, between coffee and snacks, imagining what Western cities might look like in the near future.

Sandnes has now almost joined Stavanger, and shares its oil-oriented businesses. The western part is more

Stavanger–Bergen Scenic Bus

To travel from Stavanger to Bergen, you can take an express and scenic bus *(norway.no)*, with large windows, seats next to the driver, an all-glass upper deck, and a computer work area. It takes about five hours to travel the coast, along which you can admire the incredible natural landscapes. It is called Kystbussen, meaning coastal bus. The trip also includes two ferries, which are an opportunity for a snack break.

Preikestolen

Preikestolen, or "the Pulpit," is Scandinavia's most famous and spectacular viewpoint and one of Norway's most iconic landmarks, located just 25 miles (40 km) east of Stavanger.

This 1,904-foot-tall (604 m) rocky outcrop overlooks the Lysefjord and cannot be missed. What's special is the flat top that looks as if it was made specifically for looking down on the fjord, the essence of Norway, from above. To say it's worth a stop is an understatement. The wide-open view frames the majestic natural landscape with the waters of the fjord below and the mountains rounded out by the green and gray striped glacier. It's a two-hour walk to reach it and walk back for a total of 5 miles (8 km) and 1,640 feet (500 m) of total elevation gain. You can also join a guided tour and rent equipment. You start at the Preikestolen Fjellstue hut, at 885 feet (270 m), near the village of Forsand, which can be reached by car and ferry. There is also an express bus departing from Stavanger.

Preikestolen, a scenic viewpoint over the Lysefjord

industrial, while the eastern part has a rural setting. Check out **Vitenfabrikken,** an interactive science museum which focuses particularly on mathematics, energy, astronomy, and natural science. The parts related to the town include the DBS Bicycle Museum and the Figgjo Pottery Museum.

Moving a little farther east, it is worth mentioning the Nasjonalturistveg Ryfylke, another highlight. This scenic road from Lysefjord to Sauda, northeast of Haugesund, crosses the Røldal mountain pass. The region displays the essence of Norway: islands and archipelagos, plains, fjords, and high mountains. There are three experiences you must try: a stop in Flørli, a village that is famous for the world's longest wooden staircase, 4,444 steps, to see the Lysefjord, which can also be explored by bike from Forsand; the incredible Lysevegen road, which climbs along a cliff face from Lysebotn to Sirdal, snaking around a total of 27 hairpin bends to a 3,116-foot (950 m) peak, a beautiful and frightening experience; and finally a salmon safari on the Suldalslågen River.

On the west side of Stavanger is Tananger, near the airport, a lobster fishing port with an old village. To the north is Mosterøy, an island housing the Augustinian monastery of Utstein, dating from the 13th century and converted to a museum in 1965. It preserves a magnificent medieval cloister. Finally, to the northwest is Kvitsøy, whose lighthouse offers a splendid view of the archipelago. Also worth seeing are the church from 1620, a Viking-era cross, the ruins of the fort, and the old village.

The Suldalslågen River

To reach Haugesund from Stavanger, follow the E39 toward Randaberg, then take the Byfjord Submarine Tunnel, which at its opening in 1992 was the world's longest and deepest at 3.5 miles (5.8 km) long and 731 feet (223 m) deep, to Sokn and then to Mortavika on the island of Rennesøy. From here, you have to take a ferry to Arsvågen and finally take the E39 again to Haugesund. Alternatively, the route can be done by bus in about two hours.

Vitenfabrikken ✉ Storgata 28, Sandnes ☎ 477 76 020 🕒 Hours vary; check website **jaermuseet.no**

Train Travel along the Southern Coast

For those who do not wish to take the coastal route by car, there is the Sørland Railway, with the Sørtoget train. It leaves from Oslo and arrives in Stavanger in about eight hours after many stops. There is also an overnight train with beds, but the daytime train has all the amenities you might want: large windows, a café, comfortable seats, and the chance to hop off at intermediate stops, so you can visit the southern coast. The rail route does not follow the road route, passing more inland. Instead of offering only the sea and the coast, it traverses green valleys, mountains, viaducts, and long tunnels. It is a five-hour trip to Kristiansand. From Oslo, it goes to Drammen, where another line skirts the sea to reach Larvik, then rejoins in a loop at Nordagutu, the Vestfold line. After Hokksund (northern detour, Hønefoss line), it passes by lakes Fiskumvatn and Eikeren, and goes all the way to Kongsberg. Branch off here for Lake Heddalsvatn and Notodden. Here, you enter the Telemark region, with the train running halfway up the mountainside, with Mount Gausta and Mount Lifjell on the right. From here, you will find a vast countryside, as well as rivers and forests. At Nelaug, the train connects to the line to Arendal, Arendalsbanen, then it follows the Setesdal road to Kristiansand. After Audnedal, the train turns toward the mountains again, travels through a series of tunnels then along the hills beside the sea, and finally down the fjord to Stavanger. You can also get there by taking the spectacular Jærbanen rail from Egersund, which runs alongside the sea. Tickets are booked on the Entur app.

Haugesund

This city experienced growth during the herring fishing era, and integrated fish processing and preservation with shipbuilding and oil extraction. Today, there are no ships but many more services. Although it has a population of less than 40,000, it is the main center for the Haugaland District. More importantly, for those who decide to go there, it is the starting point for some wonderful excursions.

In August, the city becomes a center of film and music with the Norske Filmfestivalen and Sildajazz. The same month hosts the Harbor Festival, in Smedasundet, with markets, festivals, gastronomy, old boats, and ships.

See the pleasant downtown with its beautiful quay (Indre kai), the town hall, and the old houses of Smedasundet. Not far away is the **Dokken,** an open-air museum that reconstructs living and working environments of the region in the past, during the herring period. To get there, cross one of the bridges over the Smedasund, which offer a view from above.

One and a half miles (2 km) north of the town is Haraldshaugen, the place that Snorri's *Saga* recognizes as the tomb of Norway's first king,

Harald Hårfagre, to whom a statue in the town center is also dedicated. An obelisk was erected at Haraldshaugen in 1872, symbolizing the unity of the nation a thousand years after the battle that unified Norway. The obelisk is surrounded by 29 stones representing the states unified by King Harald.

Nearby is the 22-mile-long (35 km) Åkrafjorden, which collects the waters of the Folgefonna Glacier. This area, which can be reached in an hour and a half's drive from Haugesund, following the E134 toward Bergen, is mostly composed of steep mountains, villages, farms, and impressive waterfalls, such as Langfoss. Take a cruise or step into a hot sauna overlooking the fjord.

From Haugesund, take a ferry to the island of Utsira–the smallest Norwegian municipality by population–on which 300 species of birds roost in spring and fall. It is an ideal place for an uncrowded vacation. Special features include a still functioning lighthouse from 1844 with an attached keeper's house and the fact that in 1926 it elected the country's first female mayor. It sits at the West Cape of Norway and has recently become a popular street art spot, with houses, mills, and rocks covered in the works of international artists.

The Hair of the King

You know when a vow is made to accomplish something very difficult? The year was 872 and Norway, divided into small kingdoms, principalities, and fiefdoms, was proving reluctant to any sort of unification. The Viking kingdoms could not agree to stand together. There were many attempts; all failed.

A man with rather long hair, thus called Hårfagre, or "fair hair," at the time King of Viken, made his own attempt. The decisive battle, against captains and nobles, took place in the Hafrsfjord. It was, as usual, a very bloody fight, but Harald emerged victorious and unified Norway under one crown, and in keeping a vow he had made, he cut off his hair after the victory.

Karmøy

Much larger than Utsira and closer to the city, the island of Karmøy is home to Haugesund Airport. It is full of beautiful beaches with white sand and turquoise sea, like Åkrasanden in the fishing village of Åkrehamn. It is truly a must-see if you want to understand a little more about this country.

On the east coast of the island is Avaldsnes, a small village that was once the stronghold of choice for Viking sea captains, since it overlooked the Karmsundet Strait. From there, one could control navigation on the coast and set out on voyages of exploration. It was the northern route, Nordvegen, that gave Norway

Dokken ✉ Brugata 1d, Hasseløy, Haugesund ☏ 527 09 360
🕒 Open only in summer
haugalandmuseet.no

The Olavskirke, in the village of Avaldsnes, dates back to 1250.

its name. Also, as is demonstrated by the royal farm of King Harald Hårfagre, this was where the first idea of a united country was born. That is why the Court of Norway was initially based here. The Olavskirke (St. Olav's Church) dates from 1250 and is connected to the **Nordvegen Historiesenter,** which uses videos, films, pictures, smells, and objects to show what this center of control for the sea route was like in the past. There is also a reconstruction of a Viking farm. Next to the Olavskirke is the so-called Needle of the Virgin Mary, a 20-foot-high (6 m) stone monolith that hangs toward the church wall. According to legend, when the stone touches the building, Judgment Day will come.

Avaldsnes is also home to the Visnes copper mine, opened in 1865 and closed in 1972. It provided the raw material for New York's Statue of Liberty. Today, it is a copper museum, with about 2,000 photos, exhibits, work quarters, and miner houses. A 15-foot (5 m) statue stands above the canal, a reminder of its American twin. Father south, at the entrance to Boknafjorden, is Skudeneshavn, which has a beautiful, well-preserved 18th- to 19th-century center with more than 200 white wooden houses. Many were built around 1850, and the village markets itself as Norway's best for seeing this type of building. Most of today's owners live in Stavanger. Also worth seeing is the **Skudeneshavn Museum,** which illustrates life there 200 years ago, with a merchant's house and a house by the sea, where tales of boats and farming are shared. It is small but effective. ■

Nordvegen Historiesenter ✉ Kong Augvalds veg 103, Avaldsnes ☏ 528 12 400 **avaldsnes.info • Skudeneshavn Museum** ✉ Holmen 16, Skudeneshavn ☏ 900 51 039 **skudenes.no**

ITINERARY: DISCOVER TELEMARK

Pristine landscapes, wooden houses and churches, traditional decorations, and old boats: a drive through Telemark can really take you back in time. Discover one of the most spectacular routes in Norway, departing from Skien by boat and reaching Dalen by bike.

Before setting out, it is best to point out that the combinations of transportation and routes vary, since navigation on the lakes and canal alternates with bus and bike sections. The entire proposed route can be done by bus, or by round-trip boat, or half by boat and half by bus. If you wish to follow the route by bike, you will have to stop at Ulefoss on the way back since the bike must be returned to the rental company. There are numerous campsites and hostels along the canal, so splitting the route into several days is quite easy. You can also opt for a boat+bike package, combining pedaling and boating sections. For safety reasons, e-bikes cannot be taken on the boat, so if you rent one, you will have to return it before you can get on the boat. With that said, let's get started!

From **Skien** ❶ leave by boat early in the morning, and after a 45-minute boat ride you will arrive at the three locks at **Løveid** ❷. This point, carved into the rock, was the first section of the canal, built in 1861.

Hovedgaard manor house was built in 1807 in Ulefoss.

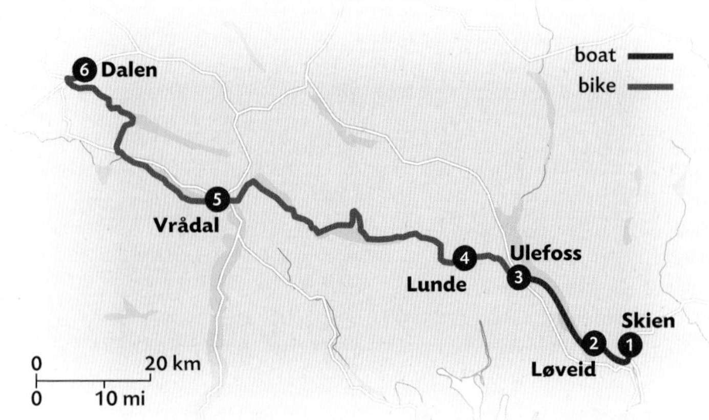

The locks make it possible to clear a 32-foot (10 m) drop. If you opt for a day's stop, you can experience the 2.3-mile (3.7 km) Skotfoss Trail, which runs alongside the river, passes through the forest, and reaches the old abandoned Skotfoss Bruk paper mill, opened around 1900. You can also see the old warehouses and the settlement that stood around it. You then glide by boat on Lake Norsjø among beautiful green landscapes, arriving after an hour and a half at **Ulefoss** ❸. Worth seeing here are Hovedgaard, an 1807 mansion built in the imperial style and open only in summer, and Øvre Verket, the old ironworks district, with colorful little houses that tell of the working conditions of those days.

In Ulefoss you can rent a bike and start riding the Kanalruta, which connects the town to Dalen via Lunde and Vrådal in 70 miles (113 km) (Ulefoss–Lunde 8 miles [13 km], Lunde–Vrådal 34 miles [55 km], Vrådal–Dalen 28 miles [45 km]).

You will ride on small roads that often run along the canal, which passes over undulating terrain and beautiful scenery, surrounded by the stillness of nature. But perhaps the most interesting moment is the spectacular locks, like those at Vrangfoss.

Pedal on to **Lunde** ❹. Here, you can take time for a canoe or kayak excursion and possibly stay overnight at First Camp. Then hit the road again for **Vrådal** ❺, which professes to be the ideal place for walking and swimming in nature. Boats, canoes, and kayaks are rented at the tourist office. The 19th-century Straand Hotel is also biker-friendly. The nearby lakes Flåvatn, Kviteseidvatn, and Bandak are home to timber towns on their shores, where, even today, lumber production is the main activity. But what fills the journey are the coniferous forests, the rocky outcrops, and the clear, green waters.

Back in the saddle, head to **Dalen** ❻, the final point of the circuit. Here, find Dalen Hotel, a magnificent historic hotel built in 1894, which was restored a few years ago, enhancing the romantic "dragon-inspired" architecture of the late 19th century and the furniture of the period. It is worth visiting the hotel, its verandas, rooms and salons, library, and billiard room, to relive a little piece of the belle epoque, Norwegian style. It is like visiting a museum, and the lights, fabrics, and decorations say a lot about the tastes of that period. You can also see old cars: a 1959 Jaguar, a 1928 Ford, and the Hotel bus Fleur de Lys, also from 1928, which make the setting feel even more real.

For a moment of relaxation, take refuge in the Soria Moria sauna on Lake Bandak, an important architectural landmark made of wood with golden tiles. An excursion to the village and *stavkirke* of Eidsborg, one of the oldest preserved in Norway with simple architectural lines and beautiful decorations, is strongly recommended. It is from the 13th century, later remodeled but always keeping the original design visible, and is dedicated to St. Nicholas. Legend has it that it was brought there by higher forces. Nearby is the Vest-Telemark Museum, consisting of an open-air area with 30 old buildings, and an indoor section telling of the cultural history of the region, from pagan cults to today's technology in electricity. After some hiking in the surrounding area, take the boat back from Dalen, or the bus if you are in a hurry, to return to Skien.

An old wooden building that is part of the Vest-Telemark Museum

Bergen, with its wooden houses overlooking the port, is Norway's second largest city. From here, you can reach the two major fjords, Sogne and Hardanger

BERGEN & AROUND

Norheimsund lies at the mouth of Hardangerfjord.

BERGEN

A former capital city, Bergen is now driving the country's growth. It has discovered the value of tourism and built a small industry from it, a new economic engine supporting the resources that come from oil. Commerce is thus the common thread linking the city's past, present, and perhaps future.

When you think of Bergen, the first thing that comes to mind is probably the fjords, especially magnificent Hardangerfjord and Sognefjord. That is its international brand. But the city is not just there as a gateway, or even a showcase. Consider two other images: Bryggen's beautiful row of warehouse-houses with their pointed facades seemingly pointing north, toward the origin of the cod industry; and Edvard Grieg's mansion in the hills where he composed his music. The most famous, "Morning Mood," is a set of poetic notes that spurs you to spend your day wisely. If you are lucky enough to experience a summer evening with the midnight sun bathing the old harbor houses, the experience will stay with you.

Bergen is the capital of Hordaland County and has a population of 255,000 (400,000 in the metropolitan area). The city and coastal climate

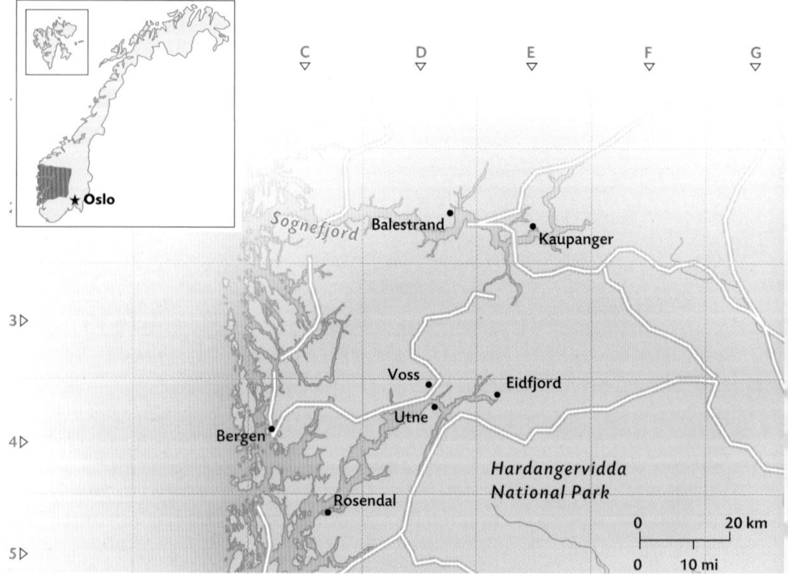

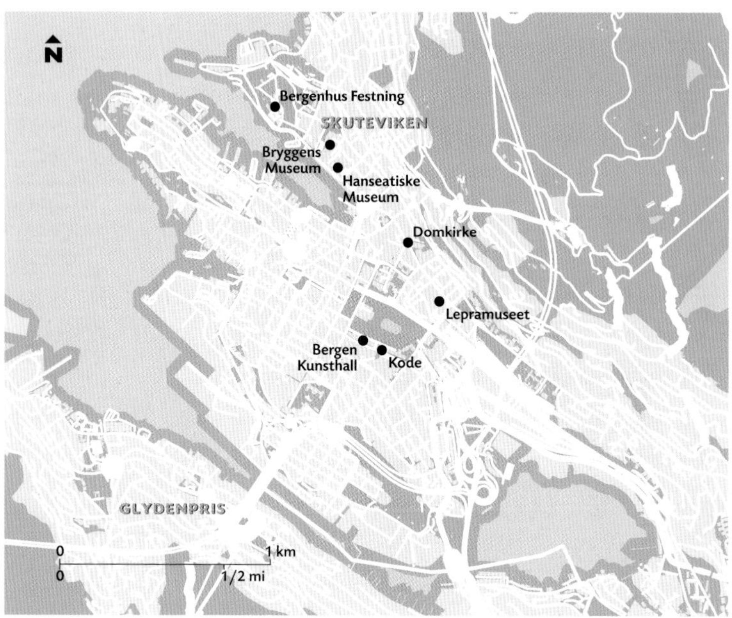

is tempered by the Gulf Stream but subject to Atlantic storms, which give it an average of 88.5 inches (2250 mm) of precipitation per year. This means there can be many consecutive days of rain or sudden changes in the weather, but also days of crystal clear skies and long summer evenings with incredible light, filtered by droplets suspended in the air. When this happens, the extraordinary landscapes of the fjord, islands, and mountains open up before you: it's the prototype of a certain Norway, that of the coast, fish, and commerce, as opposed to the gentler Norway of farms and forests.

The city is polycentric. Given the contours of the land, it had no other choice. Its founder, King Olav Kyrre,

NOT TO BE MISSED:

The Domkirke is Bergen's cathedral.

had named it Bjørgvin, meaning "land of the mountain," to emphasize the narrow space that rock and sea left for man's invention. Starting from Vågen, the old harbor, the city grew outward wherever it could, up the slope toward Fløyen and the nearby fjords, linking the various centers with an excellent road network. But, as is always the case, Vågen is still what draws people, as opposed to Bryggen and Bergenhus Festning, the local fortress. The triangular harbor district stretches between Torget Market, Torgalmenningen and Lungegård Pond. Bergen is also the starting point for an excursion on the Hurtigruten mail ship, which travels the entire Norwegian coast to Kirkenes on the Russian border every day of the year. The city also shines with its many festivals and concerts; it is home to banks and insurance companies, especially related to the

The House in the Middle of Nature

There is another place that shows Bergen's true colors, its other soul, a symbiotic complement to its commercial side: Troldhaugen, the home of composer Edvard Grieg, the fjord singer. This bourgeois home is simple but rich in culture and a model of a Bergenian home, the archetype of a home as hearth, which was replicated hundreds of times on the hills and even in the city. The mustachioed and long-haired Edvard Grieg (1843–1907) is considered Norway's greatest composer. Born into a family of musicians, he studied in Leipzig, influenced by early 19th-century German symphonies. In 1882, he bought the house in Bergen as his spring and summer residence. "My Troldhaugen, my Norway ... they form concentric circles. As an artist, I sit in the center and, fortunately, my piano is there with me," he wrote. If you listen to "Morning Mood" from *Peer Gynt* (1876), you can almost feel the fresh air coming toward you, the tree canopies swaying, your mood shifting with the start of the day.

A Train to Oslo

The Bergensbanen—the 292-mile (471 km) Oslo–Bergen railway line—is many things: a link between the two main cities, as well as a link between the sea fjord and the ocean fjord. Its track starts at the sea, rises more than 3,200 feet (1,000 m), and then dips back down. When thinking about its symbolic route, it should not be overlooked that between the two cities, the line crosses the Hardangervidda, a huge glacial plateau, considered the alter ego of civilization, the wild half of Norway, the primal soul of the country. The journey is six and a half hours, with a unique sequence of landscapes: forests and lakes, then plateau and glacier, and finally sea and fjord. The plateau section is perhaps the most scenic, running 17 miles (28 km) between snow guards that must be repaired each summer. Finse is the center of this part of the route, a ski resort just below the glacier and gateway to hiking in the Hardangervidda.

merchant navy, of which it is a hub; it boasts Europe's second largest oceanographic research institute and the country's first business university, as well as schools of art and architecture; it is the main base of the Navy and the heliport of choice for offshore platform workers and technicians.

Bergen was founded by King Olav Kyrre around the port of Vågen in 1070. The cod trade with coastal settlements to the north dates back to that time. The Bergenhus fortress, Norway's first royal residence, dates from the 13th century, back when Bergen was the capital of the kingdom. Around the 16th century, the city became a *kontor* (trading post) of the Hanseatic League, which dominated trade in the North. As early as 1536 these Germans were naturalized as Norwegians. It was through the city's port that Lutheranism, which arrived with merchants from Germany, spread to Norway. Over the next century, Bergen became the largest Scandinavian city with 15,000 inhabitants. In 1777, the rule of the Hanseatic League ended. In the 1970s, the metropolitan area formed, and in 1980, Europe's largest oil field was discovered in the North Sea, west of Bergen.

Today, the city invests heavily in tourism, as evidenced by the beautiful building near the fish market in which the **tourist office** is located. Here, you can ask for information in several languages and book activities, tours, fjord cruises, tickets to various attractions, and trains, as well as reserve rooms.

Bergen Tourist Office ✉ Strandkaien 3 ☎ 555 52 000 🕒 9 a.m.–4 p.m.
visitbergen.com

Downtown Bergen

Vågen, the old harbor, is a natural inlet that gave rise to the city and today is its own central, sentimental, and touristic destination. Around this branch of the sea rise the symbols of Bergen: the king's castle, the merchants' houses, and the best routes for visiting the city. This is where trips to the fjords depart, and this is where everyone, locals and visitors alike, hangs out. On the north side is Bryggen, or rather, Tyskebryggen, the German Pier, the name for the Hanseatic part of Bergen. It is a UNESCO World Heritage site, as are the **Hanseatiske Museum** (Hanseatic Museum), housed in one of Bryggen's oldest buildings, which recounts the lives of the merchants of the League, and the **Schøtstuene,** the room that housed the merchants' assembly.

The 12th-century Mariakirken

Next door is the **Bryggens Museum,** the cultural-historical museum based on excavations following a fire that destroyed part of the town in 1955 and housed in a reconstructed Hanseatic house. It is divided into various sections: health, trade, goods, beer and fish, shipping and daily life, the economy, festivals, and religion. There are also pottery, runic inscriptions, objects, and documents. Opposite the museum stands Mariakirken, a 12th-century church in Romanesque–Norman style, with three naves, used at the time by Hansa merchants. Note the baroque furnishings, the pulpit, the 15 statues of saints from the 17th century, and the 16th-century triptych above the altar. Farther toward the sea is the **Bergenhus Festning,** built in the 11th and 12th centuries but remodeled several times. Within the fortress area, it is possible to visit Håkonshallen (Håkon's Hall). Built between 1247 and 1261 by King Håkon Håkonsson in the Gothic style as a venue for feasts and receptions, it

Hanseatiske Museum og Schøtstuene ✉ Øvregaten 50 ☎ 53 00 61 10 🕒 June–Sept. 11 a.m.–5 p.m., Oct.–May 11 a.m.–3 p.m. **hanseatiskemuseum.museumvest.no • Bryggens Museum** ✉ Dreggsallmenningen 3 ☎ 55 30 80 30 🕒 Hours may vary; info on the website **bymuseet.no • Bergenhus Festning** 🕒 6 a.m.–11 p.m. **forsvarsbygg.no/festningene/finn-din-festning/bergenhus-festning**

Themed Routes

A quick visit or a longer stay in Bergen can be elevated by some of these themed walks, which cover the most interesting sites in the city.

1. Merchants & Markets: The Hanseatic houses, with their pointed facades caressed by the golden light of sunset, are an unforgettable sight. And they still bear the evidence of five centuries of trade. Explore their history in the Assembly Hall, the Bryggen and Hanseatic Museums, as well as the Mariakirken. And compare them with the modern fish market in Torget, where trade has been combined with tourism.
2. Downtown Walk: The center of any seaside town is its harbor, but Bergen has many harbors, and Vågen is both a touristic and symbolic place. The streets that run from the harbor include Torgallmenningen, toward the university, and Kong Oscars gate, toward the station. The first is a great place for shopping, meeting, and strolling, with the Ole Bull plass, the Festplassen, the Lille park lagoon Lungegårdsvannet, the rich picture galleries of Lars Hilles gate, and the pleasant Torggate that leads up to the Johanneskirken. The second, more inconspicuous street leads to the quiet cottage district of St. Jørgen.
3. Medieval Bergen: The starting point for this route is Håkonshallen within the imposing walls of the Bergenhus fortress. Following Øvregaten, you reach the cathedral, St. Jørgens Kirke, the Leprosy Museum, and the ruins of a Cistercian monastery. Then, outside the city, visit the ruins of Lysekloster Monastery and the newly rebuilt Fantoft Stavkirke.
4. Music of the Fjord: To explore Norway's long lasting relationship with music, you can start by visiting Grieghallen and maybe listening to one of the concerts held here. Troldhaugen, the home of Edvard Grieg, with its relics and concert hall, is the next stop. Then, head to the island of Lysøen to see Ole Bull's house museum, and finally to Fana, where the sonatas are those of the peasant tradition. In fact, the music of the fjord, set to the rhythm of the *hardingfele,* a special type of violin, are the inspiration for Grieg's chief works.
5. Bird's-eye View: Going up to Mount Fløyen is a unique experience. You can take the trails that run alongside the tracks. From the top, the view takes in the old city, the new neighborhoods, the fjord, the islands, and the buzz of marine traffic. If you feel tired, hop on the cable car to the peak.

The Hanseatic houses in Bryggen

was restored in the late 19th century with paintings by Gerhard Munthe recounting ancient sagas. Although under military administration, it hosts concerts, events, and festivals. Next to it stands Rosenkrantztårnet, the tower built in 1560 by Governor Rosenkrantz as a fortified residence on the earlier 13th-century building erected by King Magnus VI.

Not far away is the market square, Torget, overlooking the old harbor of Vågen. When we say market, we are mainly referring to fish. Since the 13th century, the square has been a place of exchange, and it now hosts the Fisketorget outdoor market throughout the summer from 10 a.m. to 6 p.m. In addition to fresh fish, shellfish, and crustaceans, you can savor ready-made sandwiches of smoked salmon or herring, and magnificent fjord strawberries. On the other hand, the Mathallen, or covered market, is open year-round, featuring fish, fruit, and vegetable stalls. There are also numerous small restaurants.

Moving slightly to the east is the Domkirke, the cathedral on Kong Oskars gate, built as a chapel in the 12th century and later enlarged and modified. The choir and the lower part of the Gothic bell tower remain from that period. Kong Oskars gate is one of the city's oldest arteries, along which sit the Cathedral School and the Danckert Krohn Cultural Center. It is then worth taking a walk on Torgalmenningen, a pedestrian promenade and shopping street, along the

A cable car takes you up to Mount Fløyen.

street that leads from the harbor to the university. Not far away, at Nedre Korskirke allmenningen 20, stands the Korskirken (Church of the Holy Cross), built in the 12th century but almost completely redone in the 17th century in the Renaissance style.

Also not to be missed is the Fløibanen, the cable car that climbs from Øvregaten to Mount Fløyen in just six minutes. The 1,049-foot (320 m) mountain is like a balcony overlooking the old city. From the top, you can see all of Bergen: the fjord, islands, and especially Vågen and downtown. Mount Fløyen can also be climbed on foot, on the trails running alongside the railway.

Returning to the museums, a must-see is the **Kode,** which groups four of them in different buildings, thus housing the second largest national art collection. The main one, Rasmus Meyer, displays paintings by Norwegian painters of the 19th and 20th centuries, such as Dahl, Werenskiold, Krohg, Astrup, and, most importantly, some works by Edvard Munch. Next door is the Lysverket, a museum housed in the former power company building from 1938, which lends itself to temporary international

Kode ✉ Rasmus Meyers allé 3, 7, 9 & Nordahl Bruns gate 9 ☎ 530 09 700
🕒 Hours vary by building **kodebergen.no**

art exhibitions. On the same street, right next to the Rasmus Meyer, stands the Stenersen, which boasts a collection of 250 works by 20th-century painters such as Ernst, Miró, Klee, Mondrian, and Picasso. Finally, visit Permanenten, the former Vestlandske Kunstindustri Museum, which houses a collection of European-level applied arts, mica wax, glass, contemporary furniture, and metalwork, as well as antique silverware and the Munthe collection of Chinese art. In addition to the four museums mentioned above, the Kode operates the art homes of Troldhaugen, Lysøen, and Siljustøl.

Along Rasmus Meyers allé is the **Bergen Kunsthall,** home to exhibitions, concerts, and events featuring contemporary international artists. Down the street is **Grieghallen,** the modern concert hall that hosts all kinds of music while also serving as a conference center. The building is also home to the Bergen Filharmoniske Orkester, among the oldest orchestras in the world, with a history dating back to 1765. From here, one need only cross the street to reach the Lille Lungegårdsvannet, a pond in the shape of an irregular octagon located in a city park. It is one of the most popular walks, ending at Festplassen,

Bergen Kunsthall ✉ Rasmus Meyers allé 5 ☎ 940 15 050 🕒 11 a.m.–5 p.m., except Thurs. until 8 p.m. (closed Mon.). **kunsthall.no**
Grieghallen ✉ Edvard Griegs plass 1 ☎ 552 16 100 **grieghallen.no**

The octagonal pond of Lille Lungegårdsvannet

where fun fairs, banquets, bands, and events are held.

When exploring downtown Bergen, stop in the St. Jørgen District, a labyrinth of old town alleyways with neat little wooden houses, for a restful walk away from the crowds. Here stands St. Jørgens Kirke, a medieval church rebuilt in 1702 following the great fire of 1624. Next door is St. Jørgens Hospital, housing the **Lepramuseet** (Leprosy Museum), which tells the story of the disease and of Dr. Gerhard Armauer Hansen, who devoted his life to fighting it and discovered its cause in 1873.

Moving to the opposite side of Bryggen, you enter Nordnes, the neighborhood that lies on the peninsula between Vågen and Puddefjorden. Here, 19th-century houses divided by narrow streets, cats, and embroidered curtains set the stage. The peninsula is home to the Magic Ice, a venue that offers a true exploration of the world of ice, with sculptures, themed lights, and music, and the Nykirken, a 600-year-old church rebuilt in the 18th century and then again in the 20th century following an explosion in 1944. At the far end, toward the sea, you can visit the **Akvariet i Bergen–Nasjonale Akvariet,** one of Europe's largest aquariums, which showcases the fauna of the northern seas and also explores the rainforest and rock of the shoreline and deep sea.

North Bergen

Moving to the north, one of the major attractions is undoubtedly **Storeblå,** the aquaculture center, which explains the practice through a digital exhibit on salmon farming. Afterwards, you can see the fish farm in person from a boat.

Next, head to the **Norges Fiskerimuseum,** a museum dedicated to the history of fishing along the Norwegian coast, its origins, and what it has meant for the city. Construction techniques, aquaculture, seal hunting, herring preservation processes, and the stockfish trade are narrated and illustrated. It is a contemporary museum with digital exhibits, set in an old 18th-century warehouse whose foundations rest on piles, located on the Sandviken Canal.

Then, of course, you must stop at the **Gamle Bergen Museum,** an open-air museum featuring 30

Lepramuseet ✉ Kong Oscars gate 59 ☎ 553 08 037 🕒 Open only in summer **bymuseet.no • Akvariet i Bergen–Nasjonale Akvariet** ✉ Nordnesbakken 4 ☎ 555 57 171 🕒 May–Aug. 9 a.m.–6 p.m.; Sept.–Apr. 10 a.m.–6 p.m. **akvariet.no • Storeblå** ✉ Sandviksboder 1G ☎ 530 06 160 🕒 11 a.m.–4 p.m. **storebla.no • Norges Fiskerimuseum** ✉ Sandviksboder 23 ☎ 530 06 160 🕒 Jan.–Aug. 11 a.m.–5 p.m.; Sept. 11 a.m.–4 p.m.; Oct.–Dec. Tues.–Sun. 11 a.m.–3 p.m. **fiskerimuseum.museumvest.no • Gamle Bergen Museum** ✉ Nyhavnsveien 4 ☎ 479 79 576 🕒 Open only in summer **bymuseet.no**

Norges Fiskerimuseum

houses from the old town, reconstructed around the small square. This is 18th- and 19th-century Bergen, with wooden buildings and narrow paved streets. Note the workshops, the baker, the dentist, the barber, the photographer, the 16th-century town hall, and the 17th-century *manufaktur*

Southwest Bergen

In the southwestern part of the city, visit **Damsgård Hovedgård,** a 1770s manor house that is a symbol of rococo in Norway. Even the garden harks back to that era with its unique choice of flowers, plants, and herbs. There is also no shortage of fountains, statues, and a swan pond.

Southeast Bergen

To the southeast, the **Bergen Sjøfartsmuseum** (Maritime Museum) celebrates Norwegian shipping by displaying ship models, shipboard objects, and paintings. Next door is the multipart **Universitetsmuseet i Bergen** (University Museum). The cultural history building is currently closed, awaiting renovation. Its collections of archaeology, anthropology, Norwegian sacred art, rural history, and folk art are available at the Natural History Museum, dedicated to botany, zoology, and geology.

For an interactive experience, move farther east and visit **VilVite,** a science museum with experiments available for adults and children.

Lastly, don't miss Ulriken, which at 2,109 feet (643 m) is the highest of the seven mountains around downtown Bergen. It can be easily reached on foot or by bus, but the ride on the Ulriksbanen, the cable car from Haukelandsbakken 40 to the top, is much nicer. The mountain offers a beautiful view of the fjords. Take a break at the cafés and restaurants. ■

Damsgård Hovedgård ✉ Alléen 29 ☎ 553 08 033 🕒 Open only in summer for guided tours **bymuseet.no • Bergen Sjøfartsmuseum** ✉ Haakon Sheteligs plass 15 ☎ 555 49 615 🕒 May–Sept. Mon.–Fri. 10 a.m.–4 p.m., Sat.–Sun. 10 a.m.–5 p.m.; Oct.–Apr. daily 11 a.m.–3 p.m., Thurs. until 6 p.m. **sjofartsmuseum.museumvest.no • Universitetsmuseet i Bergen** ✉ Muséplassen 3 ☎ 555 80 000 🕒 Tues.–Sat. 10 a.m.–4 p.m., Sun. 11 a.m.–5 p.m. **uib.no • VilVite** ✉ Thormøhlens gate 51 ☎ 555 94 500 🕒 Tues.–Fri. 9 a.m.–3 p.m., Sat.–Sun. 10 a.m.–5 p.m. **vilvite.no**

THE HANSEATIC LEAGUE IN BERGEN

Wherever there was some flow of trade, some particular product or object that had to be shipped to its rich cities, the Hanseatic League would be there. And Norway had indeed something unique to sell: stockfish, or cod that had been caught and air-dried in the Lofoten Islands.

The Hanseatic League had a strong interest in Norway. This was undoubtedly dictated by the fact that the Norwegians produced stockfish, a very important food since it could be stored for a long time, as the Vikings had demonstrated on their long sea expeditions.

The relationship between the Hanseatic League and Norway began in the 13th century, when the Germans were granted permission to trade in Bergen, where they remained until the late 18th century. Lübeck, the capital of the League, was where everything important was decided for the allied cities, including the administration of Bergen's *kontor* (trading post) and the appointment of its senior merchant and the curate of Mariakirken. The Germans lived in a special area of the city, an extraterritorial district that did not fall under Norwegian law. This area is still called Tyskebryggen, or German Pier, today.

The Hanseatic warehouse-houses, which mimic the architectural, structural, and customary models present in other cities of the League, are built of wood and arranged in rows of up to 15 buildings. Each of these consists of two floors—the upper one was reserved for living spaces and the lower was used as a storage unit, with an external staircase and gallery, and a granary. Each town in the League also had its own communal house, where all those who worked there gathered to eat together, discuss business, and teach apprentices during the calm winter months. This was called the Schøtstuene, and from his little *scrivekamer*, or office, the merchant could supervise the work and take care of inventories and accounts.

It's worth pointing out that in the Hanseatic community of Bergen, as in other kontors, only men were allowed. These merchants, clerks, apprentices, laborers, and artisans were only devoted to the religion of trade and were not to be distracted by women. In addition, German novices arriving fresh off the boat in Bergen were subjected to the so-called *Bergener spiele* by veterans: they were thrown into the sea several times, sentenced to various penances amid the laughter of older men, or stuffed into chimneys. Beginning in the 16th century, however, the Norwegian rebellion imposed a different status on the district, reducing it to a mere trading branch.

AROUND BERGEN

Bergen's land is fractured by fjords and islands. In the immediate vicinity, to the north, a disused textile factory now houses a museum, and to the south are the house where Edvard Grieg lived, a museum about local agriculture, fishing, and crafts, and an old industrial village.

Troldhaugen was the home of composer Edvard Grieg.

About 12 miles (20 km) north of Bergen is the **Tekstilindustrimuseet,** a museum located inside a textile factory from 1859, celebrating the history of the textile industry in western Norway. You can tour the factory to see the machinery in action, the carded wool, and the working environment, all accompanied by films.

Heading south, 3 miles (5 km) from town, is the Fantoft Stavkirke, a church erected in 1170 in Fortun i Sogn and transported here in 1883. The structure was razed by fire in June 1992 and later rebuilt. Today's appearance supposedly replicates the original. Continue in the same direction to reach **Troldhaugen,** literally

Tekstilindustrimuseet ✉ Salhusvegen 201, Salhus ☏ 552 51 080
🕒 Guided tours available; hours vary by season **muho.no**

"Troll Hill," the house where Edvard Grieg and his wife Nina lived for 22 years, which opened as a museum in 1928 and is now part of the Kode (see p. 149). Built in 1885 near Lake Nordås, with a magnificent view of the fjord, it was the composer's hearth, the inspiration for his poignant music. The house remains as it was then, including photos on the walls, the piano, books, and household objects.

In Stend, about 10 miles (16 km) from Bergen, is the **Hordamuseet,** a museum that illustrates the region's agriculture, fishing, and crafts while collecting old houses, boats, textiles, and objects from the rural part of Hordaland. The site also consists of an open-air area with 30 buildings and a warehouse with 26 boats.

Even farther south, on Bjørnafjorden, are the ruins of the English Cistercian monastery of St. Mary, dating from 1146, and a 17th-century wooden church. The island next door is Lysøen, or the "island of light," which houses the villa of musician Ole Bull, a violin virtuoso and one of Grieg's mentors. Bull's summer residence was built in 1872 in a cosmopolitan style. Furniture, objects, and mementos were left there by the musician when he died in 1880. There is also a network of paths on the island designed by Ole Bull himself. Like Troldhaugen, this site is also part of the Kode.

Heading southwest 10 miles (16 km) from Bergen, you find Alvøen, an old industrial village where paper and gunpowder were produced. Here is the 18th-century mansion of the Fasmer family, with a rich collection of furniture, textiles, silverware, and porcelain. If you're looking for beaches, you'll find Grønevika and Mjølkevika to the south, or Helleneset and Tommervågen to the north, all accessible by local buses. ■

Fantoft Stavkirke was first erected in 1170 and rebuilt after 1992.

Troldhaugen ✉ Troldhaugvegen 65, Paradis ☎ 530 09 700 ⏲ summer Tues.–Sun. 11 a.m.–5 p.m.; rest of the year 11 a.m.–4 p.m. **kodebergen.no**
Hordamuseet ✉ Hordnesvegen 24 ☎ 553 08 035 **bymuseet.no**

THE GREAT FJORDS

The word "fjord" comes from the Old Norse *fjorðr,* which translated means "to go," "pass," or "cross." Bergen is the gateway to Norway's two main fjords, or fjord systems: the Sogne and the Hardanger. The fjords can be visited by car, with some ferry crossings, or by bus, express boat, bicycle, and, in some parts, by train. It depends on the time you have available, your preferences, and, if you opt for biking, your physical condition and degree of training. It's best to use the app Entur, a Norwegian travel planner.

Sognefjord is the deepest fjord in Norway.

Sognefjord

The first thing to know about this fjord is that it is long—127 miles (204 km) to be precise—and deep. Its many branches multiply its features and views. It deserves attention, and that means it deserves time. If you only have 1 to 3 days, you might want to opt for a cruise that would take you to a few of the main points of interest. If, on the other hand, you want to truly savor Sognefjord's wealth, take your time. You can hop from ferry to ferry, pedal along the coast, paddle a kayak, or experience a sauna on its waters. Maybe treat yourself to a seaplane flight. Then dig into its many nuances: the villages and *stavkirker,* the small museums, and even a climb up to one of the branches of Jostedal Glacier, for fresh vantage points. It's not a figure of speech: this fjord is a universe that contains different worlds. The very coexistence of sea and glacier is something special. What's unique are its many faces, such as the steep or rounded mountains, the valleys, and the small, cultivated plains. Nærøyfjord, a UNESCO World Heritage site, clearly demonstrates this diversity among the branches.

Of course, when planning a trip to Norway you might be tempted to leave out the fjords, since they have been seen over and over and may be perceived as an overly touristy destination. Yet this fjord has a unique appeal, and it's not one that attracts a rowdier demographic. There must be a reason that these lands were a cradle of tourism, with the British coming here to fish and the King of Prussia using it for rest. The area is dotted with historic hotels, built in the late 19th century to accommodate the traveling aristocracy. But the fjord has another voice, that of the villages, which remained isolated for centuries, maintaining their own traditions. The land here is also known for its apple and cherry groves, and raspberry and strawberry production.

To drive from Bergen to Sognefjord, follow the E39 to the north and stop in Brekke. Otherwise, to the east, follow the E16 heading to Vangsnes, a town located on the same fjord but much farther inland. In the first case, you will pass through the Romarheim Valley, which joins Osterfjord with Matresfjorden, and arrive at Brekke and the port from where the ferries leave, Ytre Oppedal. On the opposite shore is Lavik, with its 19th-century, octagonal church. From here, drive along the north shore of the fjord to arrive in Balestrand after a little more than 55 miles (90 km). Note that the E39, at Vadheim, continues north to Førde. This is another way to get to Fjærland and Jostedalsbreen National Park, instead of following the fjord to Balestrand. Near Førde visit the interesting **Sunnfjord Museum,** to discover what life was like in the fjord villages: wooden houses are visible in the open-air area and collections in the main building.

Balestrand & Around

One of the large tourist centers in Sognefjord, Balestrand has the atmosphere of an international resort town. There are Viking graves near the pier, and two other mounds are located outside the settlement. On one of these is a statue of King Bele, wanted by none other than Wilhelm II of Germany, a frequent visitor. Here, it seems, he received news of the Sarajevo bombing in the summer of 1914 and thought no more of the fjord. Born with the abundant tourism of the late 19th century, the village is surrounded by an extraordinary landscape of mountains and sea, making it ideal for hiking, kayaking, and water sightseeing. You can also rent a bike.

Sunnfjord Museum ✉ Jølstravegen 107, Førde ☎ 577 21 220 **misf.no**

Balestrand, on Sognefjord

A must-see is the Kviknes Hotel, a local institution. Built in the 19th century in the Swiss style, with turrets, arabesque designs, and small columns—all in a dazzling white—it hosted English and German royalty and is still well preserved today. Try the delicious Norwegian buffet in its beautiful dining room, then admire the Høyviksalen hall, with dragons carved in wood by Ivar Høyvik.

Balestrand is also home to the **Norsk Reiselivsmuseum,** a unique museum chronicling the birth and development of tourism in the area and in the whole country. Another draw is St. Olav's "English church," a chapel commissioned in 1897 by Margaret Green, wife of a local hotelier, in a style that imitates the stavkirker. It matches the "Swiss style" popular at the time—there is nothing authentically Swiss about it, but Switzerland, then, was the premier mountain tourist destination for the British.

From Balestrand, take a boat trip along the beautiful Fjaerlandfjord, between steep mountains and greenish water—the color is due to the nearby glacier—to the town from

Norsk Reiselivsmuseum ✉ Holmen 12, Balestrand ☎ 474 53 053
🕒 May 1–June 23 Tues.–Sun. 11 a.m.–4:30 p.m. **misf.no**
Norsk Bremuseum ✉ Fjærlandsfjorden 13, Fjærland ☎ 576 93 288
🕒 Apr.–Oct. 10 a.m.–4 p.m.; June–Aug. 9 a.m.–7 p.m. **bremuseum.no**

which the branch takes its name. Here, stands the **Norsk Bremuseum,** entirely dedicated to glaciers and full of interactive exhibits–the building has received numerous international architectural awards. Also not to be missed is Bøyabreen, a branch of the great Jostedalsbreen, where you can kayak, walk on Haugabreen Glacier, or experience a sauna on a floating platform in the fjord.

Opposite Balestrand is the village of Hella. From here, the Sognefjordvegen road runs eastward along a very pretty part of the fjord, between steep walls, meadows, and orchards. Leikanger, for example, is a sea of fruit trees, with an oak tree said to be a thousand years old, and a 26-foot (8 m) Viking stele. Take a pleasant walk through the orchards, then sample the local cider and snack called *vestlandslefsa*. You can try it at the **Henjatunet** farm. Continuing on, you reach Nornes, with the monument commemorating the 1184 Fimreite naval battle between King Sverre and King Magnus, and Sogndal, a beautiful village with old wooden houses and a relaxed fjord atmosphere.

Past Sogndal is Kaupanger, where a 12th-century stavkirke has a rather distinct style. Compared to the others, it has a slenderer upward design and less decoration. It looks almost like a raised hut, yet it is harmonious and

Henjatunet ✉ Henjavegen 40, Leikanger ☎ 415 11 774
henjatunet.no

Soaring Over the Blue

One experience in Norway is worth more than a thousand words: riding in a seaplane. You will take off from the fjord in a small plane and fly over the waters sandwiched between steep mountains. From there, you can see villages, valleys, snaking roads, farms, and waterfalls. Then you will thread through a beautiful valley leading to the great Jostedalsbreen Glacier. Maybe combine the flight with a cruise or a kayak trip. Seaplanes are based in Bergen, Aurland, and Eidfjord; flights last from 25 to 85 min.

elegant. In the old sawmill, you can admire Sogn boats and fishing boats, then visit the workshop, which explains the construction techniques of each.

Close to Kaupanger, continuing on Route 5, is Mannheller, where you can board for Fodnes, on the eastern side of the fjord, and from there reach Lærdal, which rejoins the E16 to Fagernes and Hønefoss or Route 52 to Hemsedal and Gol. Both roads lead to Oslo. Part of the municipality of Lærdal is Borgund, which boasts one of the most outstanding stavkirker in all of Norway, dating from 1180 and excellently preserved.

Route 55 from Sogndalsfjøra runs into the Arøyelva River and the great waterfall of Helvetesfoss. Because of its strong current, the river is ascended by large salmon—45-pound (20 kg) specimens are not uncommon. Proceeding northward, in the small village of Solvorn, see the historic Walaker Hotel and cross Lustrafjorden by ferry to the Urnes Stavkirke on the other shore. This church, a UNESCO World Heritage site, dates from the 12th century and gave rise to the Urnes decorative style, with stylized zoomorphic motifs. It is testimony to the assimilation and adaptation of Christianity by Viking culture.

From Solvorn, continuing on 55, you arrive at Gaupne, a village in the municipality of Luster. Here, you can take the scenic Jostedal road, which ends at Breheimsenteret, the visitor center of **Jostedalsbreen Nasjonalpark,** with architecture inspired by glacial formations. There you can book guided walks or climbs on the glacier and reach the lake below the ice flow to cross it by boat. Jostedalsbreen Glacier is the largest in continental Europe, a massive force of nature: 183 square miles (474 sq km), 37 miles (60 km) long, 1,873 feet (571 m) thick at its thickest point and rising from 196 to 6,470 feet (60–1,957 m) above sea level. Numerous hikes depart from both the valley and the access points of Fjærland and Veitastrond. One of these is to the spectacular Nigardsbreen.

Sognefjellet Scenic Route

Nasjonal Turistveger 55, or Sognefjellet Scenic Route, runs from Gaupne to Lom. It's 67 miles (108 km) of everything you could wish for: green valleys, the blue fjord, snow-studded mountains, and remarkable light. As if that were not enough, there are several viewpoints. The road is also bikeable, except in winter.

Start in Skjolden, where you bid farewell to Sognefjord to take on the 4,704-foot (1,434 m) climb up the Sognefjellet road. The section from Fortun to Turtagrø is famous for its sharp turns and splendid views. Turtagrø, below Mount Store Skagastølstind, was the birthplace of Norwegian mountaineering—although it was an

Jostedalsbreen Nasjonalpark ✉ Njøsavegen 2, Leikanger
jostedalsbreen.no

A stretch of the Sognefjellet Scenic Route

Englishman who got the ball rolling in 1876—and is still a hub of mountain sports today. Shortly afterwards, you come to Oscarhaug, a service area where a pillar commemorating the 1860 horseback visit of the future King Oscar II stands.

The next destination is Sognefjellet, the highest point of the route and a mountain pass that has always been used by inland people to transport their products to Bergen. Many hikes are possible from here, for example to Skogadalsbøen or Vettisfoss Falls. Over the pass, the road descends to Bøverdal, with mountain cabins in Bøvertun and Bøverkinn. Alternatively, Elveseter offers a nice hotel and an old farm with buildings from the 17th century. Next comes Galdesand, birthplace of Norwegian-American entrepreneur Jørgine Slettede Boomer. She is buried at her Storhaugengard farm, the property she bought right next to the one where she was born in 1887. She emigrated to New York in search of fortune in 1903, later becoming the owner of the Waldorf-Astoria Hotel, hanging out with presidents, explorers, stars such as Charlie Chaplin and Frank Sinatra, and having a house built by Frank Lloyd Wright.

From Galdesand, make the climb up to Galdhøpiggen—the highest mountain in Norway at 8,100 feet (2,469 m). Summer skiing is possible on the glacier: the Galdhøpiggen Sommerskisenter offers equipment, season tickets, a bar, and restaurant. This area is part of Jotunheimen Nasjonalpark, with high mountains, glaciers, lakes, and reindeer. In addition to Galdhøpiggen, the park also includes the 8,044-foot (2,452 m) Glittertind. One of Norway's best trails runs through here.

The route then follows the Besseggen, a 10-mile (17 km) high ridge. It is recommended to take the boat in Gjendesheim to Memurubu, and

EXPERIENCE: Fjord Cheese

From a culinary perspective, the Norwegian land is best known for its fish, but many dairy products are also produced on the shores of its fjords. One of the oldest is called *gamalost,* meaning "old cheese," and is made from skimmed cow's milk—made of 50 percent protein and only 1 percent fat—and then aged. Some say it dates back to Viking times. To try it, you must travel to Vik, where there is still a farm that produces it.

Some goat cheeses, on the other hand, are made from raw whole milk exclusively by some licensed producers (Norwegian law requires the pasteurization of milk), found in the villages of Undredal and Aurland. These are called *geitost,* and they have been produced for at least 500 years (today, they are a Slow Food presidium). There is a white-colored version and the brown-orange *brunost,* which has a caramel flavor.

Brunost is a typical brown-orange cheese.

then take the trail back to the start while enjoying the view of the colored glacial lakes. Once past Galdesand, the Sognefjellet reaches its final destination: Lom.

Lom

Lom is the municipality of the park, the village of Fossbergom being its base. In town are a beautiful medieval stavkirke, modified in the 17th century and featuring acanthus decorations typical of Gudbrandsdal, and the Storstabburet, a large old granary. A must-see is the Lom Bygdamuseum, an open-air museum that illustrates the ancient life of the valley through wooden houses and farms. Another recommended stop is the **Norsk Fjellsenter,** which tells the story of Norway's mountains and glaciers, as well as offering guided tours and trail information. A point of interest in Lom is the historic Fossheim Hotel. A late 19th-century post station, the hotel has preserved its old chalets and boasts a magnificent dining room, with stained glass windows overlooking the church. Lom is an ideal place to explore the surrounding nature. Local agencies offer hiking in the mountains and to glaciers, summer ski trips, rafting in the Sjøa, hunting, and fishing. Attractions include Prestfosstraversen, the 656-foot (200 m) zip line above the Prestfossen Waterfall.

Norsk Fjellsenter Brubakken 2, Lom 612 11 600 10 a.m.–4 p.m.
norskfjellsenter.no

Hardanger's Violins

Norway's national instrument is the *hardingfele*. The shape is that of a traditional violin, but the strings are different, allowing for a special range of sounds, a unique resonance. The oldest known specimen comes from Jåstad, in the Ullensvang District, and dates from 1651. It is the hardingfele that accompanies Norwegian folk dances and music, especially along the fjords. It is thus more than an instrument; it is a kind of historical memory of the country's peasant and seafaring traditions. Ole Bull, a virtuoso of the instrument, and Edvard Grieg also used it in their music linking folk and classical traditions.

One of the most extraordinary experiences is Klimapark 2469: walk along a human-made, 230-foot-long (70 m) tunnel dug into Stone Age ice to learn about biology and geology, nature, human and wildlife in the highlands, the melting of snowdrifts, and permafrost. Also not to be missed is Tidsaksen, a half-mile-long (1 km) geological trail along which panels and stones show the changes that have occurred on Earth and in the solar system over 4.6 billion years.

From Lom, on route 15 eastward, head to Otta, where you can take the E6 from Oslo-Lillehammer to Trondheim. If, instead, you follow route 15 northwest, you are confronted with Mount Dalsnibba, with views at 4,842 feet (1,476 m) over the town of Geiranger. If, however, you take the E16 from Bergen, you first reach Vinje, where the road continues to Gudvangen and then to Flåm, with the option of taking the scenic road from Aurlandsvangen that ends at Lærdalsøyri. If you later opt for the 53 toward Øvre Årdal, you can hike to Norway's highest waterfall, Vettisfossen, with a 902-foot (275 m) drop. Returning to Vinje, instead of continuing on E16, you can take route 13 and climb the 3,234-foot (986 m) Vikafjell, in a region of mountains and lakes that forms the border between Hordaland and Sogn og Fjordane Counties, and then descend to Vikøyri. Along the way visit Hopperstad Stavkirke, dating from 1130, and Hove Steinkyrkje, Romanesque masonry church dating from the 12th century. Once you arrive in Vangsnes, take a ferry to Dragsvik (20 min) to reach Balestrand and Fjærland, or Hella (15 min), continuing to Jostedalsbreen Nasjonalpark and Lom.

Hardangerfjord

According to legend, the fjord got its name from Harder, a maiden who came to these parts with her Germanic tribe during the migration period. The girl probably came to these parts following the wild reindeer who had settled on Hardangervidda, the plateau overlooking the fjord. The Vikings descended from those peoples. Over the centuries, many others visited the fjord. For example, in the Middle Ages, the

English Cistercians passed through and introduced the cultivation of fruit trees; the Scots traded in timber in the 16th-18th centuries; and English and German noblemen started tourism on Norwegian soil here and in Sognefjord in the 19th century.

Hardangerfjord is an 111-mile-long (179 km) fjord with many branches and an area of 2,432 square miles (6,300 sq km). It has a subpolar oceanic climate with mild temperatures and average precipitation of 53 inches (1,350 mm) per year. Glaciers, like the massive Folgefonna, remain on the highlands, shaping the fjord. The lands between the sea and the mountains consist of moraines, or sand and gravel deposited before the last ice age. At the same time, the area contains fertile soil suitable for fruit growing up to 984 feet (300 m) above sea level: 2,718 acres (1,100 ha) covered with half a million plants. Salmon also finds a suitable environment here. The clean, cool waters coming down from the plateau encourage its breeding, along with rainbow trout.

The Hardanger District also retains a fondness for tradition and craftsmanship. Its costumes, fiddle making, embroidery, wood- and silverwork

The *hardingfele,* the national instrument, is similar to a violin.

dating from the 17th century are still active today, as is boat building, passed down in the schools of Jondal and Norheimsund. In all this, there's also tourism, which is increasingly important to the local economy.

A classic way to get from Bergen to Hardangerfjord is by car, following the route to Dale, Granvin, Kvanndal, and then along the west coast of the fjord to get to Folgefonna, detour to Odda, and go up the eastern branch. A more inconvenient, but much more enriching, way is to board an express boat in Bergen and in two hours arrive in Rosendal. From there take the bus to Odda and then to Lofthus and Kinsarvik. Then reach Utne and Kvanndal by ferry, board a bus to Norheimsund, and finally one last bus to Bergen. The route can also be done the other way around, or by replacing bus routes with bike.

Again, as with Sognefjord, the length of stay depends on how much time you want to devote to the fjord. In general, Folgefonna and Utne are must-sees, so consider 5 to 7 days. Otherwise, there are buses to Eidfjord, from which cruises in Hardanger depart. Finally, we recommend a trip on the Hardanger scenic route, which explores the fjord.

Fjord Cider

Apple orchards are a feature of the landscape here. First cultivated by Cistercian monks in the 13th century, apples have been popular with Norwegians ever since. But only recently has apple cider become a commercial product. The cider is made by a consortium of 50 fruit growers that have obtained a Sider frå Hardanger certification, the first in Norway for an alcoholic beverage. Juices from different apple varieties are blended to balance the acidity with the fruitiness. Alcohol by volume ranges from 3 to 12 percent, and, depending on the sugar, the cider can be sweet, semi-dry, or dry. In May, the air buzzes with the Internasjonale Siderfest, in Odda. And in Ulvik there is Cider Road, which has three farms that can be visited.

Rosendal

This village is quite interesting. You can see **Baroniet Rosendal,** a castle from 1665 surrounded by a rose garden, which holds events in summer. Then there's Salmon Eye, a floating cultural center by the architecture firm Kvorning Design. Seen from afar it looks, as the name implies, like a salmon's eye, but perhaps the meaning is more symbolic, a reference to how fish see aquaculture and its environmental sustainability. Last, be sure to stop by the Steinparken, which highlights

Baroniet Rosendal ✉ Baronivegen 60, Rosendal ☎ 534 82 999
🕒 Open only in summer 10 a.m.–5 p.m. **baroniet.no**

Baroniet Rosendal is surrounded by a lush rose garden.

the art already present in nature—a uniquely Norwegian trend. Here, you can explore the geological diversity in an artistic way, with carved boulders and sculptures.

The Steinparken offers a taste of **Folgefonna Nasjonalpark,** as well as Folgefonnsenteret, a research center that explains and illustrates Hardanger's aquatic life, the planet's water cycle, sustainable resource use, and climate change. You can rent bikes and boats or book a guided tour.

Folgefonna is Norway's third largest glacier and is divided into three parts: Nordre, Midtre, and Søndre. There are ice tongues, melt streams, waterfalls, and valleys. The main activity, besides the obvious admiring of magnificent views, is guided glacier hikes with crampons. Another, although unusual, is glacial kayaking on the Møsevatnet, between small icebergs.

On the road from Rosendal to Odda, Jondal is the gateway up to **Fonna Glacier Ski Resort,** where

Folgefonna Nasjonalpark ✉ Skålafjæro 17, Rosendal ☎ 534 84 280 **folgefonna.info • Fonna Glacier Ski Resort** ✉ Jondal ☎ 941 00 000 🕒 9 a.m.–3 p.m. **visitfonna.no**

summer skiing can be enjoyed. A 12-mile (19 km) scenic road leads from the fjord to the glacier. Odda, which has been part of the municipality of Ullensvang since 2020, is the end point of Sørfjorden, a branch of Hardangerfjord. It is a center for hiking and has five spectacular waterfalls in the valley, the best known being Låtefoss. One of the most fascinating hikes is to Trolltunga, the "tongue of the troll," a rock jutting 328 feet (100 m) out over a lake.

Nearby is Lofthus, with the open-air Skredhaugen Bygdetun, worth seeing, and many trails leading to local viewpoints. The main attraction, however, is the apple orchards, so much so that there are walks organized during blossoming season and a cider cruise from Eidfjord to Odda. In Kinsarvik, the Husedalen Valley is home to four roaring waterfalls. To see them all requires a 5- to 6-hour walk along the Hardanger Fossasti footpath, a shuttle taking you to the starting point and picking you up at the finishing point. From the village you can finally reach Utne by ferry or take a bus to Eidfjord.

Eidfjord

This beautiful village at the foot of the Hardangervidda Plateau, which has its own scenic road, is situated on the eastern end of the fjord, with a lake behind it that formed by separating from the fjord branch. The motto here is "active days and lazy days," and as soon as you experience the atmosphere, you'll understand what that means. Nearby, there are many trails. You can also go sea kayaking, rent bikes, visit the fjord on speed boats, or participate in guided tours. Don't miss Vøringfossen, a powerful waterfall with a 597-foot (182 m) drop into the Måbødalen. A narrow bridge crosses over the valley at the drop point, allowing you to admire it in all its beauty. A little higher up along Route 7, at Øvre Eidfjord, is the interactive **Norsk Natursenter,** illustrating Norwegian nature and climate.

Utne

This idyllic town sits at the tip of the headland separating the two main branches of the fjord, condensing some of the views of Hardangerfjord, viewed best from the historic Utne Hotel, built in a unique style that is recalled in the Utne Kyrkje. This is also home to the **Hardanger Folkemuseum,** which displays with careful dedication small details that are often overlooked, for example embroidery, simple, yet elaborate costumes, and a collection of *hardingfele,* the fiddles of the fjord. All are near the open-air section with old log buildings. There are numerous walking and hiking trails in the sur-

Norsk Natursenter ✉ Sæbøtunet 11, Øvre Eidfjord ☎ 536 74 000 🕒 10 a.m.–6 p.m. **norsknatursenter.no** • **Hardanger Folkemuseum** ✉ Museumsvegen 36, Utne ☎ 474 79 884 🕒 Sept.–Apr. Mon.–Fri. 9 a.m.–3 p.m.; May–Aug. daily 11 a.m.–17 p.m. **hardangerfolkemuseum.no**

Steinsdalsfossen, in Norheimsund, boasts a 164-foot (50 m) drop.

rounding area; alternatively, you can take a ferry to Kvanndal. From here, Route 13 leads to Granvin and then to Voss. Going southwest instead leads to Norheimsund, with a bus to Bergen. Before boarding the bus, however, check out the Steinsdalsfossen Waterfall, with a 164-foot (50 m) drop. It is special one because you can walk behind the sheet of water. ■

ITINERARY: HARDANGERVIDDA, AURLANDSFJORD, VOSS

A wonderful and essential representation of the area around Bergen, this itinerary offers a fitting historical and geographical snapshot of Norway, from highland and fjord to wild reindeer and the cod trade. The Hardangervidda Plateau sits at an altitude of 3,280 feet (1,000 m) and is the largest in Europe, the extreme result of glacial erosion, which has left its traces not only in polished stone, but also in lakes and ponds, pools and streams. The local fjord is called Aurland, a branch of the Sognefjord, which shows how the ice ended up as part of the ocean. Above, reindeer move in large groups. Below sits Bergen, with its historic market and centuries-old traditions of stockfish and exports. To see all this in just over 186 miles (300 km), by train, catamaran, and bus (or bicycle) is extraordinary.

The starting point of this trip, which in its entirety takes about four days, is **Bergen** ❶. From here, head by train to **Voss** ❷, suspended between Hardangerfjord and Sognefjord, between sea and mountains, a collection of villages with the administrative center in Vossevangen, which managed to revive its tourism some time ago. Considered the capital of safe extreme sports, Voss is also working to become a certified Sustainable Destination. Its destruction in 1940 during World War II has left it with only a minimum of historical monuments that form the basis of tourist activity. The landscape, however, remained intact, with about 500 lakes, as well as rivers, streams, and mountains.

See the Voss Folkemuseum, with 16 old buildings around a large courtyard. The 17th- and 19th-century houses were inhabited until the 1930s. The museum also includes other sections, such as the old vicarage of Oppheim and the Dagestadmuseet, dedicated to a local woodcarver, with rich collections of handicrafts. Also not to be missed are Finnesloftet, the oldest nonreligious wooden building in all of Norway, with a banquet hall from 1250, and Vangskyrkja, a 13th-century church with an octagonal tower and interior balcony. Before leaving, it is worth trying the Voss Gondol, the cable car that takes just a few minutes from the train station to 2,690-foot (820 m) Mount Hanguren, offering magnificent views of the region. After having finally made a trip to the two spectacular waterfalls Tvindefossen and Skjervsfossen, all that remains is to get back on the road.

Reboard the train at Voss and get off at Myrdal. From there, take the Flåmsbana, the railway that gracefully traverses the steep route to the fjord.

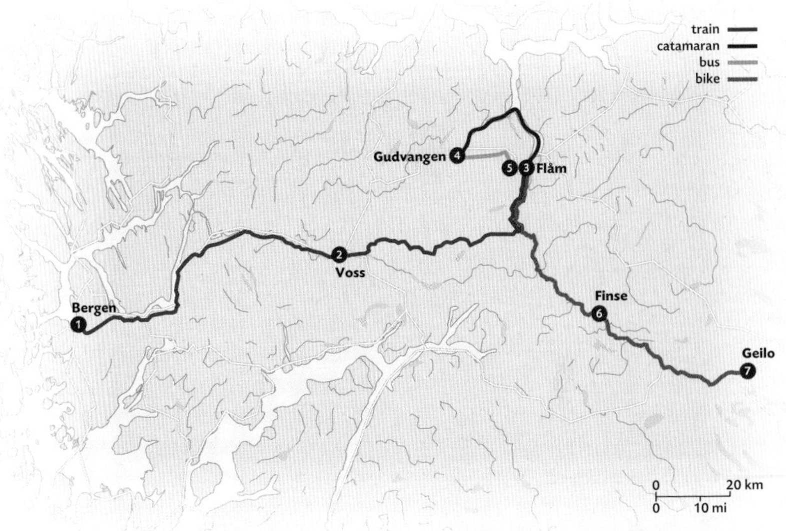

It is 12 miles (20 km) through 20 tunnels, most of them dug by hand—say a prayer for the diggers. The train offers a view of Kjosfossen Waterfall with a short stop and, in autumn, the deep valley in a show of colors. An hour later, you arrive in **Flåm ❸**, proving the conviction that travel is best done unhurriedly.

A world opens up here: mountains and fjords are no longer an obstacle, but an asset. You can choose hikes in Aurlandsdalen, called "Norway's Grand Canyon," with a full tour of about 37 miles (60 km) divided into several legs with stops at huts along the way. Or enjoy the mountains by following the scenic road between Aurlandsvangen and Lærdalsøyri, passing through the 15-mile-long (24.5 km) Lærdal Tunnel. The road is open year-round up to the Stegastein Lookout. To tackle this part of the route, you can rent a car in Flåm. But it can also be done by bike if you are sufficiently trained.

With a nice cruise on an electric catamaran along the Aurlandsfjord and Nærøyfjord, from Flåm, you can reach **Gudvangen ❹**. No words are needed to describe the beauty of the landscape, full of sheer mountains and waterfalls; suffice it to say that both branches have been designated UNESCO World Heritage sites. In Gudvangen, a true Viking experience is a must: immerse yourself in the Viking Valley, a reconstructed village where you can explore the life of these ancient people. From here, return to **Flåm ❺** by shuttle.

Once in Flåm, hop on a bike for **Finse ❻**. The cycle route is called Rallarvegen, which means "railway workers' road," after those who built the Oslo–Bergen railway in 1904. it became a cycle path in 1974. Alternatively, since there is cycling in the next section as well, you can reach the city by train or, in winter, by ski.

Finse was the training ground for explorers such as Nansen and Amundsen ahead of polar expeditions. There are magnificent views from here. To the northeast is Hallingskarvet Nasjonalpark, which encloses the 22-mile (35 km) mountain range shaped by several ice ages, with the highest peak at 6,341 feet (1933 m). To the south is Hardangerjøkulen, the sixth largest glacier in Norway. Farther on is Haugastøl, both a station and the arrival/departure point of Rallarvegen and the beginning of the Hardangervidda Scenic Road, which connects the village with Eidfjord via a 41-mile (67 km) route with 4,101 feet (1,250 m) of elevation gain. What can you see? Well, the fjord, the impressive Vøringsfossen Waterfall, the Måbødalen Canyon, the many lakes on the plateau, the Hardangerjøkulen Glacier in the background and, if you are particularly lucky, wild herds of reindeer.

With a final effort, you arrive at **Geilo** ❼, the destination of this itinerary. Geilo is a place that must be felt. At first glance, it is ordinary, with no special attractions or vantage points, especially when compared with the spectacular views of the Alps or the Rocky Mountains. But the

Hardangervidda

Hardangervidda is the largest plateau in Europe, nearly 2,702 square miles (7,000 sq km) of fascinating and desolate landscape dotted with lakes and marshes. Thousands of wild reindeer live here, competing for grazing with sheep, goats, and cows. The plateau lies about 3,937 feet (1,200 m) above sea level, with peaks, like Mount Jøkulen, exceeding 5,905 feet (1,800 m). The arctic flora and fauna are more varied and interesting than elsewhere, for here western and eastern species coexist. The landscape varies from the west, where there are deep, narrow valleys, glaciers, and large waterfalls, to the east, where the plateau is gentler and more uniform. In one of the lakes on the plateau, the first traces of humans in Norway were found.

A dense network of trails traverses the plateau far and wide, bearing witness to the hunting, fishing, and grazing of animals that have been its main resource for centuries. Outdoor activities and a renewed interest in nature have reopened this area to people and tourism. A 1,312-square-mile (3,400 sq km) national park, Hardangervidda Nasjonalpark, covers a good half of the area, protecting the local flora and fauna. Trails and refuges are available for exploring, hunting, or fishing.

Biking on the Rallarvegen Trail

ordinary ends there. It is a sustainable destination, lies exactly halfway between Norway's two urban centers, Oslo and Bergen, and is in the middle of the highlands. So what's left to do? Try new things, challenge yourself, explore deeper, and learn. Available activities include mountain biking, rafting, canyoning, hiking, lake exploration, bike trails, zip lines, guided glacier tours, and horseback riding. In winter try downhill skiing, cross-country skiing, snow biking, snowshoeing, sledding (including horse- and dog-pulled), snowmobiling, and ice bathing. Or hop aboard the Oslo–Bergen railway line, which offers remarkable views. Because of its location, you can decide where to head for your next adventure.

As you travel up the Atlantic coast, you encounter Ålesund and Trondheim, before reaching the Arctic Circle, beyond which lies the land of the Sami

THE CENTER-NORTH

Kylling bru railway bridge crosses the Rauma River.

THE CENTER-NORTH

The geographical borders of the Center-North, to simplify, cover the 621-mile-long (1,000 km) section of Norway between Ålesund and the Arctic Circle, via Molde, Kristiansund, and Trondheim. It is a lesser known and less prized region than others, but as a whole it has great potential for outdoor tourism.

Musk oxen dwelling in Dovrefjell-Sunndalsfjella National Park

Norway is not a monolith. It has great diversity and an abundance of nuance. You might think that a fjord is always a fjord, and likewise for every island or national park. But think again. The Center-North region shows how considerably diverse the terrain can be within the same territory. After all, its southern end, Ålesund, is at 62° N, while its northern border, Bodø, is at 67° N, a driving distance of about 621 miles (1,000 km).

At the heart of this vast territory lies Trondheim, one of medieval Norway's cradles and a vibrant city of culture. Then there is Ålesund, in art nouveau style, and a myriad of fjords, the most famous and visited of which is undoubtedly Geirangerfjord. We can't, however, forget to mention Kristiansund, with its four islands. Or the unique coastline full of fjords to the south, the remarkable mountains, and the national parks.

North of Trondheim up to the Arctic Circle is a jagged landscape of thousands of islands, islets, and rocks, like crumbs scattered in the sea. The strengths of the northern half are undoubtedly its magnificent

NOT TO BE MISSED:

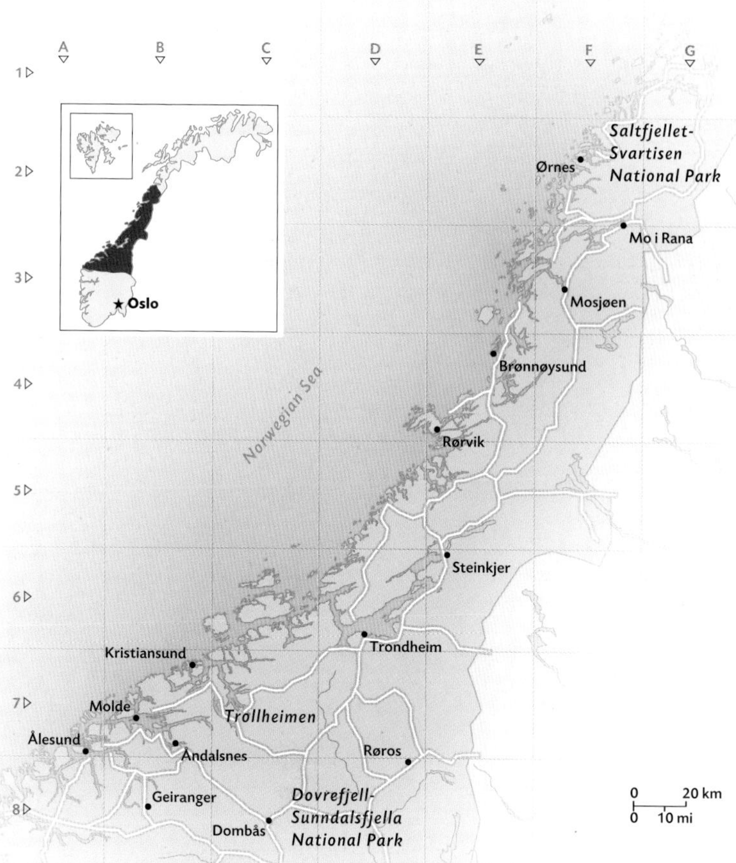

vistas and the endless opportunities to enjoy the outdoors. Cycling and mountain biking, hiking, rock climbing, zip-lining, kayaking, canoeing, sailing, speed boats, and ferries are the best ways to visit this slice of Norway. That's not to mention the railway lines: the Nordland and Rauma, as well as the Oslo–Trondheim provide an invitation to leave the car behind. As is the Hurtigruten, the mail ship, which calls at many of the ports in the area. All of these options are valid and wonderful. But there is one route that gives you a true reason to visit this region more than any other: the Atlantic Road. Built like a ribbon connecting a myriad of little islands, it defies the reach of the ocean—or chases its ebbs and flows. There, perhaps, you will find the true identity of this territory. ■

FROM ÅLESUND TO TRONDHEIM

After admiring the great fjords of Bergen, get to know those farther north, between Ålesund, Molde, and Kristiansund. Nordfjord, Storfjord, Romsdalsfjord, and the massive Trondheimsfjord offer a different perspective of the delicate relationship between mountains, sea, and islands. Three places can give a good understanding of the significance of this area: Ålesund, a Jugendstil city; Geirangerfjord, a UNESCO World Heritage fjord; and Dovrefjell-Sunndalsfjella National Park, the home of the musk ox.

Ålesund lies on the Atlantic coast of Norway.

Ålesund

When the fire broke out, fueled by a severe winter storm, no one in Ålesund thought about the possibility of giving the city a new look. That January night in 1904 wiped out 800 houses and left 10,000 people homeless. Within three years, the town was rebuilt in the Jugendstil or German art nouveau style with Norwegian influences, thanks to strong financial contribution from the Kaiser of Germany, Wilhelm II. The leaders of this revival were 50 young Norwegian architects who had studied in Germany and the United Kingdom, as well as figures of local society, wealthy from the trade, fleets, and shipyards. It was an opportunity for everyone to move from a city made of wood to a new 20th-century urban center. Plus, given that the country had just separated from Sweden three years earlier, it was time to encourage Norwegian pride. Ålesund's houses, built with this in mind in 1907, still look just as good today with careful restoration. The colorful facades, towers, and spires towering over the sea give the city an incomparable fairy-tale feel.

Ålesund, which today has a population of about 67,000, has ancient roots, as witnessed by some settlements dating back to the Stone Age, as well as by the Viking Borgundkaupangen, a medieval center of trade that later declined with the arrival of the Germans of the Hanseatic League, who monopolized trade. The marble church on the island of Giske, dating from the 12th century, is one of the earliest signs of nascent Christianity and was once the private chapel of the powerful family that ruled the region. Ålesund is also connected to the story of Gange Rolv, later called Rollo in Rouen: the son of a Viking king, he ventured south and in 911 received the lands of Normandy (*norrman* in fact means "man of the north") from King Charles III, called the Simple, of France.

Just a quick look at a map—with the intricate and fractured coastline of fjords, islands, and islets—will give you an idea of why Ålesund is so spread out. The name itself–*sund* means "strait"–recalls the passage between the islands of Norvøya and Aspøya, which form the heart of the modern city. It is one of the largest fishing ports in the country, equipping a sizeable and rather technological deep-sea fleet active year-round at various points in the Arctic and Subarctic region. The area is also home to food preservation and refrigeration businesses, as well as shipyards

The New Ålesund

Sometimes crises can present great opportunities. When its wooden buildings burned in 1904, Ålesund was already suffering from the urban restrictions of the province. So, inspired by the urban canons of Camillo Sitte's Vienna, engineer Frederik Næsser designed a new city that respected the irregularities of the terrain, while a school of young architects designed 350 buildings, all different. The result, achieved in three years, was spectacular, and propelled a small, unknown city to the center of European attention. The project manager, Henrik Nissen, set certain standards, such as height, material, amount of light, and hygiene, but the architects responded handsomely, not only finding multiple solutions for houses, stores, and warehouses, but also designing decorations, interiors, and furniture, so much so that their style became known as Ål Stil, "style of the city." Everyone was thrilled because the Germanic Jugendstil was embellished with Viking elements in full "dragon style," inspired by the local *stavkirke*.

The Jugendstilsenteret complex and KUBE museum

that have adapted to the oil business and new technologies. All this in a region, Møre og Romsdal, that sits in the middle of the network of famous fjords, such as Geiranger.

After a stop at the **tourist office,** explore the city's main attraction: its fabulous buildings in full Norwegian Jugendstil. They have been restored so well that they earned the 1988 Houen Prize for the preservation of urban environment. Particularly worthly is the **Jugendstilsenteret og KUBE.** The complex includes the national art nouveau center, the Jugendstilsenteret, situated in a 1907 building in which the old Swan Pharmacy was housed (the interiors are authentic), and the KUBE, a museum focusing on applied art, design, architecture, and visual arts. Like a time machine, it will take you back to the time when the city was burned. Then move on to Brosundet, the canal that separates the two main islands. Try the experience of crossing it in a kayak to see the buildings from below *(guided tours available).*

To enjoy a bigger picture, climb Aksla, the nearby 623-foot-tall

Tourist Office ✉ Skateflua, Ålesund ☎ 703 09 800 ⌚ Open daily in summer 8:30 a.m.–6 p.m.; rest of the year Mon.–Fri. 8:30 a.m.–4 p.m. **fjordnorway.com • Jugendstilsenteret og KUBE** ✉ Apotekergata 16, Ålesund ☎ 702 39 000 ⌚ Tues.–Sun. 11 a.m.–5 p.m. **vitimusea.no**

(190 m) hill reached by 418 steps from Byparken. Here, admire the magnificent panorama of the city, the fjords, and the mountains of Sunnmøre. The scenery is so exciting that almost all photographs of Ålesund have this perspective. The summit can also be reached by car, the Bytoget train, or a via ferrata. On the summit is a restaurant with a viewing terrace.

Next, stop at the **Fiskerimuseet,** a museum located in an old harbor warehouse from 1861 that escaped the fire. It is dedicated to the art of fishing, from the modern, hypertechnological facilities to the history of the activity on the Atlantic coast, the processing of dried cod, and the extraction of its oil. Near the canal, the **Aalesunds Museum** celebrates the city's history, its founding, development, and milestone events, including the 1904 fire.

About 3 miles (5 km) east of the center is the **Sunnmøre Museum,** which boasts an open-air section with 56 old buildings, and a rich collection of boats in the indoor section. Next door is the interesting **Middelaldermuseet,** a museum dedicated to the Middle Ages, illustrating daily life in the region at the time.

Other local curiosities include Ellingsøytunnelen. Opened in 1987, the two-mile (3.5 km) underwater tunnel connects the center with the island of Norvøya.

Moving on to the island of Hessa, visit **Atlanterhavsparken,** a large aquarium and marine science center. Located on the Atlantic coast, it was expanded in 2021 and is preparing for more work as it has been named a marine center by the Norwegian government. Amid islets and rocks, the depths of the Storfjord are explored, with the ocean bringing in herring and mackerel.

Just to the west, on the island of Godøya, you can see a prominent rocky outcrop with a beautiful view of the region, and then admire the Alnes lighthouse, built in 1876.

Also nearby is Runde, the most important bird island in southern Norway. A guided boat tour is available in the summer to see the half a million birds that crowd the rocks. Some 240 species live here, including puffins *(Fratercula arctica).*

Heading inland, stop in Stordal, 28 miles (45 km) from Ålesund, and visit Rosekyrkja (Church of the Roses), dating from 1789, with its

Fiskerimuseet ✉ Molovegen 10, Ålesund ☎ 702 39 000 **vitimusea.no** **Aalesunds Museum** ✉ Rasmus Rønnebergs gate 16, Ålesund, 905 71 260 🕒 summer Mon.–Fri. 11 a.m.–3 p.m. , Sat.–Sun. noon–3 p.m. **aalesunds.museum.no • Sunnmøre Museum** ✉ Museumsvegen 12, Ålesund ☎ 702 39 000 🕒 Tues.–Fri. noon–6 p.m., Sat.–Sun. noon–4 p.m. **vitimusea.no • Middelaldermuseet** ✉ Borgundgavlen 21, Ålesund ☎ 702 39 000 **vitimusea.no • Atlanterhavsparken** ✉ Tueneset, Ålesund ☎ 701 07 060 🕒 Open daily in summer 9 a.m.–5 p.m.; rest of the year 10 a.m.–4 p.m. **atlanterhavsparken.no**

interior decorated with *rosemaling,* and the old farms Løsetstova and Ytste Skotet.

Geirangerfjord & Around

One of the greatest tourist spots in Norway, this fjord was awarded UNESCO World Heritage status in 2005—along with Nærøyfjord—as archetype of all fjords: sheer green cliffs, peaks reaching 5,577 feet (1,700 m), waterfalls at every bend, and the sea like a mirror. At 9 miles (15 km) long, Geirangerfjord, a secondary branch of Storfjorden, offers mind-blowing views when crossed by boat.

What makes this fjord so special are its steep walls and the waterfalls that break the silence. The landscape is beautiful and varied, offering all kinds of experiences, from kayaking and speed boating, e-biking and hiking, to zip lines, via ferratas, and Tibetan rope bridges. But if you're looking for truly unforgettable experiences, try a cruise with live music and food on board, or hear the voice of the waterfall on a hike along the Fosseråsa Trail to the Storsæter Falls, where you can stand behind the falling water. The music of the waterfall is impressive. Don't miss the exceptional viewpoint from the

The Dalsnibba viewpoint

skywalk at Dalsnibba. Built in 2016, this observation deck suspended 4,921 feet (1,500 m) above sea level is reached by the fabulous Nibbevegen, a winding road built in 1939 that climbs the mountain. Just 2.5 miles (4 km) from the village, on Route 63, the Flydalsjuvet viewpoint is another great spot for photos.

Ørnevegen, or the Eagle Road, also offers a lot for visitors. It is a mountain road–officially, Route 63–that connects the village of Geiranger, overlooking the fjord, to Eidsdal. Opened in 1955, the road, which passes through eagle habitats, winds through 11 hairpin turns as it climbs from Geirangerfjord to Korsmyra at 2,034 feet (620 m). Stopping at Ørnesvingen, the highest point of the hairpin bends, you can see the fjord, the Seven Sisters Waterfall, and cruise ships and other vessels floating by. The viewpoint was redesigned in 2006 by a firm of architects when the road was included in the Turistveger.

In the village, the **Norsk Fjordsenter** also doubles as a separate tourist office in summer, as well as a hub for the western branches. It tells how the fjord was formed geologically and what the landscape looks like today, as well as the biological diversity of animals and plants. In season, there are many cruise ships passing through. From the Atlantic to Geiranger is 74 miles (120 km), which is a 3-hour cruise if you do it by catamaran, with audioguides dedicated to the landscape. E-bikes or electric cars can be rented at the village. There is also a boat that sails from town to town on the fjord year-round, giving the perfect opportunity for an off-season cruise. The ferry from Geiranger to Hellesylt operates year-round too.

Alternatively, you can travel to Geiranger by train from Oslo or Trondheim, with a stop in Åndalsnes, then by bus, or directly by bus from Oslo, Bergen, Trondheim, Ålesund, or Åndalsnes. There is also service by ship: the Hurtigruten postal ship stops in Geiranger in summer and Ålesund in other months.

By car from Ålesund, follow the E39 to Sjøholt, and then the E650 to Liabygda, where you can take the ferry to Stranda, which offers remarkable hiking opportunities in the Sunnmøre Alps and the Stranda Skisenter, one of the best ski resorts in the country. From there, Route 60 leads to Hellesylt. Another option is to follow the E650 to Linge and then ferry to Eidsdal, to reach Geiranger on the Ørnesvegen, the Eagle Road.

At Hellesylt, the scenery is magnificent, with a large rushing waterfall cascading into the fjord and a stream with crystal-clear water but black reflections from the ferrous rocks over which it flows. A green sea and a village cling to its

Norsk Fjordsenter ✉ Gjørvahaugen 35, Geiranger ☎ 702 63 810
🕒 summer 9 a.m.–7 p.m.; rest of the year 10 a.m.–4 p.m. **fjordsenter.com**

The Seven Sisters Waterfall, in Geirangerfjord

mountain. Here you can experience kayaking in the fjord, but you can also try a boat or zodiac cruise to Geiranger. On the sea journey, you will turn into Geirangerfjord after a few minutes to admire the sharp, high mountains on the left, Devil's Gorge, and then the waterfalls: the Bride's Veil, the Seven Sisters, which are light and melodic, and the Suitor (Friaren), on the opposite shore, strong and rushing. The sea of the fjord is their nuptial bed. The fjord's curiosities also include the farms of Skageflå and Knivsflå, with their captivating location at the edge of the cliffs.

From Hellesylt, take a beautiful detour on Route 60 and then 655, to the wonderful and lonely Norangsdalen Ravine that runs to Hjørundfjorden. Overlooking the fjord is the village of Øye, with the magnificent late-19th-century Hotel Union, one of the hotels that made tourism history in Norway because it was frequented by royalty and nobility. Beneath the peaks of Skruven and Jakta, the Swiss-style building conjures the atmosphere of the past.

From Øye, proceed on Route 655 to Leknes, where you take the ferry to Sæbø, which offers magnificent views of the fjord and serves as a gateway into Bondalen, a beautiful mountain valley that leads to Ørsta. Before the latter town, a side road on the right heads to Kolås, a valley that allows you to approach the sharp peaks of the Sunnmøre Alps. These were formed by the movements of the fjord and glaciers, which have left peaks up to 5,249 feet (1,600 m) rising out of the sea. A six-hour tour of Urkedalen Glacier also departs from Ørsta. Finally, the valley of Molladalen offers a crown of spectacular pointed peaks, such as the Bladet (Blade). It can be reached by bus from Ålesund or by car from Ørsta, following the E39 to Barstadvik.

Åndalsnes

Moving farther north, stop at Åndalsnes, a village on Isfjorden (at the end of Romsdalsfjord), at the mouth of the Rauma River with a valley of steep mountains behind it. Here you climb to the viewpoint of Rampestreken, about 1,801 feet (550 m) above the fjord. Don't miss the **Norsk Tindesenter,** opened in 2016, which towers over the fjord in a pointed diamond shape. It is a mountaineering center and tells the story of this sport in Norway. It offers the country's highest indoor wall and a special via ferrata, the Romsdalsstigen, available also with a guided tour.

Norsk Tindesenter ✉ Havnegata 2, Åndalsnes ☎ 712 23 300
🕒 Mon.–Fri. 10 a.m.–5 p.m. **tindesenteret.no**

The "Troll Road"

Of the many scenic roads of Norway, all different in setting and landscape, this one stands out for its 11 hairpin turns and 2,300-foot (700 m) climb. Part of Route 63, the 64-mile-long (104 km) Nasjonal turistveg Geiranger-Trollstigen—or "Troll Road"—reaches a maximum peak of 3,405 feet (1,038 m). If you start from Langvatnet, you first pass Dalsnibba and Flydalsjuvet, then tackle Ørnesvegen, a ferry crossing from Eidsdal to Linge, and finally Trollveggen to Sogge Bru. Trollveggen, meaning "wall of trolls," is also the road up to Trollstigen Pass, which divides two valleys. The road was built in 1936 between high mountains, such as Bispen (4798 feet/1,462 m), Kongen (5,295 fee/1,614 m), and Dronninga (5,065 feet/1,544 m) to the west, and Storgrovfjellet (5,344 feet/1,629 m) to the east. Each of the bends in the road has a name, and the crossing is either cut between rocks or reinforced with low walls. Open from mid-May to autumn, the Troll Road can also be traveled by renting an e-bike in Åndalsnes. The visitor center on the Trollstigen Plateau has a cafeteria as well as two steel-and-glass viewpoints designed by the Reiulf Ramstad studio.

The Romsdalsgondolen, on the other hand, is a cable car that leads to a platform with a restaurant and magnificent views of Mount Nesaksla. E-bikes can be rented in Åndalsnes with an already programmed GPS track to climb the Trollstigen Pass. We must also mention the Romsdalseggen chain, which perhaps offers the most in terms of views, including the Åndalsnes Fjord below, Trollveggen, the peaks of Nordre Trolltind, and, in the distance, Molde and the ocean.

There is also Rauma Valley, of course, with a 6.2-mile (10 km) ridge trail, an elevation gain of 3,182 feet (970 m), and an average hiking time of eight hours. You can walk up from the parking lot in Vengedalen, but there is also a bus that leaves from the train station. There are also guided hikes with the Norsk Tindesenter and Hotel Aak *(hotelaak.no)*. One tip is to try the Raumabanen, the Rauma railway line, which is considered one of the most spectacular. It runs from Åndalsnes to Dombås, and from there connects with the Oslo-Trondheim line, from the fjord to the mountains, or vice versa, crossing the valley of the green Rauma River.

If you continue westward over Romsdalsfjord on the E136, you will first encounter Veblungsnes, with Grytten Kirke, the octagonal 18th- to 19th-century church, and then, crossing the new Tresfjord Bridge, Vestnes, which stands on two peninsulas. Here, the late 19th-century, white, wooden Vestnes Kyrkje is worth seeing. A few miles farther north a ferry to Molde departs.

Around Nordfjord

From Hellesylt, Route 60 continues south to Hornindal, with the Anders Svor Museum, dedicated to the late 19th-century sculptor, and Lake Hornindalsvatnet, the deepest in Europe at 1,686 feet (514 m) and the clearest in Norway. Then take Route 15 to Stryn, a beautiful village on a branch of the Nordfjord, at the outlet of the Stryneelva River. The first thing to see here is the Visnes Hotel, a testament to the birth of tourism in Norway: made of wood and pseudo-Swiss in shape, it brings you back to a different dimension of travel. There is plenty to explore in the area, including fjords, valleys, glacier hikes, and small towns that expand the offerings.

In nearby Loen, however, we move on to the present day with the Loen Skylift, the fast cable car that opened in 2017 and takes just minutes to reach the 3,316-foot (1,011 m) Mount Hoven. Trails depart from there, or you can stop for a lunch with a view. If desired, the summit can also be reached by a via ferrata. From Loen skirt the green Lake Lovatnet and go up the Lodalen to Kjenndal to get a closerlook at Kjenndalsbreen, a branch of Jostedal Glacier.

About 4 miles (6 km) from Loen is Olden, where you absolutely must ascend Oldedalen, a valley with a magnificent lake and green pastures, to the rock wall at Briksdal. From here, continue on foot to the base of Briksdalbreen, once one of the most spectacular glaciers in all of Norway, which today forms a glacial lake. Since 2000, the glacier has been retreating.

Lake Hornindalsvatnet is the deepest in Europe.

We are then at the gateway to **Jostedalsbreen Nasjonalpark,** whose **Oppstryn Visitor Center** is housed in a replica building of a Viking longhouse. It illustrates the geology and history of the glacier and the fjords around it, their life and biodiversity, with exhibits, models, an aquarium, and a botanical garden.

Also of note is the Gamle Strynefjellsvegen Scenic Road, which in 16 miles (27 km) connects Videsæter to Grotli. There are several hairpin bends up to the Strynefjell Pass, with sharp pieces of rock marking the roadway. Along the way, the mighty waterfalls of Videfossen and Øvstefossen, both of which have special scenic viewpoints, will leave you in awe. For trained sportsmen, the route can also be done by bicycle.

On the southwestern shore of Nordfjord is Sandane, which houses the **Nordfjord Folkemuseum,** a fjord museum with 44 18th- to 19th-century farmhouses and related furniture, as well as the last remaining local boat, *Holvikejekta,* dating from 1881. Also worth seeing are the churches in the district. In Gimmestad, there is the old one from 1692 made of wood, with walls and ceiling decorated with traditional paintings, and the new one from 1910, also made of wood, with many details and a glass mosaic; in Vereide, you can visit one

Oppstryn Visitor Center (Jostedalsbreen Nasjonalparksenter)
✉ Strynevegen 1932, Oppstryn ☎ 480 02 997 **visitjostedalsbreen.no**
Nordfjord Folkemuseum ✉ Gota 16, Sandane ☎ 480 63 234 🕒 Feb.–June 16 & Sept.–Dec. 20 Tues.–Fri. 11 a.m.–4 p.m.; June 17–Aug. daily 11 a.m.–5 p.m. **misf.no**

from the 12th century, with a large stone cross in front. In Sandane don't forget to see the Gloppen Hotell, another historic Norwegian hotel, built in 1866 with a beautiful dining room known as the "hunters' hall." If you go south from Sandane toward Byrkjelo, following the E39, you will encounter farms and enjoy beautiful scenery, especially in June, when the many fruit trees bloom.

Moving north instead, you reach Anda, where you can take the ferry that arrives in only ten minutes to Lote. From here, it is easy to reach Nordfjordeid, on the branch called Eidsfjorden, where the "fjord" breed of horses live. Then continue on Route 15, which skirts Nordfjord and Almenningen—the "mountain of witches"—to reach Måløy via the long, spectacular bridge to the island of Vågsøy. Here is home to the **Måløy Raidsenteret,** which chronicles the British raid on the town on Decem-

Fjord Horses

This is an ancient breed of horse, found in Norway since the last ice age. Based on Viking finds, these specimens are known to have been selected and used in fighting. Along the fjords, they have been used as working animals for centuries. The horse has a brown, gold, or gray coat of many shades; its hooves are dark, and the body is large and muscular with a strong neck and legs.

Måløy Raidsenteret
✉ Heradsheim, Gate 1, 93, Måløy,
☎ 948 16 904 🕒 summer
10 a.m.–5 p.m. **maloyraidsenteret.no**

Fjord horses in Nordfjordeid

Peer Gynt Road

The Peer Gynt Vegen, which links all the places where the character in Ibsen's 1867 play wandered, is a series of roads that run through the mountains, from farm to farm. It is an alpine route framed by Jotunheimen, Dovre, and Rondane, and dotted with scenic viewpoints. It starts in Skei and leads to Fagerhøi, then to Gålå-Fefor, and Espedalen. About 37 miles (60 km) long, it is open only from early June to fall and is a toll road *(peer gyntvegen.no)*.

Peer Gynt Road

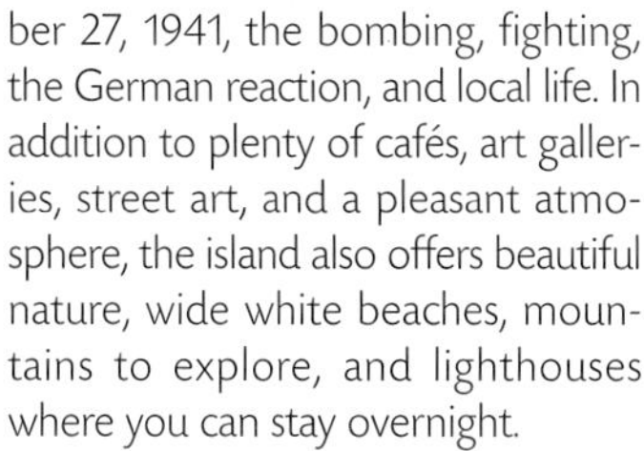

ber 27, 1941, the bombing, fighting, the German reaction, and local life. In addition to plenty of cafés, art galleries, street art, and a pleasant atmosphere, the island also offers beautiful nature, wide white beaches, mountains to explore, and lighthouses where you can stay overnight.

Dombås & Around

Dombås is an important junction between the central valleys, the western fjords, and the great North toward Trondheim. It is at the outlet of Gudbrandsdalen, a vast valley that runs 143 miles (230 km) northwest from Lillehammer to Romsdalen and then to Åndalsnes Fjord, traversed by the Lågen River, which is the main tributary to Lake Mjøsa. This valley is rich in landmarks, starting with Ringebu with its *stavkirke* from 1220, among hills and cultivated fields, with a red bell tower added in the 17th century that is a bit jarring. Around it sits the cemetery. Not far away is the 18th-century rectory.

About 37 miles (60 km) to the northwest is Heidal, where the Sjoa, one of the best rivers for rafting, flows between rock walls and forests, with blue-green water. Continuing up the valley, you reach Vågåmo, which introduces the Ottada len. There are at least three stavkirker to see: the Vågå Kyrkje, the Garmo Kyrkje, and the Lom Stavkyrkje in Fossbergom, with dragon figures on the roof that served as protection against the devil.

Moving on to Dovre, a road in the hills leads to Tofte, a property that housed all the Norwegian kings until the 19th century. The rest is waterfalls, forests, and farms. Let us not forget that the valley is part of the St. Olavsleden (St. Olav's Way), the old E6 or Gudbrandsdalsvegen—not to be confused with the modern

E6—which allows for better visits to the local villages. Running parallel in the nearby mountains is the Rondane Nasjonale Turistveger, which runs from Venabygd to Folldal, for a total of 46 miles (75 km), much of it skirting Rondale Nasjonalpark.

Once past the Dombås junction, the E136 opens to the northwest, running through the western part of Gudbransdalen, following the Lågen Valley. Just off the road is Lesja, which boasts a beautiful 1749 church with acanthus decorations and the Lesja Bygdemuseum, an open-air museum with a collection of 13 rural houses.

Musk Oxen

The Dovre Mountains are the only place in Norway, and one of the few in the world, where the mythical musk oxen can stil be spotted. An 800-pound (400 kg) ungulate with very long and odorous fur—musky, in fact—it is more closely related to sheep and goats than to oxen. It can charge at 37 miles an hour (60 km/h), lives up to 20 years, and moves in groups of 20 or more individuals. The dominant male, in the June–July mating season, fights with rivals for females. Although it is an arctic animal, it was reintroduced to this environment in the 20th century after attempts at introduction in the Svalbard Islands. A few hundred remain in the area. You can see them up close on guided tours.

Continuing on E136, you reach Bjorli, a center known for its alpine ski slopes. From here, the road travels along Romsdalen, which ends in the fjord at Åndalsnes. The valley is enclosed by high, almost perpendicular walls and offers several viewpoints. Slettafossen, for example, a 131-foot (40 m) waterfall in a gorge, or the Kylling bru, a bridge that accompanies the Raumabanen railway across the Rauma River. After Marstein, on the right, is the spectacular south face of the 5,085-foot (1,550 m) Romsdalshornet. Dombås is also a railroad hub on the Oslo–Trondheim line and the terminus of the Raumabanen, which runs to Åndalsnes. Near the station you can rent bikes, mountain bikes, and e-bikes for a tour, free or organized, of nearby Dovrefjell.

If, instead of taking the E136, you take the E6 northeast from Dombås, climb to the 3,280-foot (1,000 m) Hjerkinn, a pass and the first refuge, opened in the 12th century for pilgrims on the Nidaros Route, for the worship of St. Olav and for Norwegian kings. From the pass you can see the Snøhetta peaks, with herds of wild reindeer, and Svånåtindene, both over 6,500 feet (2,000 m) high.

The Dovrefjell Range marks the division between northern and southern Norway. In the national imagination, it is a repository of myths, with

Dovrefjell-Sunndalsfjella Nasjonalpark
✉ Hjerkinnhusvegen 33, Hjerkinn
dovrefjell-sunndalsfjella.no

Snøhetta Viewpoint

Located in Hjerkinn, this building overlooks the Tverrfjellet mountain range, which accounts for its proper name: Tverrfjellhytta. Everyone, however, calls it Snøhetta, perhaps as a tribute to the highest mountain in the range (7,500 feet [2,286 m]) or to the architectural firm that designed it. From the observatory, you can watch the park's wild reindeer without disturbing them. Toward the north is a panoramic window, of the cinematic kind. Lined with wood, it embraces visitors, as if seeking to bring people together to admire the beauty. The building is not large, with a 968-square-foot (90 sq m) base, and blends perfectly into the surrounding environment. It has won numerous awards and, in 2011, was named World Building of the Year. It is open from June to mid-October, when there is no snow, and can be reached in 20 minutes from the parking lot on a hiking trail.

a history of hunting, mining, travelers, and military activities. These peaks were part of a national park as early as 1974, under the name Dovrefjell Nasjonalpark, but in 2002 Sunndalsfjella, eight protected areas, and two biotopes were included in the jurisdiction. Thus was born **Dovrefjell-Sunndalsfjella Nasjonalpark,** one of the most beautiful in Norway. It is home to wild reindeer and musk oxen, distinctive flora, with endemic species such as Dovre poppy and mugwort. Hiking, safaris,

The panoramic window of the Snøhetta Viewpoint

bird-watching, rafting, horseback riding, and mountain biking trails are available in the park.

Continuing along the E6, you find Oppdal, a center for downhill and cross-country skiing and, in summer, an ideal place for hiking, with well-maintained trails. Worth seeing are the Oppdal Kirke, made of wood in 1651 and renovated over the centuries, and the **Oppdalsmuseet,** an open-air museum with wooden houses dating from the 16th to 20th century, textiles, and the work of a famous local woodcarver. Among the area's curiosities is the nearby Vang Viking cemetery; a guided tour in English tells its secrets.

From Oppdal, follow Route 70 westward into the wild Sunndal, which is furrowed by the Driva, a river rich in salmon, arriving at Sunndalsøra. From here, if you continue on the 70 northwest following the northern branch of the fjord, you reach Tingvoll, a rural center on the eponymous fjord that preserves a beautiful 12th-century church, Tingvoll Kirke, and the Tingvoll Museum, an open-air museum that also features a school, a mill, a forge, and a sawmill. If, on the other hand, you follow the southern branch of the fjord, you arrive at Øksendals Øra, a magnificent village between the creek and the sea, with old wooden houses, before continuing on to Molde.

Molde

Who can boast as many as 222 snow-capped peaks right on their doorstep? Well, Molde can. The views of the fjord are no small thing either. Less certain is the moniker of "city of roses," which sounds more like wishful thinking. Tourism here started in the mid-19th century. The town came into existence officially with the right to trade, in 1742, as much for fishing–given its somewhat inland location from the great sea routes–as for timber, generously supplied from inland and purchased by the British and Dutch in large quantities. Molde has thus benefited only marginally from coastal development related to the fish trade and has reinvented itself as a tourist center with the goodwill of two of Norway's literary fathers, Ibsen and Bjørnson, who found inspiration here.

A fire struck the town in 1916, and the Germans took care of the rest in 1940 with a bombing raid. The result is visible: the town looks straight out of the 1950s. But this makes it no less interesting. Apart from a few fine examples of architecture, the landscape and pleasantness of the area remains–the fjord with its frayed islands and the ocean.

The first stop is the **Romsdalsmuseet,** a regional folk museum located on the hill behind the town: 40 buildings display the development

Oppdalsmuseet ✉ Museumsvegen 11, Oppdal ☎ 916 44 172
🕒 summer Wed.–Sun. noon–4 p.m. **oppdalsmuseet.no**
Romsdalsmuseet ✉ Per Amdams veg 4, Molde ☎ 712 02 460
🕒 summer 11 a.m.–4 p.m.; rest of the year Tues.–Fri. 11 a.m.–4 p.m., Sat.–Sun. noon–4 p.m. **romsdalsmuseet.no**

View of the fjord from Varden hill, above Molde

of housing architecture from the Vikings to the 19th century. One section is devoted to the resistance, while another includes the writer Bjørnson's room. In addition, costumed folk performances are held in summer. In 2016, the Krona design building was added to the complex, with wooden structures, various exhibitions, a cafeteria, a bookstore, and a traditional costume workshop.

Then visit the Molde Domkirke, at Kirkebakken 2, a cathedral designed by Finn Bryn in 1957 with an imposing nave and an unusual bell tower. The Rådhus, the town hall built in 1966, has an unusual design too, made of glass blocks. Also architecturally interesting are the Aker Stadion and the Scandic Seilet Hotel, designed by local architect Kosberg.

Next, climb Varden, the 1,335-foot (407 m) hill overlooking Molde, which can be reached in 10 minutes by car or an hour's walk. From here, the famous 222 snowcapped peaks, Moldefjord, Romsdalsfjorden, and the islands facing the city are on display. Particularly worth visiting is Hjertøya, with its beaches. The island is also home to the Fiskerimuseet, a fishing museum that chronicles the daily challenges of the weather and the sea for fishermen, seal hunters, and whalers. An entire village and a whale oil refinery have been accurately reconstructed.

Moving past Molde and heading inland, one plunges into the Moldemarka, a hilly area furrowed by numerous trails and as many cross-country ski runs. The area is rich in forests and lakes, with marked trails. Then there are the often surprising surroundings, which preserve unique features. One such place is Trollkyrkja, the "Church of Trolls," a labyrinth of three marble and limestone caves, with streams and waterfalls—one with a 46-foot (14 m) drop—enriching an already special place in itself. It is located about 18 miles (30 km) from Molde, taking route 64 north.

Sixty-two miles (100 km) southeast stretches the spectacular Eikesdalen, the valley of Lake Eikesdalsvatnet. Here, there is also a waterfall, Mardalsfossen, and the starting point for the scenic Aursjøvegen, the road that climbs the surrounding mountains and overlooks the valley, stretching 75 miles (121 km).

Heading back north, in the archipelago of islands not far from Molde, Veøya, known for its small medieval mercantile center and 12th-century brick church, now part of the Romsdalsmuseet, is worth seeing. And don't forget Sekken Island in the middle of the wide fjord. A beautiful island, it is easily reached in 40 minutes by a ferry from the pier in Molde. It is also possible to rent a bicycle in town and then take it with you on the ferry; this mode allows you to get around all of Sekken in a short time while fully enjoying the extraordinary landscape that the island offers.

Moving slightly westward, you can find the curious Midsundtrappene, a system of four stone staircases leading to four different peaks on the island of Øtrøya, with vantage points over ocean and mountains. The project was made possible thanks to some Nepalese sherpas who built a total of more than 10,000 stone steps, which resulted in a trail. A somewhat crazy idea, but certainly very fascinating. The staircase at Rørsethornet, a 2,162-foot (659 m) hill, has 3292 steps and was completed in 2022.

Twenty-five miles (41 km) north of Molde lies the beautiful fishing village of Bud. Here the last Catholic archbishop brought together the Kingdom council and the third estate in the 16th century in an attempt to have a Norwegian king elected to maintain independence. By the end of that century and the beginning of

the next, Bud had become a center of the fish trade. In addition to the harbor, there is a pretty 4-mile-long (7 km) coastal path, Kyststien, and the Ergan Fortress built by the Germans during the last war. The scenic road leading to Vevang and then to Atlanterhavsvegen, the Atlantic Road, also starts from the village.

Finally, an excellent idea for exploring the surroundings is to hop from island to island with your bike. Starting from the city, you can go through Otrøya, Midøya, Dryna, Harøya, Finnøya, Ona, and Gossa–124 miles (200 km)–and then on to Averøya, in front of Kristiansund.

Kristiansund

A crown of islands, separated by canals but united by bridges is an idyllic image when seen from above. An image that, even without bridges, must also have struck the Dutch merchant Jappe Ippes, who in 1692 chose this place as a base for his trade–in fish of course. Lille-Fosen, which was the name of the town at the time, was where he loaded his ships with *klippfisk* (stockfish). He soon became rich and powerful, so much so that he wrested the city charter from King Christian VI in 1742. In honor of the

(continued on p. 197)

Kristiansund is nestled on four islands in the Norwegian Sea.

THE ATLANTIC ROAD

Who knew you could drive over ocean waves? The Atlantic Road—Atlanterhavsvegen in Norwegian—made it possible, defying the natural elements and providing an unforgettable travel experience.

The Atlantic Road connects Kristiansund to Molde.

In 1989, after six years of full-scale work, the Atlanterhavsvegen, or Atlantic Road, was opened, a spectacular string of bridges that leap from one islet to another like a game of hopscotch. It was made to run just over 5 miles (8 km), with even more crossings, leading from Vevang in the south to Kårvåg in the north, on the island of Averøya. The engineering feat is pure poetry, so much so that it has been called "the most beautiful road trip in the world."

Eldhusøya is the rest area by the ocean, and although it is a service building, it has interesting architecture and a much needed cafeteria. A metal pathway from the rest area to a viewpoint was designed by architects Ghilardi + Hellsten.

Although the most famous section is Vevang–Kårvåg, the Atlanterhavsvegen in a way starts in Bud, making the route 22 miles (36 km) long. This unique road—which traverses coastal landscapes of rocks, heather, polished boulders, and the breathing ocean—is part of the Nasjonale Turistveger and, like many other routes in Norway, is also a perfect destination for cyclists, who can pedal while admiring the majesty of the ocean, to which this country owes so much.

Danish monarch, the fledgling town was named Kristiansund.

The beautiful wooden houses that accumulated in the town over two and a half centuries of trade and its tangle of alleys leading to the sea burned in the German bombing raid of 1940. The destruction of nearly 900 period homes forced Kristiansund to convert to urban modernity. Economically, the discovery of oil off the coast of Trøndelag, and in particular the Haltenbanken gas field, were a major leap for the city. This event, in fact, prompted many companies to establish their offices in the city in order to serve the offshore locations.

The modern city sits on four islands joined by the historic Sundbåten boat. In operation since 1876, it is considered the oldest continuously operating public transportation in the world. That is why locals consider it a true institution, if not the beating heart of the city. Since this is a major center, a quick stop at the **tourist office** is recommended. After that, you can start visiting the districts that make up Kristiansund.

Start with the **Norsk Klippfiskmuseum** (Stockfish Museum) since the city owes so much to the trade. It is based in the old town, in a 1749 warehouse in Vågen, where the fishing was once done. In particular, Milnbergan rock, one of the largest in the country, was used for the drying of salted cod. The museum describes the history of the stockfish production process and daily life at the dock. The town is home to a Portuguese consulate because of the importance of *bacalhau* in its culinary culture.

Not far away is the Mellemværftet, at Kranaveien 22, part of the regional network, which explains the history of sailing shipyards in the 19th century. It is a center of maritime culture.

Then turn your attention to the two local churches, which offer different examples of architecture. Kirkelandet Kirke was built in 1964 based on a design by Odd Østby; today, it is considered the first true church built in the modern style in all of Norway. The 98-foot (30 m) chancel wall consists of 320 glass panes ranging from the intense dark colors of the earth at the bottom to the light shades of eternal light at the top. The Nordlandet Kirke, on the other hand, was built in 1914 in Jugendstil style; the stained glass and wall paintings are by Emmanuel Vigeland, brother of the better known Gustav.

When done visiting, turn to Innlandet, the main island, with the first customhouse, a hospital, and a school, all restored. At Sjursvika, on the east coast, see the old wooden houses that survived the German bombing raid of 1940. They are the last open-air

Tourist Office ✉ Kongens Plass 1, Kristiansund ☎ 702 38 800
🕒 summer Mon.–Fri. 9 a.m.–6 p.m., Sat. 9 a.m.–3 p.m., Sun. noon–5 p.m.; rest of the year Mon–Fri 9 a.m.–3:30 p.m. **visitkristiansund.com**
Norsk Klippfiskmuseum ✉ Milnbrygga, Dikselveien 20, Kristiansund
☎ 715 87 000 🕒 summer Mon.–Sun. noon–5 p.m. **nordmorsmusea.no/en**

The opera theater in Kristiansund is the oldest in Norway.

evidence of pre-1950s architecture. Also in Innlandet is Lossiusgården, a trading farm from 1780 that still retains its former appearance.

Moving to the island of Nordlandet, take time to visit Kvernberget, the 564-foot (172 m) hill that offers a complete panoramic view of the surrounding area. While in the Kirklandet District you can see the Operaen i Kristiansund, the oldest opera theater in the country, finished in 1914 in Jugendstil style, and Varden, the old observation tower from the 18th century. It served both to protect against enemies and to orient sailing ships. It offers magnificent views across the sea to the island of Grip and the mountains of Nordmøre.

Last is Grip and its archipelago, which is a collection of about 80 islands and rocks a half a dozen miles northwest of the town, where maritime architecture stands out. Grip is a strange island, surrounded by islets and rocks with equally strange names, such as "devil," "murderer," and "priest." Today it is inhabited only in summer, but retains a special atmosphere. The 14th-century stavkirke has been restored so many times that it has almost completely lost its original appearance.

From Kristiansund, take Route 70 and then the E39 northward to Trondheim, a gateway to the coldest part of the country. Alternatively, Trondheim can also be reached from Oppdal, following the E6. In this case, stop along the way in Støren, a village with a 19th-century octagonal church crossed by the Gaula, a river brimming with salmon.

Trondheim & Around

Sitting in a wide fjord at the mouth of a river, surrounded by mountains and a large lake, Trondheim has all the characteristics of the ideal settlement according to Viking and later medieval criteria. Even in the late 20th century, some researchers had elected it an "ideal city." Urban planners and sociologists evaluated this based on their own criteria, but it's true, Trondheim has more than a few strings to its bow. Seen from above, the landscape appears green. Seen from the sea, however, it is a harmonious puzzle of mountains, hills, fjord, and river. A walk through the old town, on the narrow alleys of the Christian Viking Middle Ages and the wide boulevards of Renaissance-era rationalism, will convince you of its greatness. What's more, Trondheim is vibrant and dynamic; its energy can be felt everywhere.

The city's name has changed several times: first Nidaros, after its river, the Nid; then Trondhjem, a name given by the Danes after unification; Nidaros again in 1930 by decision of parliament; and again Trondhjem, changed to Trondheim, a year later, at the behest of its citizens. And the history of the name reflects the city's own history, full of changes.

As the saga recounts, it was Olav Tryggvason who chose this bend between the river and the fjord to build the royal residence and a church. It was 997 and Olav, grandson of Harald Hårfagre, had just landed in Norway to claim the throne: he needed a residence to establish himself as king and a church to impose his new religion, Christianity. Olav I's reign lasted only a few years, but in the meantime Nidaros had become the de facto capital. Then came another Olav, the Saint, who took over the role. His burial site in the village became a destination for pilgrims from all over Scandinavia and beyond. The town built its cathedral, becoming the seat of the archbishop of Norway and the designated place for the king's coronation. In short, it was the political and religious center of the country. Then Norwegian politics and economy took a new direction, promoting Bergen and Oslo, and the Protestant Reformation delivered the final blow. In the 16th century, the last Catholic archbishop had to flee, and the city lost its primacy. After the particularly devastating fire of 1681, Huguenot general Johan Caspar de Cicignon drew its new layout: a grid plan with wide streets and space between blocks.

The presence of the University of Science and Technology, the largest in Norway, and the Foundation for Industrial and Technical Research consolidated Trondheim's reputation as a capital of innovation. But it is not only business that innovates; in fact, public services, the private sector, and civil society act as drivers of development. The arts and cultural scene are vibrant and international. With more than 200,000 inhabitants and an eye to the future, the capital of the Trøndelag Region seems eager to affirm its relevance, taking a page from the books of not only urban planners and sociologists but also Viking leaders.

Tourist Office ✉ Kjøpmannsgata 48 e Kongens gate 11, Trondheim
☎ 735 36 994 🕒 Mon.–Fri. 10 a.m.–5 p.m. **visittrondheim.no**

Given the cathedral's importance to the city over the centuries, your visit must begin there. The Nidarosdomen is the largest medieval monument in all of Scandinavia, the coronation seat of the kings of Norway, and the custodian of the crown jewels. According to tradition, it was built on the grave of St. Olav and was therefore the destination of great pilgrimages during the Middle Ages. Construction began in 1070 and was probably completed in 1320. The transept and chapter house are from the 12th century in Norman Romanesque style, while the choir with an octagonal apse and the Gothic naves are from the following century.

Johan Caspar de Cicignon

Trondheim's distinctive character can be attributed to one architect: Johan Caspar de Cicignon. His mark can be seen in the two main streets, Kongens gate and Munkegata, which intersect at Torvet, the market square, to form a perfect triangle: the king, the monks, and the merchants. Munkegata has another significance too: it opens the view from the cathedral to the island of Munkholmen, first a monastery and then a fortress.

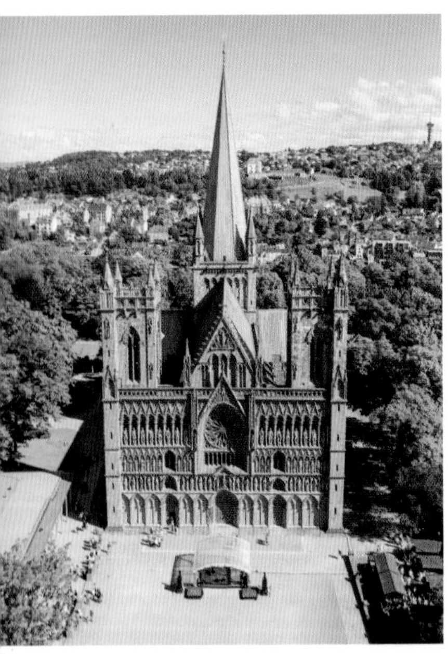

The Nidarosdomen is the largest medieval monument in Scandinavia.

For hundreds of years, Norwegian kings were crowned here, until it was decided in 1904 that the coronation should take place in Oslo. But the cathedral's glory days were short-lived: the loss of independence and the Protestant Reformation doomed it, and several fires left it in ruins. With the rebirth of the national spirit, restoration began in 1869. The project is ongoing with a team of 30 workers. In spite of this, the cathedral shines for its beauty and unique architecture, which differs depending on the season. This is why it is said that Nidaros is the symbol of Norway: first great, then decaying and submissive, before becoming independent again. Nidaros was reconsecrated in 1930 on the 900th anniversary of the death of St. Olav. Ten kings and almost all of Norway's archbishops are buried here. In the summer, the main tower is open to the public: it has 172 steps,

The Gamle Bybro connects the banks of the Nid River.

so it takes some effort to climb, but the view of the whole city from the top is well worth it.

After visiting the cathedral, move on to Erkebispegården, the archbishop's palace next door. Built by Norway's first archbishop in the 12th century, after the Reformation it became royal property and the seat of the Danish governor, then an arsenal. The Rustkammeret, one of the museums inside the palace, houses a collection of Norwegian army weapons and uniforms from the 17th century to the present day.

Not far away, the Gamle Bybro, the "old bridge," built in the 17th century and rebuilt in the mid-19th century, spans the river, linking the cathedral on one bank and Kristiansten Festning, the fortress, on the other. Erected after the fire of 1681, the fortress is placed high up to defend the city. From there, you can see the fjord, the mountains, and the whole of Trondheim. You can also visit the building and its small museum.

In the city center is the Torvet, the market square, at the intersection of Munkegata and Kongens gate. In the middle, on a high pylon, is a statue of Olav Tryggvason, the founder of Trondheim. At its base is a sundial made of pebbles and a fountain that serves as a water clock. The nearby Vår Frue Church was built in the 13th

Kristiansten Festning ✉ Kristianstensbakken 60, Trondheim
☎ 468 70 400 🕒 summer 8 a.m.–9 p.m., winter from 9 a.m. to sunset
visittrondheim.no

century in the Gothic style and restored in the 18th century in the baroque style. One of the city's curiosities is the Walk of Peace, a series of plaques set into the pavement that name the winners of the Student Peace Prize, i.e., Norwegian students or student organizations working for peace, democracy, and human rights.

There are several museums nearby. The **Trondheim Kunstmuseum,** one of Norway's leading art museums, houses important Norwegian and international collections from the 19th and 20th centuries, including Munch's graphic works. **Kunsthall Trondheim,** opened in 2016 in the old fire station, shows contemporary art at a high level. It also hosts readings, concerts, and performances. If you have time, visit the Trøndelag Senter for Samtidskunst at Fjordgata 11, an independent centre that shows the work of contemporary Norwegian and Nordic artists.

Also worth a visit are the Trondheim Sjøfartsmuseum, a maritime museum with models, ornaments, and nautical instruments; the Vitenskapsmuseet, a university institute with an archaeological section dedicated to the history of Trøndelag from the Middle Ages; and the Vitensenteret, which focuses on science and the desire to experiment, from anatomy to mechanics, electricity to geology; it also has a 3D planetarium.

Away from the city center, Skansenparken, a park at the western gate, is worth a stop. Here you can see what little remains of the city's defense system, namely the ramparts that once belonged to the Skansevollene Fortress and are now part of the public park. There is also a railway bridge over the Nidelva River. Farther along, at Brattørkaia 14, is Rockheim, the Norwegian National Museum of Folk Music. Nearby is Ravnkloa, the town square with the fish market by the harbor, known for its old clock. From here, take Munkegata to the elegant Stiftsgården, one of Scandinavia's largest wooden buildings, built in the 18th century in the rococo style, with two wings and 70 rooms. Once the private home of Lady Cecilie Christine Schøller and now the official residence of the king when he visits Trondheim, it is only open to the public in the summer; guided tours are available.

Parallel to Munkegata, just outside the old town, is Munkholmen, or Monk's Island. It owes its name to the 11th-century Benedictine Cluniac Monastery, probably the first in Scandinavia. In Viking times it was a place of execution, then a monastery, and later a fortified prison and customhouse. Today the island, reached by ferry from Ravnkloa, is also one of the city's beaches. Guided tours are available in English.

Trondheim Kunstmuseum ✉ Bispegata 7B, Trondheim ☎ 735 38 180 **trondheimkunstmuseum.no** • **Kunsthall Trondheim** ✉ Kongens gate 2, Trondheim ☎ 485 00 100 **kunsthalltrondheim.no**

Munkholmen was first a monastery, then a fort.

Heading toward the Nidelva River, you come to one of the most photographed parts of Trondheim: Bryggerekka, or Pier Row, full of warehouses and boathouses that populate the streets along the river, such as Kjøpmannsgata, Bakklandet, Fjordgata, and Sandgata. The oldest buildings date from the 18th century. If you want to see other parts of the old town, visit Hospitalsløkkan, the area around the old hospital. There is no shortage of old wooden houses here, and they offer a different insight into the city. The hospital church, Hospitalskirken, is located at Kongens gate 70a. It was designed by Dutch architect Johan Christoffer Hempel and was the first octagonal wooden church built in Copenhagen in 1706.

On your way back to the city center, stop at Sukkerhuset, Sverres gate 15, a sugar refinery built in 1754 and later converted into a brewery. It is one of the oldest surviving factories in Norway. Raw cane sugar was imported from the Danish West Indies, now the U.S. Virgin Islands, to be refined. It is now run by student associations at NTNU, the University of Science and Technology.

A little farther west of the city is the **Trøndelag Folkemuseum,** an open-air museum with 55 buildings

Trøndelag Folkemuseum ✉ Sverresborg allé 13, Trondheim ☎ 738 90 100 🕒 summer 10 a.m.–5 p.m.; rest of the year Tues.–Fri. 10 a.m.–3 p.m., Sat.–Sun. 11 a.m.–3 p.m. **sverresborg.no**

from the countryside, coast, and city, including two complete farms and a wooden church. The urban part of the museum includes a pharmacy, a dentist's cabinet, handicraft workshops, and the merchant Nissen's house. The complex stands on the site where King Sverre built his palace in 1183. Today only the ruins of the fortress remain.

If you go to the Lade Peninsula, northeast of the city, you will find the **Ringve Musikkmuseum** at Lade allé 60. At the same address is the Botaniske Hage, the university's botanical garden. Together with the Art Museum, the Botaniske Hage is one of the most interesting places to visit.

Beyond the more touristy area is the residential part of the city. In Svartlamon, for example, there are experimental houses made from reclaimed materials, an example of sustainable architecture. In Ila, a former industrial area, you can see interesting street art. There is also no shortage of microbreweries, such as Øx and Austmann, which show visitors the entire production process of their beers in bulk, cans, and bottles.

You can also take a boat trip on the Nidelva River and Trondheim Fjord. This is definitely an interesting experience, as is the chance to see the city from the river in a kayak or from a sailing boat on the fjord. Also

Ringve Musikkmuseum ✉ Lade allé 60, Trondheim ☎ 738 70 280
🕒 Summer daily 10 a.m.–5 p.m.; rest of year 11 a.m.–4 p.m. (closed Mon.)
ringve.no

The facade of the Ringve Musikkmuseum

The Living Museum

When visiting a museum, how often have you felt like trying out the objects on display to better understand how they work? Well, Russian musician Victoria Bachke and her Norwegian husband have founded The Ringve Musikkmuseum (the Museum of Music) for this very purpose.

The idea is simple and yet ingenious: to take the visitor on a grand tour of the history of music through the sounds of the instruments on display. The aim is to help visitors understand the evolution of musical discourse through the sounds and shapes of instruments. A guide leads the way, introducing the music of the time, the instruments available, and playing a short piece on them. For the uninitiated it is a pleasant experience, and for experts it an occasion of deep satisfaction. For everyone, it demonstrates the depth that a museum can go if based on new ideas and concepts. The museum displays both individual instruments (from the same period and country) and families of instruments from different cultures. There are baroque, 19th-century, 20th-century, and contemporary instruments, as well as traditional instruments from Norway and many other parts of the world.

worth a visit is Havet at Strandveien 104, the perfect place for a swim, with a sauna, restaurant and concerts.

Olavsfest, a quirky and engaging town festival, is held annually between the end of July and the beginning of August. On July 28–29, there is a prayer night in the cathedral, and then there are concerts, readings, exhibitions, and talks on human rights in various places, such as Torvet and Vår Frue Church. A medieval market is also held during the week-long festival dedicated to the patron saint, and the town comes alive with bands, orchestras, choirs, and theater performances.

On the Frosta Peninsula in the northeast, just across the river, are the remains of Frostating, Trøndelag's ancient court. The annual meeting was attended by 485 representatives from the 12 counties that made up the region, each represented by a stone placed in a circle. The medieval church at Logtun, built around 1300 and extensively restored in the 17th century, and the ruins of the Cistercian monastery at Tautra, on the island of the same name, complete this circuit.

Farther south in Stjørdal is Vaernes Church, a 12th-century church built in the Norman Romanesque style. The building has a door with bas-reliefs and a baroque pulpit carved in 1685. From here you can take the E14 into Sweden. Although many people head north from Trondheim, Røros, 93 miles (150 km) to the southeast, is another place worth visiting. Of course, if you decide to follow the E6 from Ålesund instead of the coast, a detour from Dombås will

New Worlds of Food

Why were Trondheim and the Trøndelag Region chosen as the European Region of Gastronomy in 2022? Part of the answer lies in the fjord in front of the city, which at 80 miles (130 km) long is the third largest in the country. The movement of tectonic plates created different layers in the fjord, resulting in different depths, home to around 200 species of fish and ideal living conditions for shrimp, clams, and scallops. Add to this various types of seaweed and the fact that the Nidelva and other rivers in the area are rich in salmon, and you have an interesting landscape, which explains why at least 30 percent of the ingredients used in the dishes served in the region are of local origin. This is not to mention the mountains, rich in mushrooms and herbs, and the meat of reindeer, elk, and deer, farm cheeses, pigs, lambs, vegetables, and berries. As a result, there are several restaurants, some of them Michelin-starred, that translate this magnificent breadbasket into highly recommended dishes. As for international recognition, suffice it to say that the Bocuse d'Or was held here in 2024. This means that the whole world has finally recognized the gastronomic value of Norway. On the northeastern arm of the fjord and in Beitstadfjorden is Den Gyldne Omvei, the Golden Road, where you can visit (also by bike) some of the local producers.

easily get you here. You can also get to Røros by train from Trondheim in two and a half hours.

Røros

Sometimes miracles happen. Røros is an old mining town, where copper was mined from 1644 to 1977. The town was not abandoned with the end of the mining era and has been able to build its own economy on timber, furniture, wool, and, to some extent, tourism. The old wooden town, which has not been affected by fire for over 300 years, has been preserved and restored under the protection of UNESCO, which listed it as a World Heritage site in 1980. The buildings from the 18th and 19th centuries can still be admired in all their splendor. A must-see is the Aasengården, the oldest house in town, which has been inhabited by the same family since 1644 and is now in its 11th generation. The community also participates in the Sustainable Destination Program.

After a thorough tour of the old town, head to **Rørosmuseet,** which celebrates the history of the region

Rørosmuseet ✉ Lorentz Lossius gata 45, Røros ☎ 724 06 170
🕒 summer 10 a.m.–4 p.m.; rest of the year 10 a.m.–3 p.m. **rorosmuseet.no**

and copper mining in a reconstructed old foundry, with 20 old buildings, and a modern museum. Olavsgruva, a mine 164 feet (50 m) underground, is part of this history and can be visited with a guide.

Nearby Røros Church at Kjerkgata 39, better known as Bergstadens Ziir or "pride of the miners' town," is an anomaly in this wooden town. It was built of brick in 1784, with an octagonal plan, and then restored in 2010. But it's not just the variety of materials that makes it unique, it's the unusual style, the color, the shape of the bell tower. It's the splendid great hall that, with its 1,600 seats, seems to welcome a whole community. And it's the strength and delicacy of the lights and pastel colors along with the altar crowned by its organ. Because the design and construction of the church was financed by the copper company, its logo is still prominently placed on the steeple, making the building a kind of permanent sponsor.

But Røros is not only museums and copper mines. The town also has a lot to offer when it comes to local food, so much so that in summer there is a tasting tour of typical dishes, with guides who explain the cuisine of the miners, the upper class, and the Sami. Certainly, the unique flavors that can be experienced here

(continued on p. 209)

The bell tower of the church looms over Røros.

NORDLAND RAILWAY

From the green landscapes of lower Trøndelag to the barren northern tundra, this 452-mile-long (729 km) train ride allows you to discover all the different facets of a country famous worldwide for its natural wonders.

Mosjøen lies halfway on the railway line.

Norway has developed an extensive railway network that runs through some of the country's most iconic landscapes. That's why a train ride during your vacation here is highly recommended.

The Nordlandsbanen is the longest continuous railroad in the country, and it crosses the Arctic Circle, which is symbolically important. It runs for 452 miles (729 km) from Trondheim to Bodø, with many bridges and tunnels. The entire trip takes about 10 hours but can be divided into stages thanks to the stops along the way. This is actually the recommended way to fully enjoy the journey. For example, don't miss Mosjøen Station, which is the geographical center of Norway, from where you can visit the Helgeland coast or Lønsdal and Saltfjellet National Park.

One of the most fascinating aspects of the Nordlandsbanen is undoubtedly its ever-changing landscape, from the green of Trøndelag to the brown of the tundra, through fjords and glaciers. There are also night trains, giving you the chance to see the midnight sun in summer and the northern lights and snow in winter. Part of the railroad was built during the years of German occupation using Russian prisoner slave labor. There were a number of prison camps on Saltfjellet during World War II.

The Jutulhogget Canyon, near Alvdal, is the largest in northern Europe.

are also because the low temperatures make the crops grow more slowly, making them different from those in other regions. To join a tour, visit the tourist office at Peder Hiortgata 2.

Remember: if you pass through here in winter, you can experience moving around on a *spark,* the traditional push sled that locals use to get around during the snowy months. In fact, this is one of the coldest cities in the country, so it is a good idea to bundle up in woolen clothing to make sure you stay warm and fully enjoy your visit. Constant snowfalls also make Røros one of the most popular Christmas destinations in Norway. The annual Christmas market lives and breathes the spirit of the great North.

Røros is also the perfect starting point for trips to Femundsmarka and Forollhogna National Parks, where you can go hiking, mountain biking, or fishing. In addition, southwest of the city, in Alvdal, is northern Europe's largest canyon, Jutulhogget. Formed during the last ice age, about 10,000 years ago, the site can be visited on foot, including along the upper rim. ■

FROM TRONDHEIM TO THE ARCTIC CIRCLE

From here, the barren landscapes of the great North are fast approaching. But before we cross this imaginary line and enter the Arctic, there is still much to discover. This part of the country is well worth exploring as it has many hidden wonders, especially the national parks and the coast, a world of reefs, shallow and very clear water, and islands where the term "paddling" takes on a whole new meaning. Helgeland is therefore a succession of views and opportunities, well-illustrated by its scenic routes.

Stiklestad Chapel is dedicated to St. Olav.

From Trondheim, the E6 skirts the long Trondheimsfjord, passing beaches, forests, and scenic spots, before entering North Trøndelag.

Stiklestad, the first stop on the journey, is the place where King Olav—later St. Olav—fought his last battle in 1030. A chapel and the Olavsstøtta monument commemorate him. Mære, a little farther north, also preserves medieval relics.

Only 6 miles (10 km) from Mære lies Steinkjer, the municipality of Blåfjella-Skjækerfjella/Låarte-

The Wild Harmony of Kystriksveien

The most famous and touristy places are not always the best. In this case, the less traveled Kystriksveien, the coastal road from Steinkjer to Bodø, offers landscapes that will fill your soul with joy. It is virtually impossible to remain indifferent to the rugged coastline, with rocks that seem to tell the story of time, landscapes cut by radiant light, and white beaches against transparent waters. Here lives the wild harmony that existed before humans, made of stone, sea, clouds, and sky. The 403 miles (650 km) of road, or part of it, can be traveled by car, bicycle, or bus, with the help of numerous ferries. Guided tours are also available, including one by bicycle with a support vehicle to carry luggage. Tours can be booked at the Kystriksveien information center in Steinkjer. And it should not be forgotten that the northernmost part of the road belongs to the Nasjonal Turistveger Helgeland Scenic Route.

Skæhkere Nasjonalpark, one of the largest national parks in Norway. It is a wilderness of low mountains and lakes where you can find signs of the Sami and land reserved for reindeer. Similarly, farther northeast, on the E6 to Røyrvik and beyond, is Børgefjell-Byrkije Nasjonalpark, rich in rivers, lakes, and high peaks, and populated by ermine and arctic fox.

Turning toward the coast from the E6 at Grong, you will reach Namsos, which offers breathtaking scenery both in the Namdal Valley and along the minor road that leads to Foldafjord and then to Rørvik. The latter, situated on the island of Vikna in Nærøysund, is a beautiful example of what the coast looks like farther north, from North Trøndelag to Helgeland. The islands in front of it are scattered. Sør Gjæslingan, once a bustling town, now offers overnight stays in *rorbu,* or fishermen's huts, during the summer.

Kystmuseet Norveg is a museum that illustrates coastal life from the Stone Age to today's technologically advanced fishing boats. Rørvik is home to important fishing and fish-related businesses, so the town has thoughtfully emphasized its importance with two buildings that are impossible to ignore: the abovementioned museum and the brand-new Rørvik Church. From here, you can rent a bike and explore the west side of Vikna or Abelvær, an old trading post 23 miles (37 km) south on the island of Kalvøya.

Kystmuseet Norveg ✉ Strandgata 7, Rørvik ☎ 488 80 024
🕒 summer Mon.–Sat. 10 a.m.–4 p.m.; rest of the year Tues.–Fri. 11 a.m.–3 p.m., Sat. 11 a.m.–2 p.m. **kystmuseetnorveg.no**

The island of Leka is part of Trollfjell Geopark.

Next, don't miss the Foldafjord speedboat excursion from Namsos up the coast via Rørvik to Leka, an island of oceanic crust that formed 400 million years ago. A guided geological tour is available to get a better look at the gray, red, and yellow granite. Leka has been declared a National Geological Monument and is part of Trollfjell Geopark. If you do not want to go on a hiking tour, you can use bicycles in the area.

Helgeland

It is hard to define this part of the coast. It looks as if an earthquake struck a glassworks and filled the place with its fragments. The work of plates, glaciations, and glaciers has forged a jigsaw puzzle of high, smooth mountains, spectacular rocks, and fragments in the sea, with islands, islets, reefs, and a myriad of channels. The Norwegians call it *øyriker,* or the "island kingdom," and that is an excellent way to define it.

However, Helgeland is not a place for everyone. This part of Norway is better suited for physically active people, as the landscape demands that visitors fully experience it with hiking or sea excursions. It is a bit of a challenge, yet even those who are not particularly athletic but still want to enjoy the experience can find their way, for example, by taking the Nordland train, driving on scenic roads, or even sailing. What is certain is that the views will be well worth the effort.

Start in Brønnøysund, a pleasant small town on a narrow peninsula surrounded by islands. The main attraction here has a name that is hard to forget: Torghatten, which literally means "square hat." It is

an icon of the Norwegian coast, a mountain with a naturally formed hole in the middle. And it is no small hole; it is 524 feet (160 m) long, 114 feet (35 m) high and 49 feet (15 m) deep. It is 7 miles (12 km) from the city and can be easily reached in 20 minutes by car. If you want, you can also get there by sea in fast rafts. At the site, there are panels with QR codes that tell the geological story of the mountain's birth and the hole's formation. You can imagine how the hole has inspired myths over the centuries and still fascinates

(continued on p. 215)

Trollfjell Geopark

Trollfjell Geopark has its own unique geological story to tell: the formation of rocks over 500 million years, which became islands and mountains, in other words, the coastline. That is why this area of more than 3,861 square miles (10,000 sq km) became part of the UNESCO World Heritage List in 2019.

The spectacular island of Leka is something of a symbol of the park. It shows a complete cross section of an ancient part of the seafloor that rose when Asia, America, and Europe collided. But there is also evidence of glaciers that have smoothed the rocks as they have advanced and retreated over time, or the fascinating oddity that is Mount Torghatten, famous for literally having a hole in the middle.

Perhaps the most unique and iconic feature of this park, however, is the *strandflate,* translated as "low, flat, wide shelf," a geological formation which supports stacks, reefs, and thousands of small islands washed by a shallow sea. After the last ice age, this favored the settlement of humans, who became fishermen and hunters. On the Vega Islands, another of the area's many natural wonders, the shelf extends a full 37 miles (60 km).

There are 70 marked trails of varying difficulty in the park. You can rent a kayak and let your imagination run wild as you spot 250 different species of birds, including eider ducks, black guillemots, and oystercatchers. In some areas, such as on Leka or north along the coast, you can travel by bicycle.

PADDLING WITH UNESCO

If you have enough time, devote it to discovering the spectacular views and special way of life in Vegaøyan, the Vega Archipelago. Don't miss the chance to visit this UNESCO World Heritage site!

An eider shelter

Vegaøyan, or the Vega Archipelago, consists of about 6,500 islands scattered across the geological shelf—called the *strandflate*—and arranged around the main island of Vega. Of the many ways to explore this archipelago, kayaking, either on your own or with a guide, and sailing are definitely the most rewarding. There is also a via ferrata at Ravnfloget and several bike trails.

The archipelago, which bears evidence of some Stone Age human settlements, was declared a UNESCO World Heritage site in 2004. In addition to its spectacular scenery, the site was inscribed for the symbolic value of its buildings, including the lighthouses, fishermen's cottages, warehouses, and farms, as well as the type of wooden huts that serve as shelters for eider ducks. The locals put them there not to give the birds a place to shelter, but because the sea ducks repay the hospitality with luxurious feathers—some say they fill the world's finest quilts.

However, the sustainable way of life that has been implemented here in a beautiful but harsh land must also be emphasized. The history of the place can be explored at Verdensarvsenter, the World Heritage Center in Gardsøy, which tells the story of the customs and traditions of the archipelago, including the role of women in protecting the migrating eider ducks by collecting and processing their feathers. It can be reached by ferry from Horn, 10 miles (16 km) north of Brønnøysund, in just 45 minutes.

visitors today. There is also a bike trail around the mountain. Bicycles, which can be rented at the tourist office at Sømanveien 92 in Brønnøysund, are also the ideal means for some island hopping, using ferries or fast boats to cross the sea sections. In fact, there are many trails and guided tours available.

From Brønnøysund, take Route 76 and then the E6 north to reach Mosjøen on Vefsnfjorden. The 19th-century houses on Sjøgata and the Helgeland Museum at number 23e, which is based here but has dozens of locations throughout the region, are well worth a visit. Other attractions include the Storfjellet zip line, which flies over Sjøgata and lands in

Helgeland Scenic Route

Hegelandskysten has been called Norway's longest scenic route, stretching 269 miles (433 km) along the coast, from Holm to Godøystraumen. It traverses diverse landscapes, from fjords to archipelagos, scattered islands, and sea-facing peaks, and includes crossings on six ferries: from Holm to Vennesund, from Horn to Anddalsvågen, from Forvik to Tjøtta, from Levang to Nesna, from Kilboghavn to Jektvik and from Ågskardet to Forøy. It is part of Kystriksveien, which runs from Steinkjer to Bodø. Info at *entur.no*.

Mount Torghatten and the natural hole that makes it unique

The Polarsirkelsenteret, in the Arctic Circle

the gardens of northern Norway's oldest hotel, Fru Haugans Hotel, and the via ferrata on Øyfjellet. Both are truly spectacular.

To the west, on the island of Alsta, lies the small town of Sandnessjøen, whose central attraction is De Syv Søstre, or the "seven sisters," a mountain range that dominates the landscape with peaks over 3,000 feet (1,000 m) that can be reached by hiking trails. For example, Botnkrona (3517 feet [1072 m]), the highest peak, is reached from Breimo, about 2.5 miles (4 km) south of Sandnessjøen. Just outside the village is the Viking settlement of Sandnes. A Viking longhouse—a place of trade and politics, animated with costumed characters, banquets, and illustrated daily life—has been reconstructed at the ancient site. In the southern part of the island, the **Petterdass Museet,** part of the Helgeland Museum, tells the story of the 17th-century priest-poet who first sang about these

Petterdass Museet ✉ Alstahaugveien 17, Sandnessjøen ☎ 751 10 150 🕒 summer 10 a.m.–3:30 p.m.; rest of the year Tues.–Fri. 10 a.m.–3:30 p.m., Sat.–Sun. 11 a.m.–3:30 p.m. (closed Jan.) **petterdass-museet.no**

Crossing into Sweden

From Mo i Rana, the E12 leads into Sweden, cutting diagonally southeast to Umeå. This is the tourist Blue Road, which runs from the Norwegian coast through Sweden and Finland to Russian Karelia. From Narvik, the Iron Line takes you to the Swedish border by train. The railroad skirts the fjord, the site of a World War II battle, then climbs between deep precipices to a plateau dotted with low mountains. Alternatively, you can drive from Narvik over the Rombak bridge (or Haalogalandsbrua) to reach the E6, which offers an immediate detour to Nordkalottvågen, or to the international E10 to Riksgränsen and Kiruna.

places. Near Alsta, you can kayak around the island of Herøy or cycle around the island of Dønna.

To the north is Mo i Rana, at the bottom of Ranfjorden. From here you can see Austerdalsisen Glacier, a branch of Svartisen Glacier, and Grønligrotta, a cave with an underground waterfall. Excursions also depart from the town to Saltfjellet-Svartisen Nasjonalpark, which includes the glacier, Norway's second largest at 143 square miles (370 sq km) and 60 glacier tongues, and adjacent forests and valleys, with one of the country's largest arctic fox populations and several protected plant species. It has been called "Norway in a nutshell," as the fjords and glaciers of the west are offset by the larch and birch forests of the south, while the highlands in the north and east are dotted with lakes. If you are patient and lucky, you may also see reindeer, wolverines, and eagles.

Arctic Circle

We have reached 66° 33′ N, from which extend the lands of the Arctic. It is an imaginary line, but it is safe to say that this is the threshold to the frozen North. In any case, the **Polarsirkelsenteret** (Arctic Circle Center), beyond Storforshei on the E6, almost 50 miles (80 km) from Mo i Rana, marks the dividing line. The intention is to establish a logical line that may be more significant than the nearby border between Norway and Sweden, as it defines the geographical and cultural boundary of the Sami territory. The center offers films and videos, exhibitions, models, a museum display, and other services. There is even an arctic bistro.

You can then drive through Saltdalen to Skjerstadfjord and see Sulitjelmaisen and Blåmannsisen Glaciers. From Fauske, Route 80 leads to Bodø, where you finally enter the Arctic Lands. ■

Polarsirkelsenteret ✉ Saltfjellveien 1850, Storforshei ☎ 918 53 833
🕒 open May–Oct., hours vary **polarsirkelsenteret.no**

Explore the Lofoten Islands, the Vesterålen Islands, and the city of Tromsø, before reaching—and going beyond—the North Cape, land of midnight sun and northern lights

ARCTIC LANDS

Brünnich's guillemots thrive on the island of Hornøya.

ARCTIC LANDS

By extension, the "Arctic Lands" include all areas beyond the Arctic Circle. For the purpose of this chapter, however, we have only lumped together the northern part of Nordland, Troms, and Finnmark, the latter already administratively linked to Troms og Finnmark County. North of Bodø and Narvik, you will first encounter the magical archipelagos of Lofoten and Vesterålen, then one of the capitals of the North, Tromsø, and finally Finnmark, the extreme Norwegian region bordering Finland and Russia. The unforgettable experience of the midnight sun and the northern lights will be the backdrop to your stay here.

Those coming from the south pass through Alta on their way to the North Cape, which seems to be the only possible destination of any trip to Norway. Finnmark, however, has its own character, culture, economy, and vitality that few places in these latitudes can boast.

NOT TO BE MISSED:

It is the land of the Sami, a people who have now regained their dignity and identity. It is the land of the descendants of Finnish and Russian emigrants. It is the land where many southern Norwegians have chosen to live because of its unspoiled nature.

Fishing is a big business here—just think of how many people in the world have fish sticks in their freezers. However, since the 1980s, people have started to practice aquaculture, breeding salmon instead of letting them follow their natural cycle—and this is where all the problems began, with waste in the sea and low quality fish. Anyway, the region is still producing fish in quantities that can satisfy the voracious international market.

Light industry and services have also found fertile ground here, with no lack of investment. Tourism has exploded in recent years, funneling thousands of summer

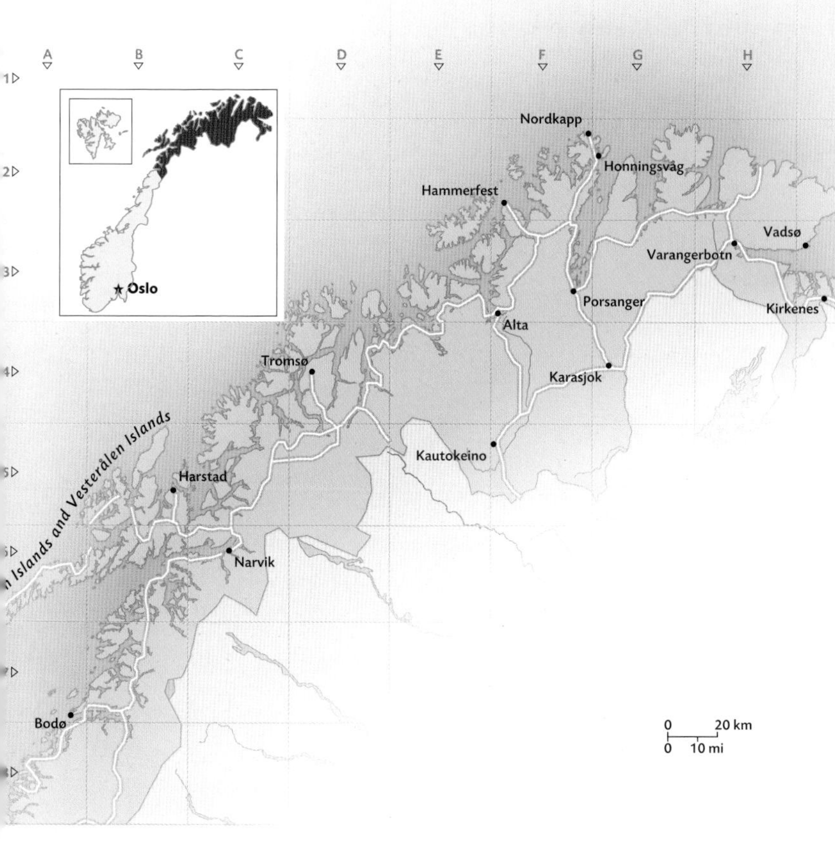

and winter travelers to these lands and spurring extensive development of hotels and service agencies. The issue of climate change, however, grows ever more pressing. Indeed, rising seawater temperatures have a number of potentially serious consequences, from the migration of traditional fish stocks to melting ice.

Finally, note that when we talk about the northeastern area of Norway, we really mean it. At the northeastern end of the Varanger Peninsula are the coastal town of Kirkenes and the peninsular town of Vardø, both of which are farther east than Istanbul.

Leaving the Center North in Bodø, you can sail slowly up the coast on the Hurtigruten, the mail ship that takes you past the Lofoten and Vesterålen archipelagos to Tromsø, and then to Kirkenes, beyond the North Cape, just a few miles from Russia. ■

THE MIDNIGHT SUN & THE NORTHERN LIGHTS

No land can rival the Arctic. Not only for its landscapes and atmosphere, but also for the two phenomena that derive from the Earth's tilted axis. These phenomena challenge our own sense of certainty: a summer sun that does not set and winter nights illuminated by colorful brushstrokes.

The northern lights are predominantly seen around the Arctic.

The Arctic Circle is just an imaginary line, but it marks the border between two worlds: the "ordinary" one and then another. In the ordinary world, an ancient pact with the gods established that day is day and night is night. In the realm of the Great Bear, however, this covenant has been broken, and Southerners can feel disoriented. A man of God who lived in these lands, not resigned to accept this truth, wanted to diligently measure the amount of light coming into the Arctic, between the bright summers, the polar auroras, the moon, and the stars. He found there was more light here than at the Equator. So the image of the twilight lands is incorrect: the light is there, it is just distributed differently.

The midnight sun over the Knivskjellodden Peninsula

The midnight sun is a puzzling phenomenon for our biological clock. It is very difficult to get used to it; the eye seeks darkness to rest, but the light gives no respite. The visual effect is that of a sun that never sets, merging directly with the sunrise and resulting in an endless day. Those who dream of having two days in one to do it all would be satisfied with Norwegian summers.

This is the Arctic 24-hour light calendar: in Alta May 18–July 27, in Andenes May 22–July 21, in Bodø June 4–July 8, in Hammerfest May 16–July 27, in Longyearbyen April 20–August 22, in Nordkapp May 14–July 29, in Svolvær May 28–July 14, and in Tromsø May 20–July 22.

The wonders of the Great North do not end there, however. This extraordinary region is also home to the famous northern lights. These quick brushstrokes paint bright fireworks across the cold sky—yellow, green, red, violet, in flashes that illuminate everything. For those who first witnessed it, this phenomenon must have been difficult to understand. It is a storm of electrically charged particles, attracted to the Earth's magnetic field. They work almost like friction with the atmosphere, lighting up as a result.

The northern lights are visible in winter months, when the sky is clear and dark. The peak time is between 11 p.m. and 2 a.m.

BODØ

Bodø forms a kind of dividing mark between the Center-North region and the fascinating Arctic Lands. The city had to reinvent itself after the German bombing in 1940 but has done so well that it was named European Capital of Culture 2024. It is also a must-see for anyone interested in ocean phenomena as it is home to the world's most powerful maelstrom: Saltstraumen.

A terrible fate befell Bodø, the capital of Nordland, whose memory was wiped out by a German bombing in May 1940. Its geographical location on the fish route had made it a base for Trondheim's merchants since the early 19th century. It then experienced a rebirth with the great herring trade in the middle of the century.

The need to rebuild a town from the ground up can be an incentive to reinvent its role, as Bodø has done, becoming a center for trade and services, while also hosting numerous oil-related activities. It leaves neighboring Kjerringøy as a reminder of its 19th-century roots and the origins of southern merchants.

Bodø has reinvented itself as a cultural hub in the 21st century.

Forget inferiority complexes: the city seems ready to strengthen its position as a "gateway" with more active self-promotion than in the past. The waterfront is part of this. On long summer evenings, when the light just won't let up, its streets and pubs fill with people. The new Bodø has become so vibrant that it was named European Capital of Culture 2024. And this title is not given to just any place, rich as it may be. So, don't underestimate Bodø because it has some important things to show.

The most important is Saltstraumen, just 6 miles (10 km) southeast of the city. It is the world's strongest maelstrom, where powerful tidal currents between the Saltfjorden and the Skjerstadfjorden swirl the water in a narrow passage, creating an enormous force.

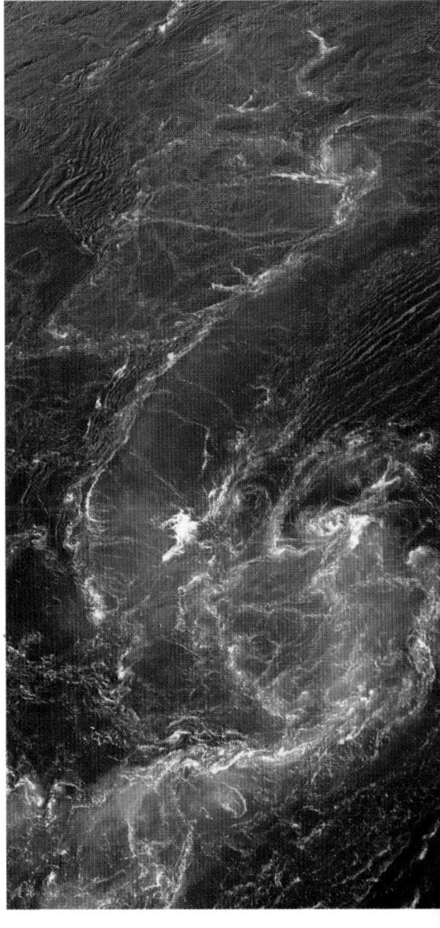

Saltstraumen, outside Bodø, is the most powerful maelstrom in the world.

The Maelstrom

A *malstrøm*, or maelstrom, is a whirlpool created by the tides. In the case of Saltstraumen, the most powerful maelstrom in the world, the tide moves over 14 billion cubic feet (400 million cu m) of water, pushing it through a 1.8-mile-long (3 km) and 492-foot-wide (150 m) funnel, centrifuging it, and creating powerful down currents. This leads to the formation of eddies 32 feet (10 m) in diameter and half as deep. The immense force reaches 25 miles an hour (40 km/h). The fascinating whirling of the water can be seen from the top of the Saltstraumen Bridge, which is equipped with walkways, or alternatively from one of the viewpoints along the shore.

After seeing this natural phenomenon, check out some of the city's more modern attractions. Not to be missed is **Stormen Konserthus,**

Kjerringøy Handelssted

Have you ever read a novel by Knut Hamsun? If the answer is yes, then Kjerringøy—with its world of fishermen in the North—must be familiar, as it is the world described by this Norwegian Nobel laureate. Anyone who has walked the creaky floorboards of the emporium will remember Mack from Sirilund and his credit sales; a glance through the windows of the manor house will surely conjure up images of Christmas celebrations and the piano that Benoni buys for his beloved Rose as a status symbol.

For non-Hamsunians, however, Kjerringøy is a pretty trade town founded in the late 18th century, like so many others along the coast, when the monopoly of Bergen and Trondheim fell. Ships left from here to buy fish in the Lofoten or elsewhere, and then sold it in Bergen. This trade was particularly active during the 19th century, and one master fisherman, Erasmus Zahl, provided employment for the entire community. The buildings are arranged around three yards: the garden, the barn and stable, and the port. The last is surrounded on one side by the shop and on the other by the three-story warehouse, the true heart of the village.

To get to Kjerringøy, follow Route 834 from Bodø to Festvåg, then take the ferry to the island. There you will find not only the open-air museum, but also beaches, nature reserves, mountains, Sami houses, and most of all, a great landscape.

the concert hall by the sea. It features clean, essential lines, geometric stained glass windows, and rooms that can accommodate classical music, ballet, and all other musical genres. Also used as a theater and conference venue, it has phenomenal acoustics thanks to special panels. Then make a stop at the **Norsk Luftfartsmuseum,** Norway's military and civilian aviation museum, which tells the story of flight with many models, including Spitfires and U2s, the famous spy planes. There are also flight simulations and guided courses for adults and children. Another interesting stop is the **Jektefartsmuseet,** a museum that shows how the *jekt,* the square Viking sailboat once used in Nordland, was essential for trans-

Stormen Konserthus ✉ Storgata 1b, Bodø ☎ 755 49 000 **stormen.no**
Norsk Luftfartsmuseum ✉ Børtindgata 35b, Bodø ☎ 755 07 850 🕒 summer 10 a.m.–6 p.m.; rest of the year Mon.–Fri. 10 a.m.–4 p.m., Sat.–Sun. 11 a.m.–5 p.m. **norwegianaviationmuseum.com**
Jektefartsmuseet ✉ Kvernhusveien 26, Bodø ☎ 930 02 950 🕒 Tues.–Fri. 11 a.m.–4 p.m., Sat.–Sun. 11 a.m.–5 p.m. **jektefart.no**

porting goods in the region for more than 400 years. It also illustrates the daily life of the poor fishermen who settled here to fish for cod and herring. From the fishing grounds, boats loaded with dried cod, herring, and redfish would set out for Bergen; the journey would take weeks, and the cargo was always at risk from bad weather. In Bergen, they loaded up with salt, flour, manufactured goods, and textiles, a vital trade for the entire Atlantic coast. In those days, up to 200 jekts sailed the seas each year, but today only one is still in operation and requires constant maintenance. Three examples have been preserved, and one, the *Anna Karoline,* is on display here. Outside you can visit Bodøsjøen, an open-air museum with 14 wooden buildings that illustrate life at the time.

If you are interested in literature, you can take the ferry from the town to the **Hamsunsenteret** in Hamarøy. Here you will find evidence of the life of one of Norway's greatest writers, Knut Hamsun (1859–1952), winner

Hamsunsenteret ✉ Vestfjordveien 1464, Hamarøy ☎ 755 03 450
hamsunsenteret.no

Kjerringøy is an ancient village about 30 miles (40 km) north of Bodø.

of the Nobel Prize for his novel *The Awakening of the Land,* which tells the story of a farming family that decides to settle in the wilderness. Another stop not to be missed is Kjerringøy, the setting for many of his novels.

Then visit Bodin Kirke, a 13th-century church and parish that once stretched from the Atlantic to the Swedish border. The south aisle dates from the 18th century, the Renaissance pulpit from the 17th century, and the baroque altar is one of the most beautiful in Norway. Then climb Mount Rønvik, about 2 miles (3 km) from the town. It offers a panoramic view of the mountains and islands surrounding Bodø, all the way to the Lofoten. It is a recommended spot for seeing the midnight sun, perhaps with a tasty local beer. Finally, stop at the **Besøkssenter Nasjonalpark Nordland,** where you can learn about the nature of the region, its geology, and the Sami people who live there. The center has beautiful wooden architecture, and outside you can practice lassoing or stonecutting. The Adde-Zetterquist Art Gallery in Storjord is also part of the center, with works that reflect Sami culture.

The road north offers unusual views of smooth, rounded mountains, white beaches with tropical-colored sea, mountain lakes with water that freezes before your eyes, and an abundance of birch and fir trees.

Ferry for the Lofoten Islands

The direct Bodø–Sørland ferry (4.5 hours) continues to Røst in the south or Moskenes in the north. Or take the Bodø–Moskenes car ferry (3.5 hours) or the Bodø–Svolvær passenger ferry (3.5 hours). If you get farther north than Bodø, there are other shorter crossings: from Bognes to Lødingen in one hour and from Skutvik to Svolvær in two hours. Your choice depends on whether you want to do more of the journey by land or by sea.

Bodø is served by an airport and a railway terminal with trains from Oslo and Bergen. There are also ferries from the city to the southern Lofoten Islands. This is the easiest way to reach the archipelago.

Once on the islands, the E10 leads to Vesterålen and from there to the mainland. With the opening of the Sløverfjord underwater tunnel in 2007, which is about 2 miles (3 km) long, you can drive all the way there. But Evenes Airport, farther north, can also be convenient. In that case you can arrive by land, first to Vesterålen and then to Lofoten. If you wish, you can rent a car, perhaps an electric one, at the airports mentioned or in Svolvær. ■

Besøkssenter Nasjonalpark Nordland ✉ Saltfjellveien 2035, Røkland ☎ 400 67 251 **nordlandsnaturen.no**

LOFOTEN ISLANDS, ARCHIPELAGO OF LIGHT

The Lofoten are fragmented islands, as if the sea was undecided about what to leave floating and what to submerge. They are rocky outcrops in the ocean, ideal for fishing. The ingenious ancestors of the locals found ways to hoard natural resources: wind and salt are plentiful, no need for chemistry. Nothing could be better suited for the cod trade than these islands.

Traditional fishermen's houses dot the Lofoten Islands.

It is hard not to wax poetic about such a landscape: the sea, the sheer peaks, beaches, rocks, verdant fields, and the ever-changing light and temperature conditions. A bewitching landscape according to Edgar Allan Poe, it was grim and thus perfect for his romantic horror stories, while for others it is very sweet. In any case, it cannot leave you indifferent.

The mountains here are at least two billion years old and were formed during the last ice age, when the ice sheet that covered all of Scandinavia receded. The Lofotveggen, or the "Lofoten Wall," is a series of peaks that tower over the sea and from a distance look like a straight line—hence the wall. Sea and mountains compete, leaving lakes of fossilized salt water deep inside, along with currents that create eddies. Likewise, the clouds bring heavy rains and changeable weather. Consider that in a single summer day you can have 77°F (25°C) and sunshine in the east, and less than 50°F (10°C) with clouds and fog in the west.

In ancient times, the archipelago prospered from cod fishing, especially in the area of the medieval settlement of Vágar, where the town of Kabelvåg stands today, until the business fell into the hands of Bergen, i.e., the Hanseatic League, in the 14th century, when they imposed taxes and had a monopoly on exports to Europe.

Arctic cod is air-dried to become stockfish.

Today, with tourism, the islands are experiencing an unusual fate. Some Norwegians say that they are overwhelmed by the number of visitors, their behavior, the garbage, and the cars parked everywhere. Therefore, it is important that you minimize your impact on the environment when you visit, so that the region can maintain its unspoiled nature.

Lofoten is pronounced Lùfutn. From north to south, the islands that make up the archipelago are Austvågøy, Gimsøy, Vestvågøy, Flakstadøy, Moskenesøy, Værøy, and Røst, surrounded by smaller formations. For more information: *visitlofoten.no.*

Austvågøy

An island of mountains—including the highest peak of the archipelago, Higravstinden (3,759 feet [1,146 m])—Austvågøy has just over 9,000 inhabitants, half of whom live in Svolvær. *Vær,* in the town's name, means "fishing port." It has existed since the Middle Ages. Its deep, branched harbor has helped it to gain an advantage in fishing over the nearby and older Kabelvåg. As the archipelago's main port, the town's fate has been tied to the fluctuating fortunes of the industry. In addition to fishing, it is also a center for the processing of dried (stockfish) or salted (salt cod) fish, export, the extraction of liver oil, and the production of flour and preserves. Tourism has also taken root here. The town and all the islands have also inspired many artists and writers,

(continued on p. 232)

THE LOFOTEN ISLANDS & *SKREI*

Arctic cod, or *skrei,* has a mythical history: it is food that moved and moves people, food of great export, food that enabled navigation, exploration, and conquest.

Lofotfiske. This is the name of the fishing season, from January to mid-April, for *skrei,* the Arctic cod. The term comes from *skrida,* a Norse word meaning "to migrate." In fact, Arctic cod species spend part of their lives in the Barents Sea and then, with maturity, return to Lofoten in winter to spawn. In the spring, young cod take the reverse route and head north.

The scientific name for Arctic cod is *Gadus morhua,* and it is one of the most useful and profitable fish for humans. Just think of the importance of dried cod. The Vikings courageously sailed their ships around the world to bring it to Russia, the Americas, the Mediterranean, and the Middle East. This trade has been going on since at least the 12th century.

In addition to the cod, the Lofoten Islands have the right temperature and humidity to process the fish in traditional ways: if it is salted and dried it is called salt cod; air-dried is stockfish. In the drying process, stockfish loses 70 percent of its water, while keeping its properties intact. This results in a high concentration of quality. The nutritional value of 2.2 pounds (1 kg) of stockfish corresponds to that of 11 pounds (5 kg) of fresh fish. Even today, cod is dried on large racks in the open air for 3 to 4 months. The preparation of salt cod is different. The fish is first crushed, then salted, and left to mature. It used to be dried on rocks, *klippe* in Norwegian, hence *klippfisk,* as it is called in this region; now it is dried in special tunnels instead. In addition to the meat, the rest of the fish is also used. The heads are dried to make flour, whereas eggs, liver, and tongue are sold separately. Stockfish is mainly imported by Italy, an import of about 50 million euros, directly from the Lofoten Islands.

In Portuguese, salt cod is called *bacalhau.* According to some, after landing on the shores of Canada in the 16th century, the Portuguese salted and dried the cod, resulting in their passion for the cheap and nutritious food, which then spread to Spain and Italy. It was not until the early 18th century that, with the availability of cheap salt, the other method of preservation began in Norway. Note that almost all producers now adhere to the Tørrfisk fra Lofoten PGI label.

some attracted by the extraordinary light, others by the great activity of the fishing season. This includes Gunnar Berg, who was born here, and Johan Bojer. Svolvær has 4,700 inhabitants and is one of the places where you can see the midnight sun (May 28–July 14).

After a stop at the **tourist office,** you can start your tour of the town from above. Climb Svolværgeita, literally "the goat of Svolvær," a two-horned spire that dominates the town; the distance between the two peaks is about five feet (1.5 m), and climbers have to jump from one to the other. Opposite is Fløya, the mountain reached by the Sherpa trail called Djeveltrappa, or "the devil's stairs." The view from the top is incredible.

Back in town, visit the **Lofoten Krigsminnemuseum,** a museum dedicated to World War II, where the years of German occupation are recalled through displays of uniforms and objects. It is part of the Museum Nord network, which operates 21 museum sites in Nordland. Another interesting museum is the **Nordnorsk Kunstnersenter,** or the Lofoten Artists' House, a center for visual arts and crafts.

In Svolvær, you can go fishing yourself, or just enjoy a meal at one of the restaurants by the sea. You can rent *rorbu* huts, bicycles, and boats, or go whale-watching to see orcas and humpbacks chasing herring. In short, there are many activities available. An absolute must is a walk to the island of Svinøya, which lies opposite the

Tourist Office ✉ Torget 18, Svolvær ☎ 760 70 575 🕒 summer 9 a.m.–6 p.m.; rest of the year Mon., Wed., Fri. 9 a.m.–3:30 p.m., Tues. 2:30 p.m.–6 p.m., Sat.–Sun. 10 a.m.–2 p.m. **visitlofoten.com**

Lofoten Krigsminnemuseum ✉ Fiskergata 3, Svolvær ☎ 917 30 328 🕒 Mon.–Fri. 10 a.m.–4 p.m., Sat. 11 a.m.–3 p.m., Sun. noon–3 p.m., all evenings 6:30 p.m.–10 p.m. **lofotenkrigmus.no**

Nordnorsk Kunstnersenter ✉ Torget 20, Svolvær ☎ 400 89 595 🕒 Tues.–Sun. 10 a.m.–4 p.m. **nnks.no**

town: it was once the center of the community, and still has dozens of rorbu huts and all the charm of the past. And then there's Gunnar Berg Galleri, which houses 70 oil paintings and numerous sketches by the Lofoten painter of the same name. While you're there, don't miss the sauna with a view of the Lofoten Islands to feel closer to the cod. Then, if you want to outdo yourself, there is a boat that will take you a little farther north to see the magnificent Trollfjord, a narrow fissure between vertical cliffs, only about a mile (2 km) long. You can get close to eagles and see underwater life with an underwater drone, ride an electric boat or go on an eagle safari with a speedboat.

Nearby is Skrova, a 30-minute ferry ride from Svolvær. This village on the island of the same name was once a center of trade and later a base for hunting small whale.

Continuing south on the E10 you reach Kabelvåg, founded by King Øystein in the 12th century. Vágar–the old name of the village–grew as a trading center and established itself throughout Nordland. The area is

Trollfjord is surrounded by vertical cliffs.

Northern Lights

There is a geographical oval area that demarcates the territory of the northern lights, called *Nordlys* in Norwegian. The Lofoten Islands lie in the middle of that oval, and thus offer a greater likelihood of seeing them. The islands also offer a number of beautiful amenities that enhance the experience. From photo tours to sailing and minibus rides, as well as bike or horseback tours in Hov, you can enjoy the magic of the colorful lights in the winter sky in whichever way you like.

home to the **Lofotmuseet,** part of the Museum Nord network. Housed in the old fishing center a stone's throw from the excavations of the medieval settlement, it illustrates the life of the fishermen with their tools, boats, houses, and the landlord's office. A few doors down is Lofotakvariet, an aquarium that houses the marine life of the islands from the beach to the open sea. There is also a pool for seals and an exhibition explaining how trout and salmon are farmed. It has a nice audiovisual element that introduces the world of the archipelago, as well as a cafeteria and a terrace. You can also book a tour on the *Nemo,* a glass-bottomed boat, to explore the seabed. Galleri Espolin houses works by the painter Kaare Espolin Johnson (1907–1994), whose brushstrokes depict the harsh life on the coast. To conclude your tour, stop at Vågan Kirke, better known as Lofotkatedralen, which was built in 1898 on the site of earlier churches. It is the church of the fishermen, a monument to the hope and prayer for incredible catches.

Continuing on, a detour from the E10 leads to Henningsvær, a village built on several islands, divided by canals and connected to the mainland by a bridge. Henningsvær is a must-see for its landscape, its architecture between the sea and the rocks, and its fishing activity. During the cod fishing season it is teeming with fishing boats and fishermen, all united by one goal. As they say here, "smell the fish, smell the money." Don't miss an orca safari from late October to late January, swimming with the whales, an eagle safari, and deep sea rafting on speed rafts.

Again on the E10, you reach the Gimsøystraumen Bridge *(toll),* which leads to the small island of Gimsøy, itself connected to Vestvagøy via the Sundklakkbrua Bridge.

Vestvagøy

The land on Vestvagøy is flatter than on the other islands of the archipelago, and therefore is good for farming: the inhabitants can raise cows, sheep, and goats, produce dairy products, and grow potatoes.

Lofotmuseet ✉ Storvåganveien 25, Kabelvåg ☎ 901 72 077
🕒 summer 10 a.m.–6 p.m.; rest of the year hours may vary
museumnord.no

Vågan Kirke is known as "the cathedral of the Lofoten."

Thus Vestvagøy is not just a fishing island like the others. This has been known since Viking times, when the chieftain's residence and farms were established in Borg, the fishing station in nearby Borgvaer, and the trading center in Kabelvåg.

Once on Vestvagøy, you can take two different routes: the E10 along the west coast, or the 815 to the east. We recommend taking one on the way in and the other on the way out.

Following the E10 will take you to Borg, home of several viking chieftains. Evidence of this can be found at **Lofotr Vikingmuseum,** where the ruins of a large settlement of the period have been found. The museum includes a 272-by-39-foot (83 x 12 m) longhouse, the largest in the world, which was reconstructed following the excavations that unearthed the original. The collection displays various types of objects, including lamps that were lit with cod liver oil. Farm animals can be seen outside. There is also the ship *Vargfotr,* a copy of a ship of the period, on which you can book a group excursion. A visit to the museum is a

Lofotr Vikingmuseum ✉ Vikingveien 539, Bøstad ☎ 761 54 000
🕒 June 15–Aug. 15 10 a.m.–7 p.m.; rest of the year 10 a.m.–5 p.m. **lofotr.no**

true immersion into the world of the Vikings; you can listen to old stories, learn how to shoot a bow and throw an axe, and see craftsmen weaving or carving wood.

From Borg take Route 815 and turn onto Route 817 to Stamsund, a fishing town with a fleet of motorboats and fish processing facilities. The old village of Steine, a few miles away, is worth a visit. The Vestvagøy Museum in Sennesvik, at Skaftnes Farm, tells the story of how families lived from fishing and farming in the 19th century. Nearby Leknes, on the other hand, should be remembered for its surrounding landscape of peaks, cliffs, and beaches.

Moving to the southern end of the island, along Route 818, you will come across the beautiful village of Ballstad, one of the largest for fishing. Here you will find rorbu rentals and several typical activities such as fishing, snorkeling, and kayaking. Heading west on the E10, you will pass through the Nappstraumtunnelen and arrive on the island of Flakstadøy.

Flakstadøy

Crossed by the E10, the rocky island of Flakstadøy has been carved by deep fjords, enchanting landscapes, long white beaches, and low-lying vegetation. A stop in Nusfjord, touted as the most beautiful village in Lofoten, is a must. The houses are from the 19th century and very well preserved. A photo of this village conveys the essence of Lofoten: the sea encroaching on the rocks, green vegetation, the deep red of the houses facing each other, the boats docked nearby, and wooden piers and walkways, all drenched with the smell of cod. Returning to the E10, you immediately encounter Flakstad, with a beautiful late 18th-century wooden church, then Ramberg, which gets its name from the large protruding rock above it. Finally, you reach the Kåkern Bridge, which connects the island to the next one, Moskenesøy.

Moskenesøy

On the E10, you first arrive in Hamnøy, a village at the mouth of the Kirkefjord, and then in Reine, which you reach by crossing three bridges. Reine is the administrative center of the island, surrounded by mountains that have inspired many painters and challenged many mountaineers. Those who like to photograph enchanting landscapes will certainly find great opportunities here. As usual, there are rorbu

A white-tailed eagle

A room in the Norsk Fiskeværsmuseum in the village of Å

rentals and a Sherpa trail, which climbs to the 1,469-foot (448 m) Reinebringen. Also worth a visit is **Lofotodden Nasjonalpark** in the western part of the island, a combination of mountain peaks, deep fjords, and open sea. Here you can see sea eagles, white-tailed eagles, and other birds, as well as glacier buttercups. The park was established in 2018 to protect the alpine coastal flora and fauna, of which the area is rich.

The E10 ends at Å, a fishing village in the south of the island. It is home to the Norsk Fiskeværsmuseum, part of the Museum Nord network, which serves as a snapshot of life in the 19th century in a place entirely devoted to fishing and fish processing, linked to the dreams and changing fortunes of one family. There is a rorbu hut,

(continued on p. 239)

EXPERIENCE: Lofoten Scenic Route

Looking for a well-rounded visit to the islands? Then drive along the Lofoten Scenic Route, a 142-mile-long (230 km) road from Raftsundet to Å, a true feast for the eyes. There are several rest stops along the way to properly appreciate the scenery, photograph the natural beauty, have a snack, and chat with other travelers. Akkarvikodden on Moskenes offers great sea views, while Rambergstranda on Flakstad has access to a beach surrounded by peaks. Then stop at Eggum on Vestvågøy to see its amphitheater-like structure, and at Austnesfjorden, where there is a pleasant woodland walk.

Lofotodden Nasjonalpark ✉ Visitor Center in Kirkeveien 52, Reine ☎ 755 31 600 🕒 summer 9 a.m.–8 p.m.; rest of the year 10 a.m.–5 p.m. **lofotoddennp.com**

RORBU HUTS

We look at *rorbu* huts—the traditional fishermen's houses—with a certain fascination for their clean lines and colors. But they are evidence of hard seasonal work, harsh living conditions, and the price paid for fishing, once the only reason to live on this stretch of the Norwegian coast.

Traditional *rorbu* huts

The importance of fishing in Lofoten, both to the nation's exports and to the crown's income, meant that accommodation had to be considered for the fishermen who, since the Middle Ages, had pinned their hopes for survival or wealth on the islands' fish-bearing sea. More fishermen meant more money, as King Øystein must have thought when he began building rorbu huts in the 12th century. The same thought must have gone through the minds of the island's lords, the merchants who owned entire villages and who prospered in the 19th century with particularly large catches. Huts were built in all the fishing areas to be rented to fishermen, who owned only their labor and paid for it in cod, of course at the price set by the merchant.

These huts were built of wood, often resting on poles fixed to rocks by the sea. The interior was divided into two rooms: one for sleeping, cooking, and eating, and the other as an entrance *(budøra)* and storage for tools. Typically, the roof of the first room was covered with grass, while the roof of the second room was made of simple planks. A chimney for the oven, which was also used for heating, had two openings, one for potatoes and the other for fish. During the cod season, a dozen men lived in a rorbu, sleeping in bunks. The main hut was also the site of parties, when the fishermen would break out into *budans,* which translates as "hut dancing."

Today's rorbu has changed with the times. Although the exterior remains much the same, the interior has been filled with modern amenities, preserving the charm of the past without the hardship and inconvenience.

Malstrøm in Literature

"The edge of the whirl was represented by a broad belt of gleaming spray—but no particle of this slipped into the mouth of the terrific funnel, whose interior, as far as the eye could fathom it, was a smooth, shining, and jet-black wall of water, inclined to the horizon at an angle of some 45 degrees, speeding dizzily round and round with a swaying and sweltering motion, and sending forth to the winds an appalling voice, half shriek, half roar, such as not even the mighty cataract of Niagara ever lifts up in its agony to heaven."

Thus wrote famous American author Edgar Allan Poe in his short story "A Descent into the Maelstrom." He was describing the Moskenesstraumen, or the Moskenes current, a giant whirlpool caused by the periodic tidal currents that push the ocean out into the inland sea and quickly fill the narrow channel between Moskenes and Værøy. The movement of the water creates huge whirlpools in the sea, with voids that produce excruciating howls, and vertical, up and down currents that swallow up everything. A romantic legend has arisen surrounding this phenomenon, fueled by the stories of Edgar Allan Poe and Jules Verne.

a bakery, a post office, a blacksmith's forge, a manor house, boat shelters, a salting plant, and an old factory where cod liver oil was processed. Staying with the theme, the Lofoten Tørrfiskmuseum is also worth a visit. The polyglot owner will tell you all about stockfish, from fishing to preparation and cooking.

All that remains of the Lofoten is the southern part, which is separated from the other islands. Værøy can be reached by ferry from Bodø, Moskenes, and Røst, while the Røst Archipelago can be reached by ferry from Bodø and Værøy, or by plane from Svolvær or Bodø.

Værøy

Værøy means "island with the fishing village" and the inhabitants here chose a puffin for its coat of arms. These birds have been the basis of the local diet for centuries, so much so that a special breed of dogs with six toes per paw, some of which still exist, were selected and trained to climb over rocks and slip into crevices to catch them. It is still an island of fishing and stockfish, and the mountains provide a magnificent backdrop. The strongest current in the world, the Moskenes current, forms between this island and Moskenesøy.

Places of interest include Punn Beach, with white sand surrounded by steep cliffs; Måstadfjellet, with its characteristic white-tailed eagles and panoramic views; and the ghost village of Måstad, evidence of a Viking fishing settlement that was permanently abandoned in 1974. Typical activities include a hike to Håheia (or Håen), a 1,437-foot (438 m) peak that offers excellent views of the island. Incredible scenery can also be found at Nordlandshagen, in the northern part of Værøy. It has a small onion-domed wooden church and a magnificent panorama: a white beach, the rocky outcrop of Mosken in the foreground and the Lofoten mountains in the background. It is experienced at its best in solitude, watching the midnight sun and listening to the cries of the seagulls recalling "the birth of the world." No cinematic special effect could make the scene as vivid as a walk.

Røst

More than a single island, Røst is an an archipelago, and a rather large one at that, made up of 365 islands and islets. The inhabitants say that "there is an island for every day of the year." In fact, only the main island–which, unlike the others, is completely flat–is inhabited. Here the storms blow away, making the winters mild and the summers longer; it has a kind of strange "lagoon" atmosphere, with canals, low vegetation, and old wood. Although the conditions are ideal for catching and processing cod, Røst's main attraction is its seabird colonies, an ornithologist's paradise that is now in trouble because of declining fish stocks in the local waters. The bird communities are settled on different cliffs and organized according to specialization: eagles on the top, puffins on the grassy terraces, guillemots on the rocky narrow ones, and cormorants and gulls at the bottom. The rocks are inhabited by waders, all kinds of gulls, ruddy turnstones, and eider ducks. ■

The island of Trenyken belongs to the Røst Archipelago.

VESTERÅLEN, THE ALPINE SISTERS

This archipelago is often overlooked, but it contains natural wonders that rival the better known Lofoten. A combination of views and activities, especially related to fishing, awaits visitors who choose to devote the time the region deserves.

A panoramic view from the Dronningruta, or the "Queen's Route"

The Lofoten and Vesterålen archipelagos could be twins. The latter undoubtedly has a less advantageous position on the international tourist map; it is less famous, less rich in fish, less frequented, and less literary than its neighbors. But it also has beautiful landscapes. Its sharp peaks tower over the sea, while on the mainland, narrow passages–through which mail ships glide–alternate with wide white beaches and clustered communities. Inland there are vast marshes with lakes and ponds.

The Vesterålen are also connected to the Lofoten through fishing, first for cod, then for herring, and all that goes with it. Every summer and fall, small cargo ships used to sail to Bergen, crammed with stockfish, liver oil, salt, beer, and other goods. Trade with the southern part of the continent was tied to the trade cycles imposed by Europe. It was also here that the Hurtigruten coastal route was first conceived–an idea that greatly contributed to the unification of the Norwegian nation.

From north to south, the main islands that make up this wild archipelago are Andøya, Langøya, Hadseløya, and Hinnøya. Vesterålen can be reached by car from Narvik by taking part of the E6 and then the E10 at Bjerkvik, or from Lofoten by taking the E10 in the opposite direction. There are airports at Evenes (Harstad-Narvik) on the mainland, and Andenes on Andøya. Finally, the Hurtigruten stops at Stokmarknes, Sortland, and Risøyhamn.

Andøya

Traces of human settlements in prehistoric times, and the much more recent presence of the Vikings, can be found all over the island. In Åse, for example, there are Iron Age sites and medieval settlements. Growth in the area came with the fish trade, both with Bergen, and with northern Russia. In the 17th century, Andenes was a Dutch whaling base. In the herring boom years of the late 19th century, 70 factories were working at full capacity to keep up with the catch. Today, fish is still important, as evidenced by the culinary culture that surrounds it, but the economy is also supported by Andøya Space, the aerospace company that deals with satellites, both civilian and military, and manages the country's only permanent launch base.

The island has a gentle landscape: imposing mountains, white beaches, islets, moors, and swamps. Everything is magnified by the unique northern light. The *multe,* or cloudberry, also grows here. It is a type of arctic raspberry with a distinctive taste, much loved on local tables and found almost exclusively in these latitudes. Saithe are caught here, too. On clear summer nights, everyone is involved in this activity, both to fill the freezer in preparation for the cold winter, or to enjoy the fish fresh, perhaps in the company of others.

The gateway to the island is Risøyhamn, a fishing town from the 18th century. From here, take Route 82 to the northernmost point of the archipelago: Andenes. A fishing center since the Iron Age, Andenes became one of Norway's most important fishing ports in the last century. Don't miss Andenes Fyr, the 130-foot-tall (40 m) lighthouse built in 1859—it is made of cast iron on the outside and brick on the inside.

(continued on p. 244)

Cloudberries grow in Andøya.

HURTIGRUTEN

Regular shipping along Norway's northern coast was, in the late 1800s, the equivalent of the railroad in the American West, a breakthrough for the country's social and economic progress.

The Hurtigruten is a communication route, but a special Norwegian one. It is the country's main artery, the vital point of contact between the more rural areas and the cities, which in this case lie to the south. The length of the journey – 1,250 nautical miles from Bergen to Kirkenes following the rugged coastline carved by deep fjords, and not getting lost among the thousands of islands and islets off the mainland– makes it an epic undertaking. It was born, of course, from the mind of a pioneer.

A Hurtigruten ship

Richard With was a captain who, on July 2, 1893, after thinking long and hard about the need to establish sea transportation from one point of the country to another in order to facilitate internal trade and commerce, began the mad quest to sail day and night, year round, through the treacherous conditions of the Norwegian Sea.

Today's tourism has taken up this challenge, which is to unite people simply by bringing them together. In this sense, the Hurtigruten is much more than just a means of travel; it is an ideal lens through which to observe Norwegian life, a great geographical essay that can be read day after day. Not to mention the intimate, meditative nature of such a cruise. You get close to nature, solitude, and the horizontal light of the North.

Born more than a century ago in Stokmarknes, in the Vesterålen Archipelago, With's project has grown to include 12 ships, 36 ports of call, and some 90 excursions. To understand its importance to Norway, the Hurtigrutemuseet tells the story of the mail ship and displays a huge model: the MS *Finnmarken* from 1956.

Once lit by oil lamps, it is now automated. From the platform you can see 15 miles (24 km) out, to where the whales swim. It has a great view of the town too, and is an excellent place to catch the midnight sun. Next door is the **Andøymuseet,** a museum dedicated to Hilmar Nøis, a famous local hunter, which illustrates the daily life of hunters and scientists in the Arctic regions.

On the western coast of the island, Bleik is also worth a visit, both for its beautiful beaches and fishing opportunities, and especially for the trip to Bleiksøya, where tourists can spot a large colony of puffins. There are said to be around 80,000 pairs here, as well as other birds such as cormorants, magpies, guillemots, and white-tailed eagles.

The Andøya Space Center

Andøya Space Center

On August 18, 1962, Norway launched Ferdinand 1, a rocket that flew 63 miles (101.5 km) into the atmosphere from Andøya Space Center. Since then, Andenes base has carried out 1,000 rocket and balloon launches, all for scientific purposes. The space center focuses on the northern lights and the interactions between the sun and the Earth. It launches research rockets in the winter and remains the country's only permanent launch base. The space center is located at Oksebåsen, just 3 miles (5 km) southwest of town, and is preparing to launch small satellites.

The Spaceship Aurora Visitor Center *(spaceship-aurora.andoyaspace.no)* is situated at Bleiksveien 46 and offers the chance to explore the northern lights, experience a virtual space mission, and learn more about space exploration.

Nordmela, another fishing village farther south, offers a beautiful wooden sauna by the sea and heated swimming pools on the beach. Nearby is Skogvoll, one of three marshy areas on Andøya that have become nature reserves. Much of the western coast of the

Andøymuseet ✉ Richard Withs gate 9, Andenes ☎ 900 76 332 🕒 noon–4 p.m. **museumnord.no**

The Light after the Storm

The decision to spend a few days of summer vacation in Andenes might be a bit of a gamble. The extreme northern tip of Andøya is in fact very susceptible to the vagaries of the weather, and it is not uncommon for weather conditions to change for the worse. Usually the changes are sudden, so you can always hope for good weather again within a few hours. However, if you are lucky, which you probably will be if you spend a few days on the island, you will experience a beautiful evening with a post-storm light show that will make the trip worthwhile. You will need a car, camera, and good company. Leave from Andenes around 10 p.m., following the west coast. Along the road, admire the breathtaking light that cuts through the mountains, caresses the houses, gives relief to the grass, and outlines the wooden frames for drying fish. It's a light that never lets up, inventing new landscapes, highlighting or obscuring some details, forcing colors to blend. The streets are clear, the houses seem empty, an intense feeling pervades even the most hardened travelers. For the driver, it is like a game, an ideal road like no other; for the photographer, on the other hand, it is a constant challenge, an invitation to capture radiant compositions, endlessly renewed by a sun that never sets.

EXPERIENCE: Whale-Watching in Andenes

Moby Dick spends his vacations in Andenes! Melville's famous whale and his friends may not know it, but there are a hundred eyes on them and perhaps as many lenses ready to capture their movements. Or maybe they do know and renew their game by waiting for the peaceful ex-whaler *Kromhout,* full of people hungry with excitement. You can't help but look for a whale, orca, or dolphin in these seas, starting from a port that for centuries was a hub for whale hunting. A mighty splash coming from the depths of the sea or a huge tail returning to the deep is indeed an impressive and unforgettable sight.

If you want to see whales up close, you can join a whale-watching trip with the top experts in Andenes, the researchers from Hvalsafari AS *(whalesafari.no).* The researcher-guide will immerse you in the underwater world with exciting descriptions of the life of this species and answer questions from the participants. The experience will bring you closer to nature and life in this part of the world. A museum tells about the biology of cetaceans and their natural habitat.

island, from Andenes to Bjørnskinn, is accessible by following the Nasjonale Turistveger Andøya, which is 36 miles (58 km) long. The views feature large beaches, mountains, and grassy dunes. The trip can be done by car, rented in Andenes or at the airport, or by bike. If you want to go even deeper, a summer ferry connects Andenes with Gryllefjord on the nearby island of Senja, which offers another scenic route.

Langøya

This large, irregular island, with a jagged coastline (especially in the west) cut by the long Eidsfjorden, is characterized by mountains, cliffs filled with nesting birds, and fishing villages. The main town here is Sortland, on the strait of the same name, connected by a bridge to Hinnøya. A fishing center in the 18th century, it developed greatly with the herring trade and later became home to shipping companies. With the birth of the Hurtigruten Route, which also stops here, it has become a central stop in Vesterålen. See the bridge of the same name, Sortlandsbru, almost half a mile long, made with a humpbacked structure for ships to pass. Then visit the **Sortland Museum** in the central Kulturfabrikken, which illustrates the importance of the sea, especially the seabed, a rather fragile ecosystem.

Sortland Museum ✉ Strandgata 1, Sortland ☎ 467 04 560
🕒 Tues.–Sat. 11 a.m.–3 p.m. **museumnord.no**

The Sortland Museum is dedicated to the ocean floor.

The bust of Richard With in the town of Stokmarknes

Follow Route 820 north to Jennestad, one of Nordland's great commercial centers, with its 19th-century emporium that has served as a meeting place, supermarket, and café in the past. It is still filled with goods, waiting for customers who maybe will never come. It paints a small picture of rural Norwegian life.

Route 821 then takes you to Myre, an administrative and fishing center. From here you can get to Stø and Nyksund, an old, restored village that is now a popular stop with its charming little colorful houses, once home to fishermen and later taken over by artists, galleries, and restaurants. You can take a boat to see seals, puffins, and other birds–and, on lucky days, some whales too. The Nyksund–Stø and Niksund–Myre boat shuttle service makes it easy to travel between the settlements. Between the two fishing villages is a special mountain trail, the Dronningruta, literally the "Queen's Route," which is considered one of the most beautiful in Norway because of its magnificent views of the ocean and the large beach at Skipssanden. It is a loop of about 9 miles (15 km) and requires an average level of fitness.

From Sortland, take Route 82 south to Skagen, served by an airport, and continue to Stokmarknes, on the island of Hadseløya, over the Hadsel Bridge and then the Børøy Bridge.

Hadseløya

The small island of Hadseløya, mountainous to the west and flat to the east, is home to the two towns of Stokmarknes and Melbu.

Stokmarknes has two distinctive features: the harbor and the bust of Richard With, the pioneer of the mail ship. The harbor tells of the fishing industry with another statue, this one in honor of Vesterålen Dampskibsselskap, the shipping company that established the Hurtigruten. In 1775, the town was granted a royal trading license, which, as had happened in the neighboring village of Melbu, boosted its fishing-based economy. In the 19th century a royal decree established an annual fair. The development of herring fishing was the final impetus that would increase the population fivefold in a few decades.

The only place to learn about the history of the Norwegian mail ship is here, where it all began. The new

The Tjeldsund bridge connects Hinnøya to the mainland.

Hurtigrutemuseet includes the MS *Finnmarken,* a ship of the postal fleet from 1956, anchored in the harbor. The museum is dedicated to pioneers, sailors, and passengers, and you can also see what remains of the earlier *Finnmarken* from 1912. In 2021, Link Architects designed a special container to go around it.

Melbu, a fish processing center, is the starting point for Lofoten, with a half-hour ferry ride to Fiskebøl on the island of Austvågøy. And it is also an up-and-coming tourist center. Visit **Melbo Hovedgård,** a restored Empire-style manor house with collections of 18th-century costumes and local memorabilia.

Hinnøya

Geographically located in Versterålen and connected to the mainland by the Tjeldsund Bridge, Hinnøya is the fourth largest island in Norway—and the largest outside the Svalbard Islands.

In the southwest part is Møysalen Nasjonalpark, a small mountain park by the fjord where the wilderness is the focus. It was established in 2003, covers an area of 19 square miles (51.2 sq km), and has some marked visitor trails. Møysalen, at 4,140 feet (1262 m) the highest peak of the twin archipelagos, towers in the center of the protected area. Heading north you come to Harstad. The town was founded in the late

Hurtigrutemuseet ✉ Richard Withs plass 1, Stokmarknes ☎ 909 96 412 ⏲ summer 10 a.m.–5 p.m.; rest of the year Mon.–Fri. 11 a.m.–3:30 p.m., Sat.–Sun. 11 a.m.–5 p.m. **hurtigrutemuseet.no • Melbo Hovedgård** ✉ Maren Frederiksens allé 1, Melbu ☎ 761 54 000 ⏲ summer only, Tues.–Sun. 11 a.m.–4 p.m. **museumnord.no**

19th century to profit from the herring trade, although the fertile plain around it had been settled for centuries. Further expansion came with the extraction and processing of oil, to which the town devoted itself, becoming a center of excellence for northern Norway. Once again, fish and oil are the foundation for the city's bright future. Despite its industrial focus, the soul of the city is still to be found in its landscape. That's why, if you visit these areas in the summer, we recommend you contact the **tourist office** and book a guided sunset tour during the midnight sun in a kayak on the fjord. It is an unforgettable experience.

In this town, which shares Evenes Airport with Narvik, everything is within easy reach. You can start with Trondenes Kirke, a fortified church built in the Romanesque-Gothic style with thick walls from the 13th century. There are three medieval triptychs in the chancel. Nearby are Viking burial mounds, Trondenes Historiske Senter—a museum about local history, the Vikings, the Middle Ages, and the post-war period—and Trondenes Middelaldergård, which has a 13th-century farm that shows its farming and living traditions. Also of interest is the Adolfkanonen gun, which was part of the Wehrmacht artillery in 1943–1945 used to defend Narvik and the coast. Guided tours are available to explain how it was used and what special features it had.

Around Harstad you can visit Nupen, 11 miles (18 km) away, a great place to see the midnight sun, and Kasfjord, overlooking the fjord of the same name. Also on its western shore is Skjærstad, a village known for Skjærstad Silde Oljefabrikk, a herring oil factory that operated from 1922 to 1928. During its six years of operation it was remarkable for its modern machinery; although it was a small factory, the entire oil production process was carried out with a steam engine. It was turned into a museum in the 1990s and can still be visited today. Finally, take a trip to Bjarkøy, a small island that was the home of Viking chieftain Tore Hund. It is the perfect place for observing large colonies of black-legged kittiwake. ■

Tourist Office ✉ Sjøgata 3, Harstad ☎ 770 18 989
visitharstad.com

Trondenes Kirke in Harstad

FROM NARVIK TO TROMSØ

Time to say goodbye to the islands, return to the mainland, and continue north on the E6 from Narvik. You will encounter wilderness areas, large islands such as Senja, and long fjords such as Vågsfjorden, between Senja and Hinnøya. This is the county of Troms og Finnmark, the last continental strip of northern Norway.

Narvikfjellet covered in snow

Narvik

It seems that most Norwegian settlements have developed around a specific activity, be it fishing, shipbuilding, or mineral extraction. Narvik is a prime example. In the late 19th century, when Sweden and Norway were a single kingdom, an idea was born in Stockholm to export Swedish iron to the world. From 1898 to 1902, workers called rallaren carved through tunnels and along cliffs to build the Ofotbanen, a railroad connected to a port on wide Ofotfjord, ice free year-round and a true highway to the sea. The town grew around the railroad, which brought wealth from Sweden, and the docks, which carried that wealth to the rest of the world.

Narvik was a primary target in Hitler's plans for Norway; iron, of course, is like bread in war. As a result, the town was the scene of several battles: first, in April 1940, German destroyers sank Norwegian ships and took Narvik; then the British fleet destroyed the Nazi ships, and Allied troops retook the town the following month. The mighty German war machine had been stopped for the first time, bringing hope. But Allied troops were soon recalled to other fronts, and Narvik was left to the Germans, who held it until the end of the war. This is well documented in the 2022 film *The Battle of Narvik (Kampen om Narvik)*, by Norwegian director Erik Skjoldbjærg.

The city has since been rebuilt and is still dependent on Swedish iron, but now it has its own university and boasts high-tech companies. It is also included in the Sustainable Destination Program. After passing by the **tourist office,** the first thing to do is take the cable car up to Narvikfjellet (2,152 feet [656 m]). The suspended platform is a great place to see the midnight sun or the northern lights. You can also ski here in the winter: jumping headfirst above the blue fjord is an unforgettable experience.

If you are interested in mountaineering, climb Mount Stetind (4,563 feet [1,391 m]), which has been declared a National Mountain. Hire an expert guide *(narvikguides.no)* from Narvik to ensure your safety while enjoying this Norwegian national heritage. It's highly recommended for the view from the top alone: a fabulous panorama that demonstrates the spectacle of the coexistence of mountains and fjords.

Back to lower altitudes, explore Narvik's two main themes: iron transport and warfare. The former is largely related to the harbor, where LKAB's wharves, some of the most modern in the world, create a striking industrial landscape. This is where the ore that arrives by rail from Sweden is shipped around the world: we are talking about millions of tons per year, loaded onto special cars. The **Narvik Museum** chronicles the construction of the Ofotbanen line and the journey of the iron from Kiruna to Narvik through photographs, models, and films. The

Tourist Office ✉ Kongensgate 41, Narvik ☎ 769 65 600
🕒 summer 10 a.m.–6 p.m.;
rest of the year 10 a.m.–4 p.m.
visitnarvik.com • **Narvik Museum**
✉ Administrasjonsveien 3, Narvik
☎ 769 69 650 **museumnord.no**

Narvik Museum

Scenic Senja

Visitors from around the world come to know the extent of the beauty of Norway's breathtaking landscapes, the kind that fill your eyes and your heart. Senja is one such treasure trove of wonders in the form of mountains crashing into the sea. The undulating island offers a glimpse of unexpected vistas, such as the green, fish-filled waters, beaches, and, to top it off, a ski resort. There are quiet and pleasant bike paths to ride and Ånderdalen Nasjonalpark to explore. Its 48 square miles (125 sq km) are home to a virgin forest with twisted pines over 600 years old, birch forests, several species of birds, and elk herds.

A must-see is the Senja Turistveger, a 63-mile-long (102 km) scenic route that allows you to explore the spectacular west coast from Gryllefjord to Botnhamn. Among the many viewpoints, the suspended platform at Bergsbotn and the white beach at Ersfjordstranda are not to be missed, but a stop at Tungeneset with its beautiful wooden walkway and a detour to the fishing village of Mefjordvær are also recommended.

building itself is worth a visit. Built in 1902 and painted red and ochre, it was the company's head office.

The other theme, as mentioned, is war. This is the focus of the **Narvik Krigsmuseum,** which chronicles a key period in the history of the town, when it was attacked by the Nazi army as a strategic target, along with Oslo and Bergen. It is a very striking museum, especially for the care put into its exhibits, which look like movie sets. Uniforms, weapons, flags, photos, memorabilia, and more are on display.

If you want to experience the infamous Iron Ore Line, a spectacular trip in itself, take it to Riksgränsen, a Swedish ski resort 26 miles (42 km) from Narvik that offers snowmobile safaris and dogsled or reindeer tours in the winter. From Narvik, the E6 continues north. After Fossbakken, a short detour takes you to **Polar Park,** where you can see reindeer, arctic foxes, deer, and musk oxen, as well as the big four of the Arctic: wolf, wolverine, bear, and moose. Passing mighty mountains, descend Bardudal valley to Bardufoss, a military air base. From there, take Route 86 to Finnsnes and then Senja. Alternatively, follow the E6 to Nordkjosbotn and then take the E8 to Tromsø.

Narvik Krigsmuseum ✉ Kongensgate 39, Narvik ☎ 769 44 426 🕒 10 a.m.–4 p.m. **krigsmuseet.no • Polar Park** ✉ Bonesveien 319, Bardu ☎ 482 40 000 🕒 summer 10 a.m.–6 p.m.; rest of the year 10 a.m.–3:30 p.m. **polarpark.no/en**

Tromsø

The Tromsø coat of arms is a white reindeer on a field of blue, a symbol of northern Europe and a testimony to the importance of this mighty animal. The central part of the city lies on the island of Tromsøya, with a western edge on Kvaløya, the "whale island," and an eastern edge on the mainland, Tromsdalen, nestled under Mount Tromsdalstinden. In short, it consists of two islands, two branches of the sea crossed by two bridges and a tunnel, and a mountain.

A statue of Roald Amundsen, one of Norway's modern heroes, stares forever into the Arctic from a public garden near the pier. It was from here that he set out in June 1928 on a last attempt to find Umberto Nobile, who was lost at the Pole after the tragedy of the airship *Italia*.

A connection between Tromsø and the polar region was established in the early 19th century with the hunting of wild animals. This was strengthened by the relationship with Svalbard and the activities that continue to flourish today. The city has developed so much that it has earned the title of Capital of the Arctic. Notable institutions include UiT, The Arctic University of Norway; Tromsø Geofysiske Observatorium, for seeing the northern lights; and Mack Bryggeri, a brewery established in 1877.

Three important events took place here in the 1940s: General Carl Gustav Fleischer moved the capital to Tromsø after the German invasion in 1940 and ordered a general mobilization, which was in vain, but it laid the foundation for the Norwegian

A panoramic view of Tromsø

The Ishavskatedralen is a work by Jan Inge Hovig.

resistance. This was the last seat of government before it was forced to flee to London. In 1942 the Krøkebærsletta concentration camp was opened, and in 1944 the famous *Tirpitz,* the jewel of the German navy, was sunk near here.

The origins of the city are ancient. Ignoring for a moment the Neolithic finds, the settlement is said to have been founded as early as the 13th century, when a church was built in 1252. It was not until the 18th century, however, that trade with the Russians and royal permits allowed the development of the region, and of Tromsø in particular. Fishing, shipyards, the brewery, and a focus on the Arctic then drove the city's growth in the 19th and early 20th centuries, as did the university, which has several campuses in Finnmark and focuses on the environment, society, technology, and culture. Like other Norwegian urban centers, it is part of the Sustainable Destination Program. For more information and local activities, contact the **tourist office.**

The city must be approached in an orderly fashion. First, cross the Tromsøbrua Bridge and visit the Ishavskatedralen, or the "cathedral of the Arctic," at Hans Nilsenvegs 41, one of the city's landmarks. Designed by Jan Inge Hovig and completed in 1965, it should be placed in the context of a quest for a Norwegian architectural style. It resembles a large white tent,

Tourist Office ✉ Samuel Arnesens gate 5, Tromsø ☎ 776 10 000
🕒 11 a.m.–4 p.m. **visittromso.no**

An old warehouse now houses the Polarmuseet.

or an iceberg, or both, representing the interaction of man and nature in the polar expanses. Victor Sparre made the stained glass window.

Back on Tromsøya, the second stop is the **Nordnorsk Vitensenter,** an interactive science center that offers challenges and experiments, such as exploring the different layers of the atmosphere with the northern lights. It covers physics, energy, the human body, and climate. It includes the Nordlysplanetariet, a planetarium dedicated to the northern lights, which offers a long audiovisual journey to learn about the phenomenon, the northern constellations, geological history, and the deep sea. An absolute must. While you're at it, familiarize yourself with the local flora at the Arktisk-alpine Botanisk hage, the university's campus garden, where alpine and Antarctic species are on display. The Norges Arktiske Universitetsmuseum, at Lars Thørings veg 10, is dedicated to nature and the Nordic people, from rocks to animal life, changes in fossils, and the adaptation of animals and plants to the Arctic climate. Sami and Vikings are also covered.

Located in an old warehouse on the waterfront, the **Polarmuseet**

Nordnorsk Vitensenter ✉ Hansine Hansens veg 17, Tromsø
☎ 776 20 945 **nordnorsk.vitensenter.no**
Polarmuseet ✉ Søndre Tollbodgate 11, Tromsø ☎ 776 23 360
🕒 11 a.m.–5 p.m. **visitnorway.com/listings/the-polar-museum**

provides insight about hunting and hunters in the polar regions, as well as research and explorers. Staying with the theme, you can also visit Polaria at Hjalmar Johansens gate 12, which has everything you need to know about the Arctic, a panoramic movie theater with environmental films, an aquarium, and a seal tank.

After visiting these places, take some time to explore the rest of the city. The **Nordnorsk Kunstmuseum** is particularly recommended, with paintings, drawings, photographs, sculptures, textiles, and Nordic art from the 19th and 20th centuries, from the Romantic painters to the present day. Also check out the Sami arts and crafts. Nearby is Tromsø Domkirke at Kirkegata 7, the northernmost Protestant cathedral in the world, consecrated in 1861.

A little farther north is the Perspektivet Museum, which focuses on art and cultural history, with exhibitions, events, and a collection of half a million photos of Tromsø from the 19th century to the present. At the southern end of the island is Folkeparken, an open-air museum of old buildings. If you are interested in legends about trolls and the world that created them, you must visit the Troll Museum at Kaigata 3. The exhibits use augmented reality.

Speaking of the city's architecture in general, its bridges are noteworthy: the first connects the mainland with the island of Tromsø, while the second, Sandnessundbrua, connects the latter with Kvaløya. Elegant and arched, they fit well into the fjord landscape and give a sense of human presence. Also worth noting is Tromsøysund Underwater Tunnel, which connects the central part of the city with Tromsdalen in the east. Of special interest are the old houses in Sjøgata, Skippergata, Grønnegata, and Strandgata. When you are done exploring, take a break at the Ølhallen Pub at Storgata 4, which is housed in a beautiful period building and offers a tasting of Mack beers, a label that was founded in 1877.

Nordnorsk Kunstmuseum ✉ Sjøgata 1, Tromsø ☎ 776 47 020
🕒 10 a.m.–5 p.m., Thurs. until 8 p.m. **nnkm.no**

The Lyngsalpene, or Lyngen Alps, rise east of Tromsø.

To conclude your tour of the city, all that remains is to reach an elevated point to enjoy some spectacular views from above. To do so, cross Tromsøbrua to the mainland and take the Fjellheisen cable car up to Storsteinen, 1,377 feet (420 m) above sea level. From this spot, considered the best place to see the midnight sun and northern lights, the mixed landscape of city, fjord, and mountains is a feast for the eyes. There is a restaurant, and you can also take a hike to the 4,061-foot-tall (1,238 m) Mount Tromsdalstinden. Alternatively, you can climb the Sherpatrappa, a 1,300-step trail built by Nepalese Sherpas that starts at the end of Fløyvegen in Tromsdalen and ends at the same spot as the cable car.

Around Tromsø

There are many places worth visiting in and around Tromsø. In particular, the two must-sees are Kvaløya in the west, with Sommarøy, and Lyngen in the east.

Kvaløya and Sommarøy have a lot to offer, from the rock paintings at Skavberg to beaches and bays such as Otervika and Sandviksletta, and plenty of activities, from kayaking and speed rafting to night hiking, a midnight sun fjord cruise, and a full Sommarøy tour. You could also take the Arctic tour from Tromsø to Senja by bus and ferry, or dine in a tent with huskies to see the northern lights. Remember that the best way to see the island is by bike. Note that before

(continued on p. 260)

REINDEER: A NATIONAL TREASURE

The reindeer is a peculiar animal that has always captured the collective imagination. For millennia, it has been the sole source of food for the peoples of the North, revered as a symbol of life in the Arctic Lands.

The reindeer is the spirit animal of Norway.

Reindeer are an integral part of Norway's economic and cultural heritage, even if currently only the Sami take care of them. Over the years, the state has passed laws to encourage reindeer husbandry, so that they can start businesses and earn enough to live on.

The number of reindeer must be kept constant, so the same amount of animals are culled as are born in the spring. This is mainly to protect the lichen, which has a relatively slow growth cycle. Sulfur pollution is a threat to the lichen and therefore to the reindeer.

From December to April, individuals remain near villages or in highland pastures, feeding on lichen, willow or birch leaves, and bark from young trees. Semi-nomadic Sami control them by moving around on snowmobiles and staying in temporary tents called *lavvu.*

In May, the reindeer are rounded up and herded to summer pastures on the coast of Troms og Finnmark. Some migrate to the islands, such as Magerøya in the North Cape. In this case, the navy intervenes to transport the calves to the sea, while on the way back the entire herd swims from the island to the mainland. This is a very old custom, illustrated in the cave paintings of Alta, which show reindeer at sea and men in boats.

From June to July, the young are branded, with special cuts on the underside of the ear to make them recognizable. In September, they return to the villages for the mating season. Five males are enough for one hundred females, and they emerge from the herd as the strongest of the group after wrestling with other contenders with their antlers. Reindeer destined for sledding are castrated. Finally, in November, large gatherings determine the number of animals to be slaughtered. Usually weaker animals, or those less than six months old, are chosen because their meat is more tender and they have a greater impact on lichen consumption. Each head yields 66 to 77 pounds (30 to 35 kg) of meat, which is sold at around 5 to 6 euros per kilo for the less noble cuts, reaching up to 20 euros per kilo for the most sought-after parts, such as tenderloin.

A *lavvu* is a temporary tent used by the Sami.

arriving at Kvaløya you can also see Håkøya, a smaller island, the place where the *Tirpitz* sank.

To the east of Tromsø is Lyngenfjord, which offers magnificent views and mountains formed of gabbro rock, with glaciers and peaks above 4,921 feet (1,500 m), plunging into the sea. It is a land inhabited by Sami and descendants of Finnish migrants, called Kven. The Lyngsalpene, or Lyngen Alps, are the rocky ridge of the peninsula of the same name between Ullsfjorden and Lyngenfjord. Almost 50 miles (80 km) in length, with 140 glaciers, valleys, glacial deposits, and the giant Jiehkkevárri (6,017 feet; 1,834 m), the highest mountain in northern Norway, the Lyngsalpene were declared a protected area by royal decree in June 2004. The Lyngsalpene protected area covers 371 square miles (961 sq km).

Lyngseidet is the administrative center of the area, with a beautiful church from 1775 that was modernized in the mid-19th century. From here begins the Lyngentrappa, a 1,200-step trail built by Sherpas that leads to Giæverlia, 1,476 feet (450 m) long, with views of the fjord and the town. Halfway between Lyngseidet and Oteren to the south is Steindalsbreen Glacier, a large tongue with a small lake.

Farther up the fjord you can stop at Storslett, where you will find the **Nord-Troms Museum** with its fishermen's houses, objects, boats, photos, and models. If you have some time, take Route 865 inland from Storslett. This will take you to Ovi Raishiin (a Kven name meaning "gateway to the Reisa Valley"), the visitor center for the magnificent Reisa Nasjonalpark, a long canyon that follows the course of the Reisa River, full of salmon and breathtaking waterfalls, such as Mollisfossen, with its 882-foot (269 m) drop. ■

The Right "Spirit"

Even at these latitudes it's impossible to not find a distillery! When owners Hans, Tor, and Anne-Lise founded Aurora Spirit, the northernmost whiskey distillery in the world, they must have imagined being at 69° N would bestow their products with a magical quality. These whiskeys, gins, vodkas, and aquavits are truly Arctic. Guided tours with tastings are available to learn about the distilling process and the vision behind the company *(Årøybuktneset 44, Lyngseidet, bivrost.com)*. The founding company is called Bivrost, a term that combines the words *biv* and *rost*, which literally means "trembling paths." It is said that the Vikings used these words to describe the northern lights. In short, a nice way to link past and present.

Nord-Troms Museum ✉ Hovedveien 2, Storslett ☎ 975 58 330
🕒 Mon.–Fri. 10 a.m.–3 p.m. **ntrm.no**

EXPLORING THE NORTH CAPE

Just a couple hundred miles to the north, the rocky outcrop that marks the northernmost point of the continent is within reach. It is like the end of a symbolic journey, full of expectation and meaning. Nordkapp, a rock overlooking the Arctic, serves as a line beyond which the land is no longer accessible, a window to the North Pole.

The architecture of Nordlyskatedralen is inspired by the northern lights.

Alta

With a population of just over 19,000, the city is the most populous center in Finnmark and the northernmost urban center in Europe, at nearly 70° N, but also farther east than much of southern Sweden and Finland. Alta has its ancient roots in the prehistoric Komsa culture, the first known culture to have existed in Norway, and in an even more mysterious people who left behind thousands of rock carvings. In historical times, this land was a frontier, populated by the Sami and good for fishing, so much so that Bergen bought the rights to it in the 17th century. It was also a land of proscription for prisoners, who had to serve their sentences working in the fishing industry. Depending on who's speaking—Norwegians, Laplanders-Sami, Kven, or Balto-Finnic immigrants—the town is called Alta, Áltá, or Alattio.

Its more recent roots lie in salmon, slate quarries, the Arctic University—which is shared with Tromsø and other cities—research, and tourism. The common denominator is always the particularly mild climate due to the currents that flow through the long Altafjord, which makes it possible to grow grain even at these latitudes—a record-breaking feat! It is also an ideal vantage point for viewing the northern lights and the fascinating midnight sun.

As you can find out at the **tourist office,** the most important thing to visit in town is Hjemmeluft, a UNESCO World Heritage site for its carvings, some of which are almost 7,000 years old. Also worth a visit is the **Alta Museum,** with exhibits on cave art, the development of trade in Alta, the northern lights, copper mining, and the history of the region from glaciation to the construction of the dam. This should be followed by a coffee with a view of the fjord and the carvings.

Then comes everything else. At Markedsgata 30 it is not hard to guess what awaits you. The building

Tourist Office ✉ Labyrinten 3, Alta ☎ 991 00 022 🕒 Mon.–Fri. 9 a.m.–3 p.m. **visitalta.no • Alta Museum** ✉ Altaveien 19, Alta ☎ 417 56 330 🕒 summer 9 a.m.–7 p.m.; rest of the year Mon.–Fri. 9 a.m.–3 p.m., Sat.–Sun. 11 a.m.–4 p.m. **altamuseum.no**

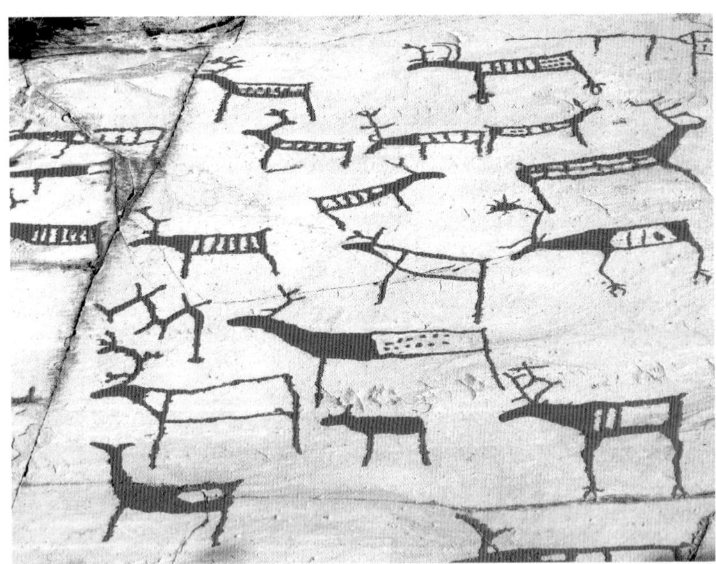

Alta rock carvings are a UNESCO World Heritage site.

Sautso Canyon is the longest in northern Europe.

looks like a roll of ribbon that spirals upward: the movement represents the northern lights, but the surprise of Nordlyskatedralen is that it is a real church. The design can also be interpreted as a path to heaven.

A little farther on you can visit **Laksen Hus,** a center dedicated to aquaculture. Here you can also see areas where salmon are raised.

Alta seems to lure visitors to its nearby excursions. Start with the great Alta River, Altaelva in Norwegian, which creeps inland from the fjord. It is one of the best for salmon, char, and trout fishing. It is home to Sautso Canyon, the longest in northern Europe, a real sight to see on foot, by bike or, when the water level is high enough, by kayak. You can also visit the famous dam at the center of the Sami people's dispute. In the 1970s, they opposed the construction of the dam, which was built to help power a hydroelectric plant, so that the river could continue to flow and the salmon could spawn there.

(continued on p. 265)

Laksen Hus ✉ Markedsgata 3, Alta ☎ 452 25 384 🕒 Mon.–Fri. 11 a.m.–4 p.m. **laksenshus.no**

UNESCO ROCK CARVINGS

Written on the rocks of Alta is a record of human prehistory, a story in pictures that goes back nearly 7,000 years and testifies to the life and culture of the ancestors of the North.

The inclusion of Alta's rock carvings on the UNESCO World Heritage List has certainly helped to raise awareness of this region on the edge of Europe and to integrate it into the continent's cultural fabric.

In the 1970s, some 3,000 carvings were discovered in four different areas near Hjemmeluft, in an inlet of Altafjord called Jiepmaluokta in Sami, meaning Seal Bay. Dating from 7,000 to 2,000 years ago, the carvings depict people, animals, boats, weapons, and unidentifiable figures. The dating was done by analyzing the location of the rocks on which the drawings were carved, as well as the differences in style and content of each. The hypothesis is that the carvings were made at the water level, probably because it was devoid of vegetation, and that the lowering of this level over the centuries gradually exposed new rocks. This means that the carvings on the higher rocks are older than those on the lower rocks.

Some of the carvings depict hunting scenes and are probably part of a magical ritual related to the killing of animals. But interpretations vary. Once at the site, for example, you can see a carving of a ship with moose heads on the bow and stern, two men and a woman in the middle holding a T-shaped object. Reindeer swim in the sea around it. For the Sami, who are used to herding reindeer, this represents the annual sea crossing that the men make with their herds to move between the villages where they live in winter and the summer pastures. According to this interpretation, what the woman is carrying is a ritual object. For others, it is a scene of hunting these animals at the time when they are easiest to catch. Other carvings depict pregnant women and female animals associated with fertility rites. Still others depict spirits and myths.

The carvings were probably made with quartzite chisels and bone hammers by shamans or chieftains on special occasions or for rituals, an assumption supported by the fact that they are most visible in the radiant light of sunset.

The most interesting scenes are those depicting reindeer trapping, bear hunting by following tracks through the soft spring snow to the den, halibut fishing from two boats, waterfowl trapping, and boats with a moose head on the bow as a ritual sign. Some of the carvings have been repainted with a red-brown color.

Also nearby is Halddetoppen, at about 2,952 feet (900 m) above sea level, the site of the old northern lights observatory, the first in the world, which operated from 1899 to 1926. It was here that the height at which the northern lights occurs in the atmosphere was determined. Today, the observatory has been restored and you can spend the night there.

Continuing west, you will come to Bubbelen at Langfjordbotn, a large river that bubbles out of the ground, a curiosity that has attracted tourists to the area since the 18th century. Here, since the town lies on a fjord, you can join a whale safari to see orcas, sperm whales, and seals, go fishing, have dinner in a Lapp tent to see the northern lights, ski on the plateau, or rent a snowmobile.

From Alta, the E6 continues relentlessly north. At Skaidi, whose name means "where the rivers meet," there is a junction with Route 94, which leads to Hammerfest. The city, located on the island of Kvaløya, is different from the one near Tromsø, and can be reached from the mainland via the Kvalsund Bridge.

The Salmon River

It is a well-known fact that Norway is the place par excellence for salmon fishing. The purity, temperature, and salinity of the water are ideal for valuable species such as salmonids, which are known to swim upstream in rivers to spawn. The Altaelva River has been popular as a salmon river since the 16th century and is still one of the best in the world. English lords used to fish here when Norway was just beginning to enter the tourist and European routes. The charm of this world, described by many English travelers and Norwegian novelists, has remained intact, or almost so. The long boats are now motorized, the slender poles are used only for docking, the materials and clothing have changed, and strict regulations have been introduced. Although expensive, you can hire a professional guide to ensure a successful fishing trip, and they will also share stories and legends around the fire.

Hammerfest

At 70° 39′ N, this is one of the northernmost cities in the world. Its coat of arms is a polar bear, and it is the seat of the Isbjørnklubben, the Royal and Ancient Polar Bear Society.

Hammerfest has been a witness to many geopolitical events. It was attacked by the British Navy during the Napoleonic Wars, helped by Kaiser Wilhelm II when it burned, and destroyed by the Germans following occupation, after it was turned into a submarine base in defense of the famous *Tirpitz*. Fish freezing helped the town survive, then oil revived it. It was a fate common to many towns along the Norwegian coast, but one that Hammerfest has managed to leverage, adding ship handling as a supporting service to fish processing.

Land of Adventure

In Finnmark, you can discover just how rich the winter season may be! Combining century-old Sami traditions with technology, ever more convincing opportunities make the cold seem like less of an enemy.

The spirit of adventure that drives people involved in tourism in this region probably stems from the realization that the area's resources are its nature and nothing else, or rather, nothing else monumental or immediately attractive. Hence the notion that the environment can be actively enjoyed, maybe through the intense thrill of a snowmobile ride over the plateau, through snow and shrubs and nothing else for miles and miles, to base camp. Or maybe it's a hike on the frozen river, on a sled pulled by a pack of beautiful, icy-eyed huskies. Or it might be participation in the life of a Sami camp, complete with reindeer, traditional tents, and a meal around the fire. Or ice fishing on a frozen lake.

Sea and harbor are the backdrop of the city. The first settlements date back to 1250, but the natural harbor was known even before that. Ottar, a Halogaland chieftain who served King Alfred of England, had passed through here in the ninth century on his expedition to the Kandalaks, or the White Sea, and was the first to write a chronicle of these areas. Then came Barents and Chanchellor in their search for the Northeast Passage. In 1789, King Christian VII gave it the title of city. It soon became the capital of the so-called *pomor,* the trade with northern Russia, which consisted of a supply of fish in exchange for grain. Hammerfest's sailing ships did not stop in the city on their return but continued on to southern Europe. From the end of the 18th century, they also set their sights on the Arctic, first for hunting, then for geographical and scientific expeditions.

In the same building as the **tourist office** is the headquarters of the Isbjørnklubben, the Royal and Ancient Polar Bear Society. The institution is actually not that old, having been founded in 1963. In any case, it offers an overview of the records of Arctic hunting, fishing, and exploration, a kind of city album.

A little farther to the west is the **Gjenreisningsmuseet,** a museum that tells about the lives of the inhabitants who were displaced during World War II by

Tourist Office ✉ Strandgata 29, Hammerfest ☎ 784 12 185
🕒 Mon.–Fri. 10 a.m.–4 p.m., Sat.–Sun. 10 a.m.–3 p.m. **visithammerfest.no**
Gjenreisningsmuseet ✉ Kirkegata 19, Hammerfest ☎ 784 02 940
🕒 Mon.–Fri. 10 a.m.–3 p.m., Sat.–Sun. 11 a.m.–2 p.m. **kystmuseene.no**

The Hammerfest Kirke is reminiscent of cod drying racks.

the fires set by the Germans after the defeat, and of the reconstruction that followed at the end of the conflict. Not far away is Hammerfest Kirke, designed by Hans Magnus and consecrated in 1961. It resembles the racks used in Norway to dry cod. Inside are objects from the city's previous churches, which were burned and destroyed.

Just behind the town is Salen Hill, about 262 feet (80 m) high, reached by the zigzag path from the town hall, which leads to the "pyramid," a small, restored tower, and some peat houses. The peak is an excellent place to see the midnight sun and the northern lights.

On the other side of the bay is the Struves Meridanbue, a monument dedicated to the scientist Friedrich Georg Wilhelm von Struve and his geodesic arch. The astronomer's intention was to map the shape and size of the Earth by measuring the distance between Hammerfest and the Black Sea. This international project began in 1845, lasted nearly 40 years, and consisted of numerous triangulation points arranged along a segment of about 1,864 miles (3,000 km). Because of their historical impact, the Norwegian geodetic points and those of other countries were added to the UNESCO World Heritage List in 2005.

The surroundings of the city are also very interesting. For example, the island of Seiland is home to Seiland Nasjonalpark, with peaks, glaciers, and mountain walls that plunge into the sea. Sørøya, another

The Road to Havøysund

Havøysund, on the island of Havøya, is a recommended detour, not least because it is reached by a scenic road of the same name. Connecting the town with Kokelv, over 40 miles (67 km) away, the route shows the wild and barren side of the coast. From Havøysund, you can reach the islands of Ingøya, Rolvsøya, and Måsøya by boat. Hjelmsøystauren, a cliff known as a nesting place for many species of birds, is also worth a visit, especially if you are a birdwatcher. Spend some time at Havøygavlen, the highest point on the island, which can be reached by a half-hour hike. Finally, in the southwest part of Havøya, you will find the cliffs of Storvika.

large island an hour's boat ride from the city, is worth a visit for the fishing village of Akkarfjord and the fertile Gamvik Plain with its farms.

Back at the Skaidi junction, take the E6 to Olderfjord and then the E69 to Magerøya. The mainland and the island are connected by the Nordkapptunnelen, an underwater tunnel opened in 1999 that is almost 4 miles (7 km) long and lies at a depth of 695 feet (212 m).

Honningsvåg

Often abbreviated to H-vag, the town of Honningsvåg on the island of Olderfjord grew around fishing and its inevitable related activities, i.e., boat building, materials, processing, and more generally seafaring culture.

Since the 1950s, in conjunction with the decline of fish in the Arctic, the number of tourists has increased. In the summer, the island of Magerøya is often overcrowded, and the fishing village is forced to cope with the tourist phenomenon, as are the Sami, who bring their reindeer here in the spring and sell souvenirs along the road in the summer.

Sights to see in this area include the **Nordkappmuseet,** a museum dedicated to the North Cape, the island of Magerøya, and the town of Honningsvåg. Settlement on the island dates back some 8,000 years, and fishing has always been the main activity of thc inhabitants, who depended on cod and "poor cod" (see p. 274). The Nordkappmuseet documents daily life in the past with re-created settings, working tools, a boat, and several photographs illustrating the village and its people.

Then head to Honningsvåg Kirke, a white church from 1884 that survived the Nazis, who destroyed many monuments during the conflict. After, visit the fishing harbor with its nearby raw material processing factories.

Nordkappmuseet ✉ Holmen 1, Honningsvåg ☎ 480 60 465 🕒 summer 10 a.m.–4 p.m.; rest of the year Mon.–Fri. 11 a.m.–2:30 p.m. **kystmuseene.no**

Kirkeporten rock arch is Skarsvåg's most famous sight.

Not far from the harbor is the area's **tourist office.**

The E69 continues into the arctic landscape of Magerøya and climbs to the plateau that precedes the North Cape. Young reindeer are brought here by ferry in the spring and return in the fall by swimming across the strait. It is a spectacle to see the animals in the water, a scene depicted in the carvings of Alta. Before reaching the northern end of Norway, you can also make a detour to Skarsvåg, the northernmost fishing village in the world. The place is known for a peculiar rock formation, an arch called Kirkeporten, which offers an unusual view of the North Cape, especially beautiful with the midnight sun. To the west, a 5.5-mile (9 km) trail leads to Knivskjellodden, a promontory at 71° 11′ N, geographically slightly higher than the cape. But there is no need to split hairs. This is a long and difficult hike (about six hours) and is only recommended for experienced hikers. Finally, continue on the E69 to reach Nordkapp.

Tourist Office ✉ Fiskeriveien 4, Honningsvåg ☎ 784 77 030
🕒 Mon.–Fri. 9 a.m.–4 p.m. **nordkapp.no**

The midnight sun in Nordkapp, at 71° 10′ N latitude

Nordkapp

Finally! That's the cry that everyone lets out on this flat rocky promontory that plunges into the Arctic Ocean at 71° 10′ N latitude. Mind you, the cry may be a chorus, given the popularity of the place in the summer.

But what is it that brings so many people to the North Cape?

"Here I am, at the extreme edge of the world, and I can safely say so as there is no place farther north that is inhabited by humans. My thirst for knowledge is now quenched, and now, God willing, I want to return to my country." This is what an Italian Franciscan monk, Francesco Negri—considered the first "tourist" who reached the North Cape for his own pleasure—wrote on his journey to these lands around 1665. How many of us recognize ourselves in this liberating statement? So, the North Cape is not merely a destination, but a mental boundary point that may be a little disconcerting and perhaps disappointing, but which must be added to the luggage of a traveler.

So what is there to see? The rocky promontory, of course, a 1,007-foot (307 m) drop into the ocean. Then there's the globe sculpture, made of steel rings, representing the Earth with meridians and parallels, installed here in 1978; the *Barn av Jorden* monument, consisting of seven medallions with drawings of as many children from different

parts of the world; and the *Mother and Child* sculpture, with the child pointing to the medallions. An obelisk commemorates the visit of King Oskar II in 1873, while a plaque commemorates the battle between the German and British navies in 1943.

Also worth seeing is the Nordkapphallen, a domed building built in 1959 and extended in 1988 and 1997. It consists of several floors with a café, a souvenir shop, a post office, and a restaurant with a panoramic view. A movie about the characteristics of the four seasons on the island can be seen on the lower floor. The building also houses St. Johannes Kapell, the northernmost ecumenical chapel in the world. Then you come to the centerpiece, the gallery terrace carved into the rock overlooking the sea. If the weather is bad, you'll have to make do with the stained glass window; if it's nice, find a spot on the terrace and gaze at the horizon: you're only 1,242 miles (2,000 km) from the North Pole! There is also a small Thai pavilion commemorating the visit of King Chulalongkorn in 1907 and a plaque in memory of Francesco Negri.

To get to the North Cape you have to buy a ticket. There is a bus from Honningsvåg, called Nordkappekspressen *(northcapeexpress.com)*.

Where Is North?

Calling it "the northernmost point" may seem simple ... But "northernmost" of what? Europe is not easily defined; there is the geographical, the political, and the economic. In addition, there is continental Europe, Europe including islands, Europe with Overseas Territories. In short, it is not so straightforward. If we look at geographical Europe with islands, it is clear that the Svalbard Archipelago is unrivaled. For continental Europe, already there is some doubt. In fact, Magerøya, where the historic Nordkapp stands, is an island; therefore, in theory, it should be excluded. But here the debate gets tricky. It is an island, but very close to the mainland, so almost mainland. In conclusion, let's just stick to Nordkapp.

Porsanger

Returning to Olderfjorden, the E6 turns south, skirting Porsangerfjorden, to Lakselv, the regional center of Porsanger and an important German air base for attacking convoys to Russia during the last war. Along the way is the beautiful Kistrand Kirke, built in 1856. As the name Lakselv, or "salmon river," implies, fishing here is often abundant with salmon, salmonids, trout, and char. In winter, in addition to organized trips to see the northern lights, the area offers husky-driven and motorized sleigh rides; in summer, the area is great for biking and canoeing. In Porsanger Fjord, near Børselv, is the Reinøya Island Nature Reserve, with unique flora and fauna and the largest dolomite formation in northern Europe.

Most importantly, southwest of Lakselv is Stabbursdalen Nasjonalpark, which contains the northernmost pine forest in the world, with trees that are 500 years old. Protected since 1970, this area of more than 270 square miles (700 sq km) offers magical hikes in the valley on skis or horseback, making the most of a landscape full of waterfalls and canyons. The 37-mile (60 km) Stabburselva River is teeming with salmon. The nature reserve also features terrain with bogs and marshes and is a place where rare plants grow and birds nest. To learn more, visit **Stabbursnes Naturhus og Museum,** the nature museum of the valley and Porsanger Fjord, which shows the life, economic activities, and culture of the region. A must-see. ■

Stabbursnes Naturhus og Museum ✉ Vestre Porsangerveien 1335, Indre Billefjord ☎ 784 64 765 🕒 June 1–16 & Aug. 17–31 11 a.m.–6 p.m.; June 17–Aug. 16 9 a.m.–8 p.m.; rest of the year Tues. & Thurs. 9 a.m.–3 p.m., Wed. noon–6 p.m. **stabbursnes.no**

Silfar Canyon, in Stabbursdalen Nasjonalpark

EXPLORING THE NORTHEAST CAPE

What does it mean to look eastward after reaching the coveted North Cape, the final destination for many? It means realizing that the world continues to the right, toward Arctic Russia. The coast of the Barents Sea, with its large peninsulas and endless fjords, accompanies us all the way to the Russian border at Kola. It is an exclave of non-Russian Europe, a point of contact. The landscape is that of a plateau, interrupted by river valleys and low elevations, and the climate is that of a tundra, with little precipitation and therefore little vegetation, except for birch trees in the more sheltered Varangerfjord.

Tanafjorden is situated between the North Cape and Russia.

The Tana River, called Deatnu in Sami, is a kind of Rio Grande of this part of the world, stretching over 186 miles (300 km). It is formed by the Karasjohka and Anarjohka Rivers and marks the border with Finland, then flows into wild Tanafjorden with a pristine delta and large sandbanks. A dramatic landscape.

From Karasjok, 46 miles (75 km) south of Lakselv, continue on the E6. The Tana Valley leads to the town of the same name. A few villages dot the 105 miles (170 km) between the confluence and the Tana Bru, a bridge. Here, the **Tana Museum,** currently closed, tells the story of life in the region, especially salmon fishing

Tana Museum ✉ Polmakveien 1599, Tana ☎ 952 62 162 **dvmv.no**

on the river. In fact, the Tana is one of the best in the world for this species. Cross the Tana Bru and continue east on the E6 to Varangerbotn, where you will enter Varangerfjord.

Varanger Peninsula

On a map, the Varanger Peninsula looks like a frayed ear on the Barents Sea. The many fjords to the northeast and west counterbalance its heart: Varangerhalvøya Nasjonalpark. To the east and south, the area is crisscrossed by a main road, the E75, while to the west there are secondary roads that follow the Tana Delta and branch off to the towns of Båtsfjord and Berlevåg in the far north.

Following the E75, you can reach the village of Nesseby, where you will find the **Varanger Samiske Museum,** or Várjjat Sámi Musea, which showcases Sami history and culture from prehistoric times to the recent revival.

Continue on to Vadsø. Have you ever heard of poor cod? This small, herring-like fish used to migrate from the Arctic Ocean to these shores in February (but now their numbers have declined, and fishing is banned), starting one of Norway's great fishing seasons. In Vadsø, poor cod oil was extracted, and the by-products were used as bait in the cod fisheries in Lofoten and along the entire coast of Finnmark. The town was also one of the centers of Finnish immigration in the last century, a stage in the colonization of Finnmark. Today, the descendants of the Finnish settlers speak Norwegian, but a monument stands as a reminder of those times.

Steller's eider in the water

Visit the **Vadsø Museum-Ruija Kvenmuseum,** which is part of the Varanger Museum, divided into three locations: Vadsø, Vardø, and Kirkenes. The museum tells the history of the town, especially Finnish immigration in the 18th and 19th centuries, Finnish architecture, and the patrician houses of the 19th century. It also includes Vadsøya Kulturpark, a cultural park on the island opposite the city with remains of medieval settlements, and Luftskipsmasta, the anchorage used by the airships *Norge*

Varanger Samiske Museum ✉ Endresens vei 4, Varangerbotn ☎ 410 70 050 🕒 Mon.–Fri. 10 a.m.–3 p.m. **dvmv.no**
Vadsø Museum–Ruija Kvenmuseum ✉ Grensen 1, Vadsø ☎ 407 04 500 🕒 summer 9 a.m.–5 p.m.; rest of the year 9 a.m.–3 p.m. **varangermuseum.no**

and *Italia* on their trips to the Pole. There are also war relics, a reserve that protects various bird species, such as the Steller's eider, and a cultural trail that connects the various points of interest. Finally, do not miss Vadsø Kirke at Amtmannsgata 1c, which was completed in 1958. The building has a unique entrance that resembles two blocks of ice.

If you take the E75 north again, you will reach Vardø on the island of Vardøya. Although Vardø was granted town status in 1789, traces of settlements from the 14th century have been discovered. If you're curious enough to come all the way up here to the northeasternmost point of the country, it was likely because you wanted to immerse yourself in nature: bird colonies, seals, whales, reindeer, the northern lights, and the crisp air of midsummer are indeed an important part of the natural heritage of this place. As for landmarks, there is Vardøhus Festning, the fortress that guards the island and the town, whose construction began in 1300 and was completed in 1738. It is a strange sight in these latitudes, seemingly incongruous with the endless natural beauty that surrounds it. Apparently, the Arctic was a contested territory even in earlier times, and so defensive structures and outposts had to be built.

Next, admire the large *Drakkar-Leviathan* sculpture (made in 2016), which re-creates a stranded Viking ship with the body of a dragon,

A cannon outside Vardøhus Festning, on the island of Vardøya

Drakkar-Leviathan is a sculpture that merges a drakkar with a dragon.

combining images of land, sea, migration, ships, myth, and history.

Next, head to the **Pomormuseet,** which tells the story of the Pomors—Russian Orthodox settlers—and their trade and contact with the Norwegians. From here, you can walk to Vardø Kirke, which looks like a rocket being launched into the sky, or, more peacefully, like a large tent being pitched. On the west side of the coast is Steilneset Minnested, a building erected to commemorate the people who lost their lives as a result of accusations of witchcraft in the 17th century. On the same theme, back on the peninsula, make a stop at Domen Hill, known in local folklore as the place where Finnmark witches met the devil. Three beautifully designed lookouts have been

Varangerhalvøya Nasjonalpark

Here, in incomparable landscapes where the Subarctic region meets the Arctic Sea, you will encounter rivers teeming with salmon, semi-domesticated reindeer, and several bird species. The park has a variable climate for an area where stratified sedimentary rock formations mix with sand dunes, rocky shores, and raised beaches, evidence of post-glacial rebound. There are cliffs along the outer coast. The park's trails are unmarked, so caution and proper equipment are of the utmost importance. The park is also surrounded by several protected areas.

Pomormuseet ✉ Kaigata 2, Vardø ☎ 407 04 510 🕒 summer 9 a.m.–5 p.m.; rest of the year 9 a.m.–3 p.m. **varangermuseum.no**

built here to provide a view of the area even in bad weather.

It is also worth stopping at Hamningberg, a fishing village that is only inhabited in the summer. It is located at the end of the Varanger Scenic Road on the Arctic Ocean and has preserved wooden houses from the 18th century. There is also a shelter for bird-watchers.

For more bird-watching, stop at Hornøya, an island near Vardø with Norway's easternmost nature reserve and protected area. Here you can see cliffs teeming with colonies of birds, including puffins, shags, razorbills, and Brünnich's guillemots.

When you're done visiting the peninsula, get back on the E6, which runs east from Varangerbotn to Kirkenes. Just before the city, however, lies Neiden, a village well worth a visit because it is home to Norway's only Orthodox chapel—dedicated to St. George—which also happens to be the country's smallest church. According to tradition, it was a certain Trifon, a monk of uncertain origin, who Christianized the Sami of this area in the 16th century.

Kirkenes

Here we are, on the border, on that line that divides three nations. It is a meeting point of peoples: first, the Sami, then the Norwegians, the Finns, and the Russians. An intersection of cultures and religions, of eastern and western flora and fauna. A small enclave in the long confrontation between Finns and Russians. In recent years, this border has become hot again, with Russian armaments just on the other side. And plans for Arctic routes made increasingly possible by ice melt increase the pressure and the presence of intelligence services on both sides.

Kirkenes sits right at the edge of it all. With a population of 3,500, this town in the far northeast of Norway, which also has a solid Russian community, is the last stop on the Hurtigruten route that began in Bergen.

(continued on p. 279)

Varanger Scenic Route

Norway's last scenic highway runs from Hamningberg to Varangerbotn, a distance of 99 miles (160 km). Last, of course, means northernmost. The landscape here is dominated by birch forests, marshland, and live rock, all bathed in a peculiar light, made of shades of gray that flatten even the sky. On one side are birds, wildlife, and reindeer; on the other is the Barents Sea, part of the vast Arctic Ocean, making it a *finis terrœ* (Latin for "the end of the world"). And what makes it even more beautiful are the small, elegant landmarks that dot the way: viewpoints and service stations, including the Hamningberg and Varanger bird-watching spots, as well as the Mortensnes cultural site, built where settlements date back 10,000 years.

THE FUTURE OF THE ARCTIC

The Earth, it is known, is not a perfect sphere: it is more flattened in the north and south than anywhere else. The melting of polar ice gives us a glimpse at what new and cheaper trade routes would look like, and it facilitates the search for minerals needed for technological innovation.

A fishing boat moored on the shore of the Barents Sea

The Barents Sea is warming faster because of its shallow waters. The ice of the Arctic ice cap and the Arctic lands cannot withstand the rising temperatures. Everyone knows that an icicle turns to water when taken out of the freezer. Not to oversimplify complex phenomena, but you get the idea.

There are several countries around the North Pole: the U.S. (Alaska), Canada, the Russian Federation, Norway, Sweden, and Finland. But it is the shadow of another that could be decisive in determining the region's fate: China. Everyone knows about the Chinese project of the New Silk Road and the Mediterranean ports on the Suez Canal run by the Chinese. Now geopolitics could follow the climate and make the Arctic routes over Siberia the new trade route, safe from pirates, unstable countries, and wars. The faster, safer routes would also require less energy to cool goods. But the Arctic has other enemies: the minerals the West and China need for future production, lithium and rare earths, the ABCs of the 21st century.

In short, the part of the world that people once sought to reach for exploration is once again at the center of international disputes. We will just have to wait and see how things turn out, hoping that the natural beauty of this part of our planet remains as intact as possible.

The Crustaceans that Escaped to the West

The new fortune of Kirkenes is a crustacean that weighs about 22 pounds (10 kg). Introduced from the Sea of Japan around Vladivostok in eastern Russia and transplanted to the Kola Sea in the 1960s, the king crab decided it liked this area. Today it proliferates in Varangerfjord, fueling an international trade. In winter, the crabs are caught by drilling holes in the ice with an auger, throwing the nets into the icy water, and pulling them up full of the crustaceans.

During World War II, the town, garrisoned by the Nazis because of its border with the USSR, was used as a base for German attempts to capture Murmansk, only to be destroyed in the clash with the Red Army.

There are many things to see and do in this multicultural place, which was deeply influenced by the 20th century. For example, you can ride an e-bike or an inflatable raft to the Russian border or take a boat out to fish or catch king crabs. You can also stay in a year-round ice hotel. But to immerse yourself in history, you must visit the Andersgrotto, the bunker where people took shelter during more than 300 air raids during the last war. Twenty-five hundred people could take shelter in this labyrinth of underground

King crabs are fished in Kirkenes.

Bjørnevatn, the Mine of Bear Lake

An immense wound in the earth, cut to search for the depths of ore, the open-pit iron mine of Bjørnevatn, or Bear Lake, is only about 6 miles (10 km) from Kirkenes. The mine was established in the late 19th and early 20th century and was of great value to the local people. Firstly, it meant job opportunities, and secondly, an identification with the commercial aims of the company that operated it. In 1944, however, these tunnels were also a source of salvation for people fleeing the destruction of the Nazis. On October 25, approximately 3,500 people ran out of the mine to greet and thank the Soviet soldiers who had liberated the city from the German occupiers.

tunnels, named after the engineer who designed it, Anders Elvebakk.

Then stop at the Saviomuseet, dedicated to John Andreas Savio (1902–1938), a painter whose brushstrokes depicted the life of the Sami people in the North, and the **Grenselandmuseet,** a border museum which illustrates the culture and nature of this part of Finnmark.

The chapel of Grense Jakobselv

As you head east toward the border, the small village of Grense Jakobselv is well worth a visit. This place is famous for the historic stone chapel of King Oscar II. The building has an important symbolic meaning as it was erected in 1869 near the Russian border to mark the Norwegian and Lutheran ownership of the area. To the south is Øvre Pasvik Nasjonalpark. It acts as a wedge between Russia and Finland, with the aim of preserving the subarctic pine forest and other rare species in Norway, as well as serving as a winter refuge for moose, a grazing area for reindeer, and a meeting point for Siberian and Western species. Hiking, canoeing, and photo safaris are available *(pasvik.no).*

Finally, to reach the national park you cross Pasvikdalen, a forested valley that is home to the largest population of brown bears in Norway. ■

Grenselandmuseet
✉ Førstevannslia, Kirkenes
☎ 789 94 880 🕒 summer 9 a.m.–5 p.m.; rest of the year 9 a.m.–3 p.m. **varangermuseum.no**

ITINERARY: THE SAMI ROUTE

To enter the vast Finnmarksvidda, with its own two towns of Kautokeino and Karasjok, is to get closer to Sami culture. Here you can breathe in those wide open spaces that convey the Arctic soul more than any other place in the country.

The Sametinget building houses the Sami parliament in Karasjok.

The desolate, endless plateau of Finnmarksvidda is freezing in winter and infested with tiny mosquitoes in summer. It is a world of wonders, full of vast expanses like a desert, with the same delicate balance and the same poetic nature. Here, the "absences" define the land, giving meaning to what is or isn't there. And it is the wind that shapes the winter forms and responds to human loneliness. The Sami have always known how to listen to the sound of the wind and have captured it in their songs, the *joik*. What's more, they have internalized it and adapted to its moods in a three-way conversation between man, animal, and nature.

Another important presence here is the dwarf birch. Small and insignificant at first glance, it is essential and omnipresent with its delicate, twisted branches. In this magnificent setting, the colors of the Sami costumes stand out: bold, obvious, almost excessive. They scream their existence.

The charm of these lands is not immediately understood. You have to listen to the voice of the wind to perceive it. But those who fall in love with it struggle to stay away. The longing for the great North is in fact a permanent feature of travel books.

Alta ❶ is the starting point of this intense and intimate itinerary. By car, follow the E45 to Finnmarksvidda, the plateau of Finnmark carved by the many canyon-forming rivers. After about an hour's drive, you arrive at the Sami farming village of **Masi** ❷, Máze in the local language, situated on the Kautokeinoelva River. Around 50 years ago, when the famous Alta Dam sparked a debate with the Sami people, Masi was destined to end up underwater but was thankfully spared. Visit the wooden Masi Kirke, rebuilt in 1965 after German troops burned down the previous one in 1944.

Then continue on the E45 to **Kautokeino** ❸, or rather Guovdageaidnu, the only town which is

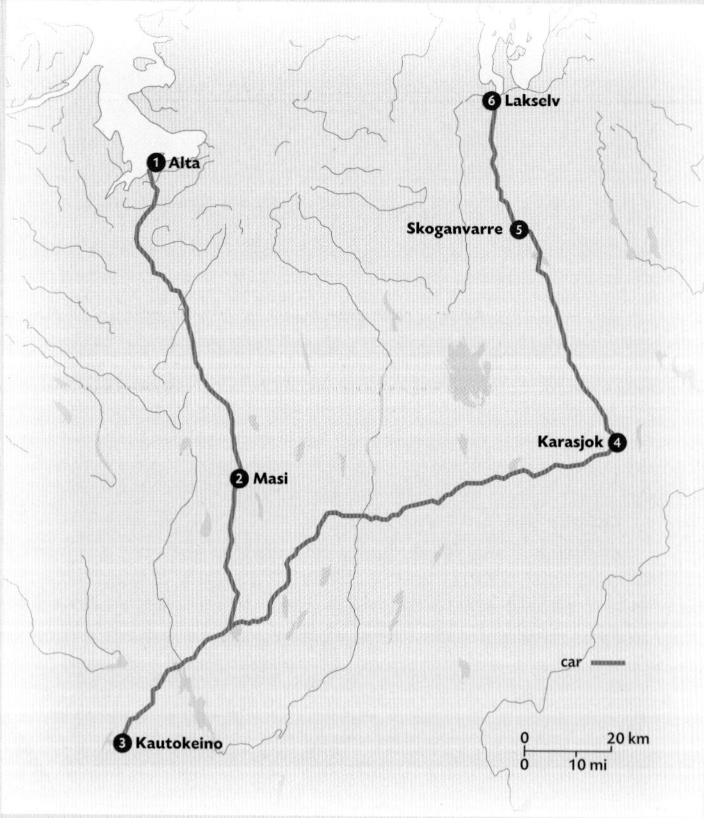

officially considered Sami. This might be enough to intrigue the average traveler, but there is more. Here, 85 percent of the people speak Sami as their first language, and there are far more reindeer than people. It is a center of Sami education and cultural research, with a state school that teaches everything about reindeer and *duodji*, or Sami handicrafts. We are about halfway through the trip: if you want to divide the trip into two days, we recommend that you stay overnight and spend some time getting to know the local culture.

In addition to reindeer being the staple of the local economy, including herding, slaughtering, and meat processing, another source of wealth is the Biedjovagge mines. Their natural and cultural heritage is put on display for the tourist market, which is the real asset now. The earliest known reliable record of this place is from the 16th century, but of course there are many earlier records from the region. At the end of the 17th century, the parish priest gathered the population in the present inhabited area, creating a permanent settlement. However, it was not until the 19th century that the presence of domestic reindeer was recorded. The herds now spend the winter on the plateau and migrate in spring to the grassy coastal pastures, as far as the North Cape.

Worth seeing is the Kautokeino Bygdetun/Guovdageainnu gilišillju, a museum with an indoor section displaying artifacts, fishing gear, and winter transportation, and an outdoor section with an old dwelling, food storage buildings, and models of peat-roofed huts. The museum is part of the Riddo Duottar Museat, a network of five sites. Also stop by the red wooden Kautokeino Kirke, built in 1958, with a bell tower rising above the flat landscape. It replaced one from 1701 that was burned down by retreating Germans at the end of the war. Weddings and baptisms are celebrated here during Sami Easter.

The Kautokeino Kulturbygg, or House of Culture, is known for being the first example of new Sami architecture to win the North Norwegian Architecture Prize in 1987. It houses the Beaivváš Sami Theater, a library, a leisure club, and the Nordisk Samisk Institutt, a research institute for Sami tradition and culture.

Duodji, the famous Sami handicrafts, are handmade objects made from natural materials such as birch wood, bones, and reindeer skins. Traditionally they have been practical items related to life in the wilderness, from clothing and shoes to knives. The only exception is perhaps jewelry, such as the magnificent silver pieces on display at the Juhls Silver Gallery.

In addition to its cultural attractions, the village invites you to take advantage of its surroundings. Tundra safaris, guided snowmobile tours, reindeer viewing, and ice fishing are all available. To fully experience the spirit of the place, consider visiting during Easter. This is when the Sámi Beassášmárkanat *(samieasterfestival .com)* is held, with weddings, communions, confirmations, reindeer races, cultural events, and joik singing, all performed in colorful costumes.

The true heart of the great Finnmarksvidda Plateau is perhaps the route from Kautokeino to Karasjok. Within these 78 miles (128 km) lies the soul of Norwegian Lapland, a world of dwarf birch trees, hilly terrain, bogs, and wind. It is the land of the reindeer, which can be seen here in winter and grazing along the coast in summer.

The Sami community of **Karasjok** ❹, or Kárášjohka, can be reached by taking the E45 north for a short distance, then turning onto Route 92.

Kautokeino Kirke was rebuilt after being burned down by the Germans.

The rebirth of Sami identity, language, and culture took place in the Norwegian part of this people's land, where the community is much larger than those found in Sweden, Finland, and Russia. Karasjok is the capital of this hypothetical united Lapland. It is also home to the Sami parliament, a political institution that has given voice to the Sami people's aspirations for independence and their demands, and to Sami radio and television, which, along with the schools, are the most important means of reviving their language. The town has all the charm of a borderland. Reindeer herding is the main activity, which in itself makes it an interesting destination. Then there is the natural landscape, which is truly magnificent, with the wide river and the fir forest. Winter temperatures can reach as low as -40°F (-40°C) , but in summer you can still swim in the river, as the water hits 68°F (20°C), and then dry off on one of the long sandy beaches in the area.

A must-see is the Sami Museum, opened in 1972, which has the largest collection of Sami artifacts in Norway and provides a better understanding of Sami culture. The museum is divided into a main building and an outdoor area, which is closed during the winter. Then continue on to Sapmi Park, a cultural park dedicated to the Sami way of life, with live performances, a theater, handicraft workshops, a café, and a restaurant. Just a few hundred feet from the park is Sametinget, or Sámediggi, a building in the shape of a *lavvu* (Lapp tent), which houses the Sami parliament, a citizen-elected advisory body with jurisdiction over matters affecting the community within Norway. Free tours are available in English.

Other places to visit include Sámi Dáiddaguovddáš, the Sami Center for Contemporary Art, which combines handicrafts with new artistic expressions and promotes their development; Karasjok Bibliotek, with the largest collection of Sami literature in existence and translations into several languages; and Karasjok Gamle Kirke, the oldest church in Finnmark, dating from 1807. Karasjok also offers outdoor activities such as snowshoeing to Halde, a magical place for the Sami, to see the landscape under the northern lights; skiing on the plateau; visiting a reindeer herding family; guided salmon fishing trips; and snowmobile, dog, or reindeer sled trips. An important event for the local communities is the Finnmarksløpet, the longest dog sled race in Europe, which starts and ends in Alta with a stop in Karasjok. First held in 1981, the event now takes place in March and the full version involves 14 dogs and a 745-mile-long (1,200 km) route.

Head north on the E6 from Karasjok through a landscape of rivers, lakes, and pine forests to **Skoganvarre ❺**, Skuvvanvárri in Sami. The village is located along the Lakselva River, surrounded by pine forests, and is a place where you can meet nomadic families with their reindeer herds. Just before reaching the town, you can stop to visit Feltlasarettet i Skoganvarre, where a military hospital was built in 1943 but never completed. Both Norwegian and German patients were treated here. When the conflict ended, the area was abandoned. Today it is possible to walk through the remains of the facility. The site is also close to Lake Gakkajávri. Opposite Skoganvarre, in Lake Øvrevann, is a small island with a Sami ceremonial site which is more than 2,000 years old

When the sightseeing is over, drive to **Lakselv ❻**, the final destination of our itinerary. The settlement is located at the southern end of Porsangerfjorden and is famous for its salmon. Considering the long journey, all you need to do now is relax, and perhaps treat yourself to a cruise along the fjord.

The Sami Knife

***Stuorraniibi* is the name of the traditional Sami knife. Children are given it when they are about 10 years old. It is an everyday tool, indispensable for outdoor life, but it also has symbolic value as a sign of initiation into adulthood. In traditional medicine, it was used to treat warts and boils and to stop bleeding. The handle is made of birch wood, seasoned for a full year, and is large enough to be easily grasped even with gloves on. The blade closest to the handle is for larger jobs such as cutting wood, the middle part is for precision cuts, and the tip is for fine cuts.**

This frozen archipelago in the Arctic Ocean—the northernmost inhabited land on Earth—is home to parks and nature reserves for polar bears

SVALBARD ISLANDS

Colorful houses in Longyearbyen, capital of the Svalbard Islands

SVALBARD ISLANDS

The coordinates of these islands, between 74° and 81° N, place them halfway between the Arctic Circle and the North Pole. The Svalbard Archipelago, in the Arctic Ocean, covers an area of 23,938 square miles (62,000 sq km), 60 percent of which is covered by ice, and has about 3,000 inhabitants, most of whom live in the capital, Longyearbyen. The climate, which can change abruptly, is arctic and harsh in the interior and more moderate on the western coast, where there are patches of tundra. The archipelago, once a land of coal mines, has no less than seven national parks and several nature reserves.

The Svalbard Islands are the only permanently inhabited land in these latitudes, and for only four reasons: their coal mines, their strategic location, tourism, and research. The frozen layer 500 feet (150 m) thick–known as the permafrost–is restrictive, but the archipelago remains inhabited and has gradually become a destination for visitors from around the world, even being included in the Sustainable Destination Program. One of the first questions visitors may have is why it has two names, Svalbard and Spitsbergen. To settle a long-standing dispute between Icelandic navigators, who discovered the islands in 1194 and named them Svalbard–meaning "cold coast"–and Dutch explorer Willem Barents, who "rediscovered" them in 1596 and renamed them Spitsbergen–meaning "sharp mountains"–the former was chosen as the name for the archipelago because of its Viking origins, while Spitsbergen was kept for the main island.

Nomenclature is not the only issue that has shaped the history of the archipelago. For centuries, the right to rule these lands has been debated. Count Fritz Wedel Jarlsberg, the Norwegian delegate to the 1919 Paris Conference that sought to end disputes on the sovereignty of the islands, eventually won it. The following year, a treaty was signed, which came into effect in August 1925 and formalized Svalbard's entry into the Kingdom of Norway. However, there were two conditions: that no military bases could be established there and

NOT TO BE MISSED:

Visit to Gruve 3 293–294
Svalbard Museum 294
North Pole Expedition Museum 294
Cruise in Magdalenefjorden 296
Pyramiden and Barentsburg 297

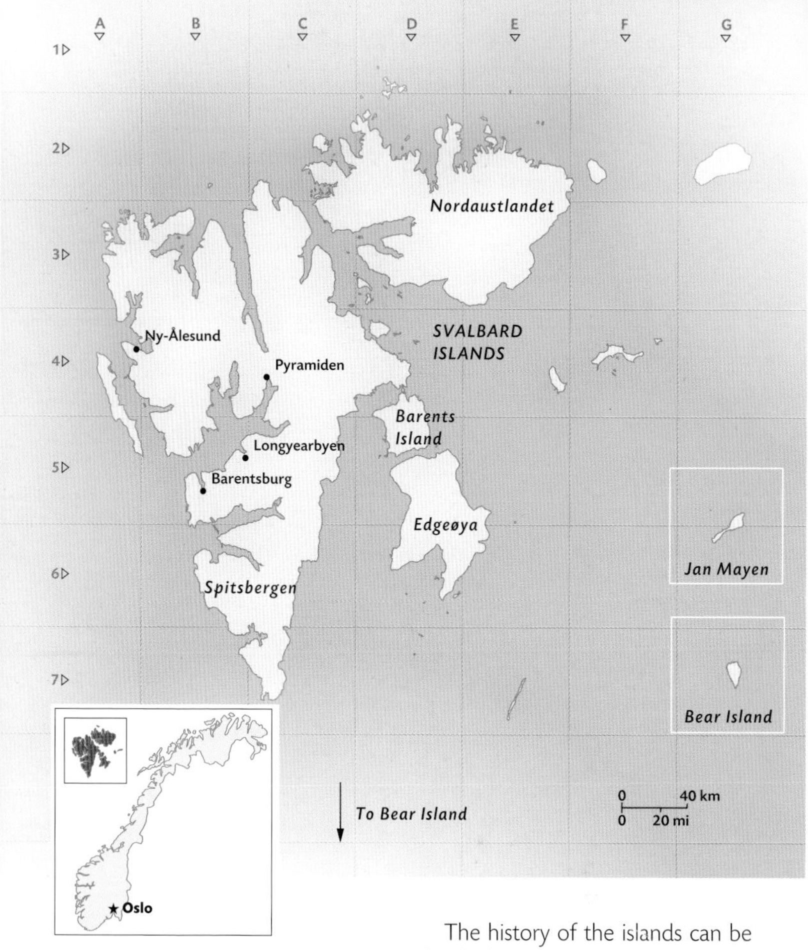

that all signatory countries would have an equal opportunity to exploit its mineral resources. Arctic wisdom, it was said, although it may not be thought of in the same way today. The USSR, which signed the treaty only ten years later, took this second clause seriously and established two settlements on the archipelago: Barentsburg and Pyramiden. Today, in addition to the Russian population still living in the first of the two towns, there are Polish, Chinese, and Indian research stations on the islands.

The history of the islands can be divided into two distinct periods: before and after coal mining. In fact, before the mines were established, the main activities here were hunting and fishing. In the 17th century, Dutch and English whalers, as well as Hanseatic and Basque whalers, came to the archipelago to hunt the great bowhead whale, which they eventually wiped out. In the 18th century, the Russians arrived to hunt reindeer and walrus and to collect bird eggs, which they also decimated. Then, in the 19th century, the Norwegians came to hunt seals. Finally, in 1899,

Unincorporated Area

The Svalbard Islands have a rather unique administration: since 1925, they have officially been part of the Kingdom of Norway, but as an "unincorporated area," i.e., an area without legal status and without its own municipality. In this case, the archipelago reports directly to the central Norwegian government through a governor, the *sysselmester,* although since 2002 Longyearbyen has had a local council, *lokalstyre* in Norwegian, which is responsible for infrastructure and public services, including kindergarten, primary, and secondary schools.

Under the Svalbard Treaty, which established sovereignty over the area, the islands have a special jurisdiction that keeps them out of the Schengen treaties, the European Economic Area, and the Nordic Passport Union. This is the same situation as the Norwegian islands of Jan Mayen in the Arctic and Bouvet in the Antarctic, which are uninhabited.

Søren Zachariassen returned from his voyage with a piece of coal found on the islands, sparking the so-called "coal fever," a frenzy similar to the one that led to the Klondike gold rush. For the surviving animals, it meant their salvation.

A plaque commemorating American entrepreneur J. M. Longyear

And thus began the second period: the aftermath. Norwegians, Russians, British, Dutch, Germans, and Americans all came looking for coal. John Munro Longyear, an entrepreneur from Michigan, wasted no time. In 1901, he passed through Svalbard on a cruise, and five years later he returned and founded the Arctic Coal Company—later bought by the Norwegians in 1916, becoming Store Norske Spitsbergen Kulkompani, SNSK—and established a stable community. This settlement, now the archipelago's largest city, was named after Longyear himself: Longyearbyen, *byen* meaning "city."

The first explorations and maps came from the whalers, and scientific research only began in the 19th century. The landscape is dominated by glaciers plunging into the sea, dark green valleys with little vegetation, flat blue-gray mountains, and sharp peaks streaked with white. Only a thin layer

Iceberg off the coast of Austfonna ice cap

of soil manages to withstand the permafrost ice, giving the arctic flora a chance to flourish. The flora and fauna are a colorful addition to the bright Arctic summer, before everything returns to the white winds.

The current inhabitants are very attached to these lands, living mainly off tourism, research, and fishing, as warming seas push fish populations northward. There is also a satellite station that receives data from polar orbit. People here enjoy longer vacations, pay lower taxes, have a university, a well-connected airport, a local TV and newspaper, and cultural and sports clubs that serve as meeting places, as well as cinemas and theaters. Is all this enough? Perhaps yes, since those who choose to settle here have a passion for the Arctic. There are three main islands: Spitsbergen, which makes up half of the archipelago, Nordaustlandet, and Edgeøya. There are also a number of small islands. All settlements are located on Spitsbergen, except for the weather stations on Bjørnøya and Hopen.

Arctic University

The archipelago has its own university, the University Center in Svalbard (UNIS), based in Longyearbyen. Courses are taught in English and focus on subjects related to the Arctic. Some of the disciplines covered are biology, geology, and geophysics, with graduate and postgraduate levels. The university is attended by Norwegian and international students who change the perspective of the archipelago.

The Red Tent

Italian engineer and explorer Umberto Nobile reached the North Pole in May 1926, flying over it in the airship *Norge*. He attempted the feat again in 1928 with the airship *Italia*, but on his return he crashed on the ice pack just off Foynøya, in Svalbard. This failure tarnished the image of Fascist Italy and cost many lives. One of the victims was the great Roald Amundsen, who set out to rescue the Italians and disappeared into the ice. The survivors of the crash of the airship *Italia* lived for 48 days in the "red tent," a silver structure dyed red with aniline to make it more visible during rescue operations, and they were brought to safety by a Soviet icebreaker. Both of Nobile's endeavors departed from Svalbard.

Sixty percent of the islands is covered in ice, thirty percent is rocky, and only 10 percent has some vegetation. The largest glacier, Austfonna, on the island of Nordaustlandet, covers an area of about 3,240 square miles (8,400 sq km). The highest mountain is Newtontoppen at 5,620 feet (1,713 m), while the longest fjord is Wijdefjorden at 67 miles (108 km). The ice comes from glaciers and icebergs that break off. It melts fairly quickly in the sea, while the 5-foot (1.5 m) layer of winter ice on the water's surface melts only from May to June.

More than 50 percent of the territory is protected by national parks, nature reserves, bird sanctuaries, or flower sanctuaries. Therefore, it is forbidden to pick flowers, hunt or harm birds and mammals, collect fossils, leave garbage, construct new buildings, or take objects within 328 feet (100 m) of a grave or cross.

It should also be mentioned that the special nature of this environment requires a number of precautions. The weather can change rapidly, so it is paramount to have appropriate clothing. More specifically, in summer, mountain gear is sufficient, but in winter you will need special suits, as well as two pairs of gloves, one silk and one wool, a hat or earmuffs, and glacier glasses. You will also need a double pair of socks, comfortable shoes in summer and rubber boots in other seasons. You must take off your shoes when entering a building, even a hotel or restaurant. When hiking, you should hire a local guide who knows the weather and ice conditions, is trained to deal with avalanches, is armed in case a polar bear suddenly appears along the route, and can use reliable communication systems. All safety regulations can be found on the Svalbard governor's website *(sysselmesteren.no)*. Read the Svalbard guidelines carefully. In practice, it is highly inadvisable to venture out of Longyearbyen alone.

It is also good to know that the city hospital, although public, does not apply international standards of medical care. This means that the European Health Insurance Card is not valid, so health services are not free. For more information and to book excursions in the archipelago, please contact the **Longyearbyen Tourist Office.**

Longyearbyen

Given what was said about the town's history and evolution, it is worth noting that Longyearbyen is not so much an actual town as it is an Arctic settlement of 1,800 inhabitants that is fully dependent on Norway. For this reason, it should be understood and explored with a keen eye. Everything that might seem normal or mundane elsewhere is not so here. Roads, transportation, houses, public buildings, even the church, services, and minor taxes must take into account the remoteness of the place and its lack of self-sufficiency.

The area is known for its long polar night, from late October to mid-February, although brightened by longer northern lights. The midnight sun can also be seen here from April to August.

The Gruve 3 coal mine, with its sedimentary rock processing plant, is still open for visits and offers a glimpse of the true essence of why people came here. During the visit, you can see all the machinery that

Longyearbyen Tourist Office ✉ Vei 221.1, Longyearbyen 🕒 summer 10 a.m.–5 p.m.; rest of the year 10 a.m.–4 p.m. **visitsvalbard.com**

Carts from the decommissioned mine in Longyearbyen

The entrance to the Svalbard Museum

was left when the mine was closed, as well as the tools and mining routes. Guided tours are available that include hotel pickup and bus transportation to the mine site, owned and operated by Store Norske, 10 minutes from town. It is the only one of the seven existing mines that can be visited, all of which have ceased operations.

Afterwards, head to the **Svalbard Museum,** which gives a detailed account of the natural, economic, and social history of the islands, with an emphasis on mining and pioneer hunting. There is an extensive collection of photographs and objects ranging from miners' tools to everyday survival equipment, diaries, and books. The **North Pole Expedition Museum** is essential for understanding the era of exploration. Here you will find letters, films, photos, telegrams, articles, objects, and models of ships and airplanes that tell the story of famous explorers such as Nansen, Andrée, and the Duke of Abruzzi. Also quite nice is the Svalbard Kirke, a wooden church built in 1958 on the site of the 1921 church that was

Svalbard Museum ✉ Vei 231-1, Longyearbyen ☎ 790 26 490
🕒 9 a.m.–5 p.m. **svalbardmuseum.no**
North Pole Expedition Museum ✉ Post box 644, Longyearbyen
☎ 913 83 467 🕒 9 a.m.–5 p.m. **northpolemuseum.com**

Svalbard Global Seed Vault

When an idea is brilliant, it must be recognized. And this one is beyond brilliant: taking samples of all the world's seeds and storing them in a safe place—always within the limits of human possibility—in order to ensure a food supply for every country in the event of a disaster. This could prove to be very useful, given the critical situations of an overheated planet in the grip of constant geopolitical tensions.

In a way, the Svalbard Global Seed Vault turns convention on its head: it is located in a land where nothing, or almost nothing, can grow, but where all the agricultural and human wisdom of millennia can be preserved. The project is the result of an agreement between the Crop Trust (formerly known as the Global Crop Diversity Trust) and the Nordic Genetic Resource Center (NordGen). The concrete structure consists of three atomic bomb–proof halls made of 120 sandstone blocks. It is located near Longyearbyen and can only be seen from the outside.

destroyed during World War II. Longyearbyen Kulturhus has two multipurpose halls, a movie theater, a bar, and a recording studio; Nordover, an arts center, has movie theaters, shops, and cafés. Nearby is the small harbor with its pioneer atmosphere, and there are always people around.

The Svalbard Global Seed Vault

The Pyramiden mining settlement was abandoned in 1998.

Then there is Adventdalen, the long valley that runs parallel to Longyearbyen, where you can go snow-scootering in the winter and see arctic flora in the summer. Down the road from the airport is Isfjord, with its summer chalets and reindeer herds, and the cliffs of Fuglefjella, which rise 1,540 feet (470 m) above the sea at the southern entrance to the fjord. It is home to 20,000 pairs of seabirds. Farther south, Sveagruva, a mine closed in 2017 with its abandoned village, allows you to overlook the great Van Mijenfjorden.

The Hurtigruten ship company offers a great way to see Svalbard: a 12-day cruise that visits the most important places in the archipelago, from Magdalenefjorden to Isfjord, and from Longyearbyen to Barentsburg *(hurtigrutensvalbard.no)*. The same company also offers an electric-hybrid catamaran excursion to Billefjorden and Nordenskiöld-breen Glacier, as well as many other packages, from dog-sledding expeditions and kayaking through icebergs to skiing in Ny-Ålesund, sea fishing, and staying in ex-miner homes. Local events include the Svalbard Ski Marathon, the Spitsbergen Marathon, and two festivals, Taste Svalbard and Dark Season Blues.

Ny-Ålesund

Located along Kongsfjorden, Ny-Ålesund consists of a wide bay in the area called "land of Haakon VII," with four large glaciers around it. There used to be an underground coal mine here. Now the only inhabitants are scientists from the Norsk Polarinstitutt and a few residents who provide services and tourism, about 20 people in total. It can be reached by boat in the summer and by snowmobile the rest of the year.

Visit the Ny-Ålesund By og Gruvemuseum, renovated and expanded in 2014, dedicated to the history of the settlement from the 17th century up to the accident that led to the closure of the mine in 1962, and subsequent scientific research. The town's history is remembered in the memorial stone commemorating Amundsen's flight to the North Pole in search of Nobile, the pylon where the airship *Italia* docked in 1928, and the stele dedicated to the miners who died in the 1962 explosion. Today, the research stations of Himadri from India, Yellow River from China, and the one from Norway are the center of the city.

Russian Settlements

After the signing of the Svalbard Treaty, the USSR established the mining settlement of Pyramiden, which was later abandoned in 1998 and is now a ghost town. The other village, Barentsburg—named after Willem Barents—was actually founded by the Dutch in 1920 and then sold to the Russians in 1936. Today, Barentsburg is the second largest town in the archipelago and has a population of 450. The company village of Arktikugol, a Russian coal company, is still in operation and can be visited. There is a hotel and a shop, as well as a school, a library, and a farm with a greenhouse. Like Pyramiden farther north, the village is built in the socialist style, and that alone is worth a visit. Those interested should know that the two settlements preserve the northernmost statues of Lenin in the world!

Please note: Due to the conflict in Ukraine, the visits to the Russian settlements coordinated by Visit Svalbard have been suspended. ■

FAUNA & FLORA OF THE SVALBARD ISLANDS

As impossible as it may seem given the arctic temperatures, there is flora and fauna in this archipelago beyond 70° N. These are special species, the only ones able to survive in the Great North.

Polar bears are a protected, endangered species.

The first report sent to the Netherlands after the rediscovery of Svalbard said: "The climate up here is so harsh that the animals are completely white." The fauna was certainly more abundant then, although only four mammal species and one bird species could (and can) survive in the Svalbard winter: polar bear, Svalbard reindeer, arctic fox, walrus, and ptarmigan. In the summer months, however, 30 species of birds come up here to nest, populating the sea cliffs and coastal lagoons. The Barents Sea provides an abundant supply of fish for the islands' millions of birds.

A walrus relaxing on the Svalbard Islands ice pack

Razorbills, guillemots, puffins, eiders, and black-legged kittiwakes are the most common. The arctic tern *(Sterna paradisea)* holds the record for the longest migration of any animal in the world: each year this bird makes its way from the Arctic Circle to the Antarctic Circle. It nests on the ground, especially on sandy beaches or rocks, and does not always stand out from its background. It fiercely defends its nest; if you get too close, the tern will take to the air, screeching, and assume an attack position with its pointed beak aimed at your head. It then swoops turning away at the last moment.

In the fjords or on the floating ice you can find seals and walruses, whereas near the ice floe you can see belugas, which "chatter" loudly when they gather.

Orcas in the waters of the Lofoten Archipelago

Svalbard poppies are endemic to the archipelago.

Seals have to defend themselves against bears, and whales against orcas. The polar bear is the king of the islands, a protected species of which only a few individuals remain, especially in the northern and eastern regions of the archipelago. They tend to be very aggressive and can attack quickly and without warning. Adults weigh 440–1,540 pounds (200–700 kg), cubs about 1.3 pounds (600 grams) at birth. There are no excursions available to see them.

As for the flora, the permafrost layer does not allow the growth of tree species. Only a small layer of soil thaws and allows plants to take root. Therefore, only shrubs, flowers, mosses, and lichens survive here, all vegetation with shallow surface roots. Svalbard poppy (*Papaver dahlianum*, an endemic species), dandelion, buttercup, yellow saxifrage, and moss campion are also found here. These are all fairly hardy plants that are adapted to the harsh climate of the Arctic. They also require a short window of time to grow, allowing them to thrive during the brief periods when warmer temperatures give the archipelago some respite.

TRAVELWISE

A sauna on the banks of a fjord

TRAVELWISE

PLANNING YOUR TRIP

When to Go

Like other countries at northern latitudes, Norway alternates between periods of intense light and periods of almost total darkness. Rather than seasons, it is more accurate to speak of "periods" and fixed dates.

More specifically, there are two main periods in Norway: one that runs from early June to early August, and another that runs from October to March. The first is characterized by the fascinating midnight sun, the peculiar Scandinavian summer, which is definitely the best season in terms of light and range of visible colors. The second is when the northern lights can be seen, especially in the Center-North region.

These make for two very different trips. In the summer, you can take advantage of the many hours of daylight to explore the southern and western coast, whereas if you choose to travel in the fall and winter, you can set your sights on other destinations such as the Lofoten and Vesterålen archipelagos, Finnmark, and the Varanger Peninsula. These are the best places to enjoy the many nuances that winter Norway has to offer residents and visitors alike.

Whatever time of year you choose, careful planning is paramount if you want to take full advantage of all the opportunities. It's worth checking out the available platforms in advance, such as the Norwegian Tourist Authority's website *(visitnorway.com)*, and apps. In addition to national sites, regional portals have also been set up, such as *fjordnorway.com, visitsorlandet.com, nordnorge.com, visitlofoten.com.* Major cities also have their own websites: see *visitoslo.com, visitbergen.com, visittrondheim.no, visittromso.no.*

Don't forget that adjusting to the Norwegian light can take some time. During the midnight sun period, remember to bring a sleeping mask to make sure you get enough rest for the next day. In winter, keep in mind that many activities may be suspended for the season, or places of interest may be closed or have reduced hours. It is advisable to decide in advance which activities you would like to do and therefore what time of year it is best to visit.

What to Bring

There is no such thing as good or bad weather, only good or bad clothing. This saying applies perfectly to the Norwegian climate. The weather can change quickly here, especially in the summer, so windproof and rainproof clothing is a must. It is best to dress in layers, as you would when hiking in any other mountainous region, so that you are prepared for all eventualities.

If you plan to do some hiking, in the mountains or by the sea, you will need the appropriate technical clothing. Also remember to bring a hat, sunglasses, and sunscreen.

In winter, thermal underwear and heavy jackets are essential. In some regions the temperature can drop to -4°F (-20°C), so it is good to be prepared. However, if you forget something, you can easily find it in major cities and most medium-size towns.

Then there's footwear: While you can safely wear sneakers in the city in the middle of summer, you'll need snow boots in winter and in more rural areas. Avoid shoes with smooth soles.

Documents

Although it is not a member of the European Union, mainland Norway is part of the Schengen area, which means that in order to enter and stay, all you need is a passport that is valid for at least three months after the end of your visit. U.S. citizens won't need a visa to visit the Schengen area—provided that the trip is fewer than 90 days, within a 180-day period. However, extra controls are carried out when entering the Svalbard Islands because they do not belong to the Schengen area. For certain types of transactions, such as bank transactions or bank transfers, you may be asked to present a passport. More information is at *sysselmesteren .no/en/visas-and-immigration.*

Digital ID

If you want to access digital services and payments remotely, you will need a BankID *(bankid.com),* which is an electronic passcode sent by your bank to your phone. This will allow you to securely access the services of interest, using the code for identification and signing. Of course, the above does not apply to normal card or payment application transactions, for which your digital identity is already registered.

Embassies & Consulates

U.S. Embassy in Oslo
Morgedalsvegen 36, Oslo
Tel 213 08 540
Outside of office hours, contact:
213 08 540
Email: *OsloACS@state.gov*
no.usembassy.gov

Norwegian Embassy in Washington
2720 34th Street, NW
Washington, DC 20008
Tel 202 333 6000
Email: *emb.washington@mfa.no*
norway.no/en/usa

Norwegian Consulate General in New York
1 Dag Hammarskjöld Plaza, 35th Floor
885 Second Avenue, New York 10017
Tel 646 430 7500
Email: *cg.newyork@mfa.no*

American Presence Post in Tromsø
Hjalmar Johansens gate 14, Tromsø
no.usembassy.gov

Customs

Norway is not part of the European Union, but it is part of the Schengen area. Customs inspections of imported goods are likely, both in luggage and in person. There are special restrictions for the Svalbard Islands.

You cannot bring in more than 25,000 Norwegian kroner—about $ 2,350 USD at the time of writing—without notifying customs. It is possible to import goods worth up to 6,000 Norwegian kroner—about $560 USD—but there are restrictions on alcoholic beverages. Specifically, the minimum age for importation is 18 years, but it rises to 20 years for spirits with an alcohol content of more than 22 percent. You cannot carry more than one liter of hard liquor, and there are various possible combinations of hard liquor, wine, and beer in relation to the quantities you can carry. However, it is not possible to import spirits with an alcohol content of more than 60 percent.

Consult the U.S. Department of State website for a complete list of types and quantities *(travel.state.gov/content/travel/en/international-travel.html)*. Also refer to the same address for specifications regarding food items that you can take with you, including meat, milk, and cheese, and for those regarding tobacco.

Medicines are only allowed in small quantities and for strictly personal use. For more information, see the customs regulations at *toll.no* and the Tolletaten app, which can be downloaded for iOS and Android.

Insurance

It is not required for U.S. citizens to obtain travel insurance when traveling to Norway. However, many U.S. health insurance plans may not provide coverage when traveling out of country so we recommend signing up for one before departure that also includes possible medical repatriation by air or transfer to another country. Several companies offer insurance coverage for a trip, for unforeseen events, or for situations such as canceled flights, lost luggage, and/or the need for medical treatment. It is a personal choice, but it can give you peace of mind when traveling in country.

HOW TO GET TO NORWAY

By Plane

Several airlines offer direct flights from the U.S. to Norway. The national airline, **Scandinavian Airlines SAS** (*flysas.com*), offers flights from Atlanta, Boston, Chicago, Los Angeles, Miami, New York, San Francisco, and Washington, D.C., to Oslo, Copenhagen, and Stockholm. Other airlines flying from the U.S. to Norway are **Norse Atlantic Airways** *(flynorse.com)*, **Lufthansa** (*lufthansa.com*), and **Air Antilles** *(airantilles.com)*.

The main airport in Norway is Oslo Airport *(OSL; tel 648 10 000, avinor.no)* in Gardermoen, about 31 miles (50 km) from the center. The airport express train connects the airport and Oslo S Central Station in just 20 minutes, with service every 10 minutes. However, many low-cost airlines fly to Torp Sandefjord Airport *(TORP; tel 334 27 000, torp.no)*, 68 miles (110 km) from the capital. This is certainly a cheaper option, but it is also a longer drive into the city, so be sure to factor in travel time when booking your flight.

In addition to the two near Oslo, other airports in Norway include Bergen-Flesland *(BGO; tel 670 31 100, avinor.no)*, Stavanger-Sola *(SVG; tel 670 31 000, avinor.no)*, Trondheim-Værnes *(TRD; 670 32 500, avinor.no)*, Tromsø-Langnes *(TOS; 670 34 600, avinor.no)*, Bodø *(BOO; 670 33 500, avinor.no)*, Alta *(ALF; 670 34 900, avinor.no)*, and Kirkenes *(KKN; 670 35 300, avinor.no)*.

By Train, Bus, or Car

If you are planning a longer European trip, maybe combining more than one country, know that Norway has flights to and from all European countries, especially the Nordic ones, but overland travel is still worth considering. It is a different way of traveling, allowing you to explore more places along the way.

Flexible train tickets can be purchased from **Interrail** *(interrail.eu)* or **Eurail** *(eurail.com)*, or you can buy multiple tickets for domestic routes.

Bus travel is also an option to consider. Several international companies operate throughout Europe, such as **Flixbus** *(flixbus.it)*.

If you choose to travel by car, you can take your car by ferry from Denmark. There are also ferries departing from Copenhagen to Oslo and from Hirtshals to Kristiansand. For more information, visit the websites of **DFDS** *(dfds.com)*, **Color Line** *(colorline.com)*, and **Fjord Line** *(fjordline.com)*.

GETTING AROUND

By Plane

Many small towns have airports with regional service. The archipelagos of Lofoten, Vesterålen, and Svalbard also have their own airports. This allows you to move freely from place to place and reach the most interesting destinations, including the islands. For domestic flights, we recommend the national airlines **Scandinavian Airlines SAS** *(flysas.com)*, **Norwegian Air** *(norwegian.com)*, and **Widerøe** *(wideroe.no)*.

By Train

The train is a convenient way to get around and a pleasant ride, especially in the south-central areas of the country. The main Oslo–Bergen line—known as Bergensbanen and operated by **VY** *(vy.no)*—is truly spectacular as it climbs the Hardangervidda Plateau and then heads into the fjords that are an integral part of the Norwegian landscape and identity.

But many other lines don't lack for convenience, travel solutions, and incredible views, such as the Oslo–Stavanger (Sørland Railway), Oslo–Trondheim (Dovrebanen), and Trondheim–Bodø (Nordland Railway). The intercity lines Oslo–Bergen and Oslo–Trondheim and the international line Oslo–Stockholm are operated by **SJ** *(sj.no)*. Also worth mentioning as some of the most fascinating railways are the Raumabanen in central Norway, the Myrdal–Flåm (Flåmsbana) in the fjords, and the Ofoten Railway in Narvik.

With the Entur app *(om.entur.no)*, which can be downloaded on iOS and Android, you can plan trips and buy tickets for different modes of transportation, such as train, boat, and bus. It also functions as a travel planner. For Oslo, you can use the Ruter app *(ruter.no)*, which allows you to buy single tickets, day tickets, and 7-day or 30-day passes.

By Hurtigruten

The Hurtigruten mail ship service *(global.hurtigruten.com)* is another smart way to get around Norway. This fjord mail ship stops at more than 30 ports between Bergen and Kirkenes. It is a sort of cruise in stages, following the rugged coastline and sometimes meandering between the coast and the islands. You can get on and off wherever you want, using it as a means of getting around. If you have the chance, do not miss this experience, even if it is just for one stop. Interesting stops include Ålesund, Trondheim, Svolvær, Tromsø, and Hammerfest. Some of the ships run on biogas and carry cars.

In recent years, the **Havila Ky Struten** service *(havilavoyages.com)* has also started covering the Bergen–Kirkenes route with cruise ships, offering a 12-day voyage that travels the entire route with scheduled stops at 34 ports of call.

By Ferry

Ferries are indispensable and ubiquitous, especially in the fjord region that basically runs from Stavanger to Tromsø. They are used to cross fjords and reach islands. There are car ferries and passenger ferries. During the summer, when certain routes are overcrowded, cars may not be accepted. Timetables and traffic conditions are available on the National Road Administration website *(vegvesen.no)*. The portal also provides information on ferry routes and schedules. See also *nordnorge.com*. You can board tourist boats on the Telemark Canal (*telemarkcanal.com*), Hardangerfjord and Sognefjord around Bergen (covered by Fjord Tours, *fjord-tours.com*), and Lake Mjøsa on the Lillehammer side to cross on the historic Skibladner (*skibladner.no*). Some of the best cruises are the one from Flåm to Gudvangen and the one across Setesdal on the 1866 Bjoren boat, which still runs on steam (*bjoren.no*).

There are also express boats, such as the Norlandsexpressen, from Bodø to Sandnessjøen, along the beautiful Helgeland coast, which works like Interrail for trains. Information can be found on the travel planner website *reisnordland.com*. The Nordland Travel Pass gives you unlimited access to express boats, buses and ferries.

By Bus

For internal travel by bus, **Vy Buss** (*vybuss.com*) and **Nor-Way Bussekspress** (*nor-way.no*) have a dense network of routes within the Trondheim–Stavanger–Oslo triangle. For the North, there are bus routes such as Bodø-Lofoten–Vesterålen–Senja–Tromsø, or Tromsø–Alta–Nordkapp, or even Vardø–Kirkenes. Tickets can be found on the app Troms Billett (*fylkestrafikk.no*) and Snelandia Mobillett.

By Car

Visitors traveling by car will find a respectable, well-maintained, and monitored road network, with numerous underwater tunnels to reach the islands or move from one island to another. The minimum age for driving is 18 years. Your national driver's license is a valid document for renting and driving a car in Norway. Highways have speed limits of 55 to 68 miles an hour (90–110 km/h), while other roads with one lane in each direction have limits of 37–49 miles an hour (60–80 km/h). Main roads are European roads, marked with an E followed by the identifying number. In cities, the speed limit is 18–31 miles an hour (30–50 km/h).

The 18 most beautiful roads in Norway have been designated Nasjonale Turistveger, or National Tourist Roads (*nasjonaleturistveger.no*). Fuel prices are high, due to environmental concerns, and gas stations are far apart, especially in the north. There are about 17,000 charging points for electric cars, including more than 3,000 fast ones. To access the stations, you need to register with the main providers using apps. A map of charging stations is available at *ladestasjoner.no*. More information is also available at *elbil.no*.

Tolls are charged on many roads, bridges, and tunnels. Your car must be registered in advance using one of two methods: the first is AutoPASS (*autopass.no*), a kind of subscription with discounts and stickers for the windshield; the second is EPASS24 (*epass24.com*), which allows individual payments by credit card.

Warning: The legal maximum blood alcohol content in Norway is 0.02%; also be aware of medications that can alter your perception and attention; and never hold a mobile phone or drink in your hand while driving. Low lights should always be used, even on scooters and motorcycles.

Always check *vegvesen.no* for temporary mountain pass closures. Also remember that pedestrians have the right of way, seat belts are mandatory for drivers and passengers, and children under 36 pounds must ride in child safety seats.

A rental car is the best choice, especially if electric cars are available. The usual international car rental companies are represented in Norway. Rent-A-Wreck (*rent-a-wreck-scandinavia.com*) rents out older cars—in good working condition of course. Arctic Campers (*arcticcampers.no*) offers fully equipped campers in Oslo and Tromsø. Rental locations can be found in cities and towns, near airports, harbors, and train stations. Book in advance, especially during the summer. You can also easily find spots that rent bicycles, e-bikes, and boats, both motor and sailing.

By Taxi

Taxis are available throughout Oslo and in larger cities. The service is more expensive than the European average, so it's not always worth it. Besides, you won't often need them, as Norwegian public transportation is efficient. In any case, the biggest company in the capital is **Oslo Taxi** *(oslotaxi.no)*, which also has maxi-taxis for up to 16 people and a fixed price to and from the airport.

By Bike

Norway is a bicycle-friendly country, as evidenced by the incredible bicycle routes the country has to offer. Den Gyldne Omvei *(dgo.no)*, in the Trondheim area, certainly stands out among the others. The starting point is reached by train, and there are bike rentals at the station, including electric bikes. Worthwhile routes include Rallarvegen, from Hardangervidda to the fjord; Kanalruta, along the Telemark Canal; and Nordsjøvegen, the North Sea route from Kristiansand to Haugesund. Then there are the great road climbs, mountain bike and fat bike routes, and the wonderful opportunity to cycle and ferry from island to island, for example along the Helgeland coast. Visit *bikemap.net* for information on the various routes. For organized tours, you can check out Discover Norway *(discover-norway.no)*.

Popular in Oslo are the Oslo Bysykkel city bikes *(oslobysykkel.no)*, which can be used with an app and are available at more than 200 locations. Syklistenes Landsforening *(syklistforeningen.no)*, the cycling association, offers several routes and is developing a Green Biking Routes project around the capital. Viking Biking & Hiking *(vikingbikingoslo.com)* and Oslo Bike Rental OBR *(oslobikerental.no)* offer city bike tours.

Helmets are mandatory and cycling in tunnels is prohibited. Bikes must have front and rear lights, reflectors on the pedals, and a bell. You can check the weather forecast at *yr.no* and on the app.

PRACTICAL ADVICE

Addresses

Addresses are written with the street name, house number, ZIP code, and city. In smaller villages, it can be more complicated to find places; therefore, it is best to consult websites, where available, to retrieve helpful directions.

Communications

Internet

Wireless hot spots are found everywhere—in cities, gas stations, bars, shopping malls, hotels, and on public transportation—but access is not always free. In more remote areas, coverage is reduced and sometimes non-existent. The main telephone companies are Telenor and Telia Norge. You can buy a Norwegian SIM card or a temporary one if you find it necessary.

Mail

The state postal service, **Posten Bring** *(postenbring.no)*, has changed services and closed many offices over the past two decades. If you need a specific service, you should consult its website, which is available in English.

Telephone

The code for calling Norway from abroad is 0047. Local numbers have eight digits, the first two of which are the area code of the city you are calling. To call abroad from Norway, dial 00 followed by the country and area code and the local number.

Although Norway is not part of the European Union, it is in the same economic area, so as of 2017 those with European SIM cards can use international roaming without activating other tariffs. If you are using an American SIM card, however, a roaming plan might be more convenient. Check with your carrier for a roaming package to avoid hefty pay-per-use fees.

Unit of Measurement

Norway uses the metric system.

Electricity

European electricity standards are used in Norway, 220V/50Hz, along with the standard Europlug (flat, non-rewirable two-pole, round-pin domestic AC power plug).

Etiquette

Although Nordic people are stereotyped as cold and aloof, it is safe to say that this is not true of Norwegians. They are easygoing and friendly people who are open to social interaction. The most important values are undoubtedly family and friends, with whom they try to spend quality time. There is even a word that the locals use to describe the state of well-being found in small pleasures: *kos*. Therefore, to be well received in Norway, all you need is kindness and courtesy, giving back what you have received.

Public Holidays

Most businesses are closed on holidays, and public transportation offers limited service. Museums may be open, but if so, they often close the Monday after the holiday. Many restaurants and bars are also open on bank holidays, but may close on Christmas and New Year's Day.

January 1–New Year's Day
Easter (varies)
May 1–Labor Day
Ascension (varies)
Pentecost (varies)
May 17–Constitution Day
December 25–Christmas
December 26–Boxing Day

Alcoholic Beverage Regulations

The minimum age for drinking and purchasing alcoholic beverages is 18 but rises to 20 in the case of hard liquor.

Media

NRK is the national broadcaster; it has four digital TV channels and many radio stations, both FM and digital. There is also the commercial TV2 and TV3, and TVNorge-Discovery. Newspapers are mostly regional; the most widely circulated national newspaper is *Afteposten,* followed by the tabloid *Dagbladet.*

Currency

The current currency in Norway is the Norwegian krone (NOK), which is divided into 100 øre (its value fluctuates with oil prices).

The country is largely cashless and supports electronic payments everywhere, even in smaller towns. Visa and MasterCard credit cards are accepted, as well as payments by smartphone, PayPal, Apple Pay, and Google Pay.

Opening Hours

In general, during peak season, stores are open Monday through Friday from 10 a.m. to 5 p.m., with an extension on Thursdays until 7 p.m., and on Saturdays from 9 a.m. to 3 p.m. The same applies to museums. Supermarkets and shopping malls are open Monday through Saturday from 10 a.m. to 8 or 10 p.m. Pharmacies operate Monday through Friday from 9 a.m. to 5 p.m. Restaurants run two shifts, one for lunch from 12 to 3 p.m., and one for dinner from 6 to 11 p.m. In the winter, hours are often reduced, and closing days may increase.

Religion

Around 65 percent of the population is Protestant and belongs to the Evangelical Lutheran Church of Norway, although active participation is low. Until 2012, Lutheranism was the state religion, according to the constitution. It still receives public support, as do other religious communities.

Nearly 7 percent of the population belongs to other Christian denominations, and 3.1 percent is Muslim. The unaffiliated make up 18.3% of the population.

Toilets

Shopping malls, train stations, and other similar places have pay toilets. The cost is between 20 and 40 kroner. In bars, pubs, and clubs you can generally use them for free. It should be mentioned that the Norwegian passion for design can be seen also in the country's public toilets: along many of Nasjonale Turistveger's scenic routes, specially designed toilets have been built and placed at scenic spots.

Smoking

Smoking is prohibited in most workplaces and indoor public places such as bars and restaurants. Smoking is also prohibited on all public transportation. Electronic cigarettes containing nicotine are banned in Norway but can be imported for personal or medical use. A regulation to legalize their sale is currently under consideration.

Time Zone

Central Europe, UTC+1, is the local time zone. Daylight saving time is also observed.

Tipping

Tipping is common in restaurants and bars if you leave satisfied, and ranges from 5 to 15 percent of the total bill. In other situations, it is unusual.

Traveling with Kids

Norway is a great place to travel with children. There are many activities suitable for them, especially outdoors, such as theme parks and wildlife areas, aquariums, whale watching, and elk safaris, or farms with horseback riding. There is also no shortage of interactive museums that combine entertainment and education and offer discounts for young children.

Travelers with Disabilities

Major cities have many accessible services. Airplanes, buses, trams, trains, and subway stations are widely equipped. Even fast boats and ferries have ramps to accommodate people in wheelchairs. Most accommodations have accessible rooms, but it is best to check directly with the hotels you are interested in.

Outdoor activities are more problematic, but some scenic spots have wheelchair-accessible trails. For 100 percent accessible tours and facilities, visit *disabledaccessibletravel.com*.

Pets

The Norwegian Food Safety Authority *(mattilsynet.no)* sets the rules for temporary entry of animals such as dogs and cats into the country. As a rule, the animal must be more than three months old and have an identification tag (special tattoos before July 2011 or microchips) and a pet passport approved by the European Union. All dogs must be vaccinated against rabies and treated for dwarf tapeworm 24–120 hours before entering Norway.

Tourist Information

The ministry of trade, industry, and fisheries has commissioned Innovation Norway *(visitnorway.com)* to create, develop, and maintain Norway's official travel guide. The website is full of useful information and travel tips for a true Norwegian experience.

For the capital, the **Oslo Visitor Center** *(visitoslo.com)*, at Jernbanetorget 1, offers maps, free Wi-Fi, and tickets for events, transportation, and tours. Also available is the Oslo Pass, which covers land and fjord transportation, museums, and discounts on sightseeing, activities, restaurants, and swimming pools. A similar solution is available for Bergen, the Bergen Card.

EMERGENCIES

Norway is generally a safe country with no major threats and a low crime rate. However, common sense rules for safe travel still apply: keep your money and valuables in an easy-to-check purse, do not leave your bags unattended, and avoid dimly lit streets at night. When traveling, carry photocopies of your passport or other important documents, and use credit and debit cards so you don't carry too much cash. The police are usually polite and helpful.

Some useful terms:

Emergency	*Nødsituasjon*
Help!	*Hjelp!*
Police	*Politiet*
Police officer	*Politibetjent*

Emergency Telephone Numbers

Emergency medical care and ambulance 113
Police 112
Firefighters 110

Health

Although Norway is not part of the European Union, it is a member of the European Economic Area. This means that a European citizen only needs to present his or her European Health Insurance Card (EHIC) to receive necessary medical treatment, even if it is not urgent, free of charge or with a required co-payment. In the absence of the EHIC card, a doctor's certificate can be used as a substitute.

If some facilities require payment, keep the receipts and documentation so that you can submit a claim for reimbursement upon your return. If you need urgent care, you can also use private services such as DrDropin *(drdropin.no)*, which has clinics in

Oslo, Bergen, Stavanger, Trondheim, and Bærum. The cost is 695 kroner for a personal visit and 350 kroner for a telemedicine visit. In the latter case, however, you must have a BankID.

No specific vaccinations are required for travel to Norway. For up-to-date information on the health situation in Norway, visit *helsenorge.no.*

Some useful terms:

Ambulance	*ambulanse*
Dentist	*tannlege*
Doctor	*lege*
Hospital	*sykehus*
Medicine	*medisin*
Pharmacy	*apotek*

What to Do in Case of an Accident

In the event of a breakdown or accident, drivers should carry a high-visibility vest, reflective triangle, and liability insurance. The first thing to do is to write down all the information about the driver and the vehicle, then contact the police.

Emergency telephones are available on mountain roads and in tunnels. For 24-hour roadside or technical assistance, contact NAF *(naf.no, tel 232 13 100)* or Viking *(vikingredning.no, tel 06 000)*. For information on insurance procedures, see *consap.it.*

RECOMMENDED READING

Fiction

Fame by Knut Hamsun (2002)
The Unseen by Roy Jacobsen (2022)

Travel

Amundsen's Last Voyage by Monica Kristensen (2019)
Shark Drunk by Morten A. Strøksnes (2015)

Outdoor & Nature

Doppler by Erlend Loe (2007)
Norway by Udo Bernhart, Rasso Knoller, & Christian Nowak (2020)

History & Culture

Heimskringla: The Lives of the Norse Kings by Snorri Sturluson (2021)
Norwegian Folktales by Christen Asbjørnsen & Jørgen Moe (2019)
The Sami Peoples of the North: A Social and Cultural History by Neil Kent (2018)

HOTELS & RESTAURANTS

The accommodation system in Norway is extensive and varied, offering different types of solutions, from historic hotels built the late 19th century to modern facilities, campsites, and guesthouses. The restaurants are equally varied, presenting traditional dishes juxtaposed with fresh interpretations, highlighting the quality of local products while experimenting with newer and creative ingredients.

Hotels

More than in other countries, Norwegian hotels have changed significantly over the past 20 to 30 years. With the exception of the historic hotels in the fjord region—those established in the late 19th century with early British and German tourism, which still preserve their charming wooden structures—both chains and independent hotels have changed their approach and the way they present themselves.

In general, you will find hotels with a contemporary design that are comfortable and offer excellent services. Some accommodations have revolutionized the concept of the traditional hotel, offering solutions with rooms in other buildings, independent cabins, or small rooms next to large common areas. Then there are campsites, traditional and innovative lodges, apartments, and guesthouses.

Particularly noteworthy are the accommodations in nature, which allow you to fully experience the natural wonders of the country. Although the average prices are high, you can find affordable accommodation for every budget. In addition, breakfast is often included in the price, which can offset the cost somewhat and provide an opportunity to sample some Norwegian dishes.

Restaurants

Today's restaurants, like the hotels, are the result of Norway's new way of presenting itself over the past two decades. Nordic cuisine is now world-renowned, thanks in part to international stars and Michelin-starred chefs, and in part to a rebirth that is deeply connected to the roots of the land, based on attention to the way it is grown and farmed, as well as experimentation with new ingredients. The high incomes of the residents have facilitated a shift to more organic and gourmet offerings, leading to Trøndelag's nomination as the European Region of Gastronomy 2022.

Visitors can sample both traditional and international dishes, united by a common quest for high-quality ingredients. Surrounded by the sea, Norway undoubtedly has an impressive range of seafood, complemented by excellent meat and dairy products.

Structure & Abbreviations

Hotels and restaurants are listed by chapter and place name, in alphabetical order by price. Hotels are listed before restaurants. The number of rooms listed includes rooms and suites. "Nonsmoking" indicates either nonsmoking rooms or a general ban throughout the hotel and, in restaurants, a non-smoking area or a general ban (which usually does not extend outdoors).

PRICES

HOTELS

An indication of the cost of a double room in the high season is given by **$** signs.

$$$$	Over $250
$$$	$170–$250
$$	$100–$170
$	Under $100

RESTAURANTS

An indication of the cost of a three-course meal without drinks is given by $ signs.

$$$$	Over $120
$$$	$60–$120
$$	$30–$60
$	Under $30

OSLO & AROUND

HOTELS

AMERIKALINJEN

$$$$–4 stars
JERNBANETORGET 2
TEL 214 05 900
info@amerikalinjen.com
amerikalinjen.com

An elegant building in the old town with a dazzling contemporary interior design. Spacious rooms with high ceilings, modern furniture, minibar, TV, bathroom, ironing amenities, free Wi-Fi, restaurant, and several bars. Perfect location for relaxation, accessible and with 24/7 reception.

SOMETHING SPECIAL

HOTEL CHRISTIANIA TEATER

$$$$–4 stars
STORTINGSGATA 16
TEL 210 43 800
stay@christianiateater.com
christianiateater.com

Opened in 1918 and located in the beating heart of the capital, this hotel boasts more than a century of history, excitement, and culture. As the name suggests, the building was once a theater and concert hall. They offer a complete package that includes a show, accommodation, and a hearty breakfast. The latter is always included and can be taken to go for those who have to leave the hotel before the morning service. A restaurant and wine bar are also available. Of course, free Wi-Fi, TV, and minibar are in the room.

102

SCANDIC HOLMENKOLLEN PARK

$$$
KONGEVEIEN 26
TEL 229 22 000
scandichotels.com

One of the capital's oldest hotels on Mount Holmenkollen, a famous venue for ski jumping competitions. Although extensively renovated, it has retained its iconic architecture with a redesigned interior. It offers free Wi-Fi, a spa with swimming pool, a 1,000-square-foot gym (93 sq m), and a restaurant and bar. The views of Oslo and the Marka forests alone are worth the stay.

376

RADISSON RED OSLO ØKERN

$$
LØRENFARET 3
TEL 242 00 300
radissonhotels.com

A red square building in a rapidly changing neighborhood, the hotel

offers rooms of various sizes, free Wi-Fi, and panoramic views from the rooftop bar and garden. Breakfast is included and lunch and dinner are available at the in-house restaurant.
204

RESTAURANTS

SOMETHING SPECIAL

STATHOLDERGAARDEN

$$$$
RÅDHUSGATE 11
TEL 224 18 800
post@statholdergaarden.no
statholdergaarden.no

Bent Stianten's restaurant won the Bocuse d'Or award in 1993. Central and elegant, housed in a 17th-century building, it offers gourmet cuisine, the highest quality ingredients, and excellent service. It's no surprise that this unique dining experience, enhanced by the beauty of the artwork decorating the restaurant's five rooms, has been included in the Michelin Guide.
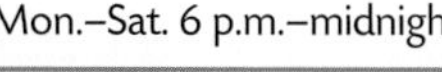
Mon.–Sat. 6 p.m.–midnight

VAAGHALS

$$$
DRONNING EUFEMIAS GATE 8
TEL 920 70 999
post@vaaghals.com
vaaghals.com

Contemporary restaurant with an old-fashioned touch: food is served on stone slabs and is meant to be shared to bring tables together and start conversations. Dishes are made with Norwegian ingredients but have an international approach and presentation.
Tues.–Fri. 11 a.m.–2:30 p.m., Mon.–Sat. 5 p.m.–11:30 p.m.

DOVREHALLEN BAR & RESTAURANT

$$
STORGATA 22
TEL 221 72 101
post@dovrehallen.no
dovrehallen.no

In a world that offers more and more new things, enhancing the old can be a good marketing strategy. Old-fashioned ambience and traditional food, even if only from the 1980s. Central and convenient.
Daily 10 a.m.–midnight, Fri. & Sat. until 2:30 a.m.

THE SOUTH

HOTELS

SOMETHING SPECIAL

DALEN HOTEL

$$$$–5 stars
HOTELLVEGEN 33, DALEN
TEL 350 79 000
post@dalenhotel.no
dalenhotel.no

Historic hotel from 1894, built in Viking style at the end of the Telemark Canal. Charming outside and beautiful inside, with all the woodwork, decorations, wallpaper, and objects from its past. Rooms and suites in the same style, so no TV or minibar, but full of historical atmosphere. There is also a restaurant (check the website for dress code), a large park, a sauna, and a vintage car showroom.
49

CLARION HOTEL ENERGY

$$$
ISHOCKEYVEIEN 2, STAVANGER
TEL 513 47 800
cl.energy@strawberry.no
strawberryhotels.com

Designed by Snøhetta, the hotel boasts cutting-edge architecture and design, with thoughtful details to make everything as comfortable as possible. The name Energy is reminiscent of the economy of the city, Norway's oil capital. There is a bar, a bistro, and a gym.
400

SCANDIC SØRLANDET
$$
TRAVPARKVEIEN 14, KRISTIANSAND
TEL 381 77 777
scandichotels.com
Located in a quiet area near the airport, with bus stops and train stations just nearby, it offers free Wi-Fi, comfortable rooms, a fitness room, and a large outdoor area with a heated pool and beach volleyball court.
210

RESTAURANTS

SOMETHING SPECIAL

RE-NAA
$$$$
NORBØGATA 8, STAVANGER
TEL 515 51 111
post@restaurantrenaa.no
restaurantrenaa.no
The dishes are innovative and elegantly presented, just as you would expect from a restaurant with two Michelin stars. The chef, Sven Erik Renaa, has an Italian father, but was born and raised in Trøndelag. The dishes are inspired by Norwegian nature, with a strong focus on sourcing ingredients that best represent the essence of the region. Book well in advance.
19 Wed.–Sat. from 5:30 p.m.

BØNDER I BYEN
$$$
RÅDHUSGATA 16, KRISTIANSAND
TEL 911 47 247
post@bonderibyen.no
bonderibyen.no
One restaurant, one concept. Well, actually two, because the restaurant has a twin in Oslo. Urban peasant cuisine, that's what the name of the restaurant literally means. An apt definition: ingredients are sourced from farmers and fishermen for dishes that are as local as possible. Don't miss the baked and marinated beets, fried cabbage, and roasted pumpkin seeds.
Mon.–Fri. 11 a.m.–10 p.m., Sat. 8 a.m.–7 p.m.

AARNES KAFETERIA
$$
STRANNAVEGEN 302, GVARV
TEL 359 55 733
post@aarneskafeteria.no
aarneskafeteria.no
Overlooking Lake Norsjø and the surrounding apple orchards, it is a casual, approachable place with a cozy atmosphere where you can enjoy traditional Norwegian dishes found nowhere else, such as meatballs in brown sauce, with peas, potatoes, and cranberries.
Mon.–Sun. 8 a.m.–8 p.m., Sat. 8 a.m.–7 p.m.

BERGEN & AROUND

HOTELS

ELVA
$$$$
NEDKVITNESVEGEN 25, SKULESTADMO-VOSS
TEL 565 10 525
post@vossactive.no
elva.no

Consisting of a main building and five smaller buildings, all named after nearby rivers, it is surrounded by vegetation that can be seen through its glass windows. Beautiful scenic rooms, a restaurant, and a peaceful atmosphere. Breakfast is always included. Charging stations for electric cars available.

SOMETHING SPECIAL

DET HANSEATISKE HOTEL

$$$–4 stars
FINNEGÅRDEN 2A, BERGEN
TEL 553 04 800
frontdesk@finnegaarden.no
en.dethanseatiskehotel.no

Located in Bryggen, in the historic center of Bergen, this property makes the historical surroundings its strong point. A memorable stay that will take you back to the days of the Hanseatic League thanks to the well-maintained furnishings. Culinary delights served in the in-house restaurants.

37

HARDANGER HOTEL

$$$
EITRHEIMSVEGEN 13, ODDA
TEL 536 46 464
post@hardangerhotel.no
hardangerhotel.no

Located in the town center, just a stone's throw from the fjord, this hotel is housed in a red timber building and has a bar and breakfast room, free Wi-Fi, and TV in all rooms. Comfortable rooms, some with views, and breakfast included. No pets allowed.

50

QUALITY HOTEL SOGNDAL

$$
GRAVENSTEINSGATA 5, SOGNDAL
TEL 576 27 700
q.sogndal@strawberry.no
qualityhotelsogndal.no

Located in the heart of Sognefjord, this modern building has a gym, a bar, and three restaurants, and is ideally situated for dozens of outdoor activities in the area. Note the facility's efforts to minimize its environmental impact through the use of solar panels, thermal insulation, and hydroelectric power from the fjord. Charging points for electric cars available. Accessibles, nonsmoking, and pet-friendly.

226

RESTAURANTS

IRIS–SALMON EYE

$$$$
HARDANGERFJORDEN, ROSENDAL
TEL 565 76 000
contact@restaurantiris.no
restaurantiris.no

A restaurant housed in the Salmon Eye Aquaculture Visitor Center, casually floating on the fjord. Enjoy a rich, high-quality tasting menu preceded by a multisensory underwater experience.

Wed.–Sat. 12:30 p.m.–9 p.m.

SJØ RESTAURANT, C/O HOTEL KLØVERHUSET

$$$
STRANDEGATEN 13, BERGEN
TEL 929 41 371
booking@sjorestaurant.no
sjorestaurant.no

Design reigns in this restaurant, from the ambiance to the service and the food. Impeccable and elegant courses with mixed techniques and preparation.

Mon.–Sat. noon–4 p.m. & 5 p.m.–10 p.m., Sun. noon–2 p.m.

PRICES

HOTELS
An indication of the cost of a double room in the high season is given by **$** signs.

$$$$	Over $250
$$$	$170–$250
$$	$100–$170
$	Under $100

RESTAURANTS
An indication of the cost of a three-course meal without drinks is given by $ signs.

$$$$	Over $120
$$$	$60–$120
$$	$30–$60
$	Under $30

ÆGIR BREW PUB

$$
A-FELTVEGEN 19, FLÅM
TEL 576 32 050
mail@flamsbrygga.no
flamsbrygga.com

A sort of troll house or *stavkirke* by the fjord, this microbrewery has good, vaguely Viking cuisine and award-winning beer, which also becomes the star of the dishes served. A casual place with charming architecture.

Daily 5 p.m.–9:30 p.m.

▶ THE CENTER-NORTH

HOTELS

SOMETHING SPECIAL

POLAR PANORAMA LODGE

$$$$
GARDTOFTVEIEN 1, FJORDGÅRD, SENJA
TEL 934 93 786
contact@polarpanoramalodge.com
polarpanoramalodge.com

On one of Norway's most spectacular islands, this is a modern, minimalist cottage with large windows offering just the perfect views of the northern lights, when they are present. Kitchen, gym, and social spaces available. Garden and parking on property.

RADISSON BLU ROYAL GARDEN HOTEL

$$$
KJØPMANNSGATA 73, TRONDHEIM
TEL 738 03 000
info.trondheim@radissonblu.com
radissonhotels.com

Right in the city center, on the river, within walking distance of the Nidarosdomen, this is a nice hotel recommended for both location and comfort. Spacious rooms, rooftop restaurant, gym, free Wi-Fi, and parking. Affordable hotel with breakfast included.

298

SMART HOTEL

$
SJØGATA 30, BODØ
TEL 415 36 500
bodo.smarthotel.no

A hotel chain that offers a different concept of accommodation in six different cities. It has a central location at more than reasonable prices, in a modern facility also equipped with a shop open 24/7. Different room sizes, large common area with co-working stations, breakfast buffet, and TV with Chromecast. Cashless hotel.

161

RESTAURANTS

TO ROM OG KJØKKEN
$$$
CARL JOHANS GATE 5, TRONDHEIM
TEL 735 68 900
toromogkjokken.no
Trøndelag ingredients inspired by Mediterranean cuisine. À la carte or 3–5–7 course menu. Beautiful setting and very thoughtful dishes, full of style and color.
Mon.–Sat. 4 p.m.–midnight

APOTEKERGATA NO5
$$
APOTEKERGATA 5, ÅLESUND
TEL 701 14 500
hei@apotekergata5.no
apotekergata5.no
Hotel Brosundet's restaurant in the heart of the Jugendstil city. Mainly seafood cuisine in a classic early 20th-century setting.
Mon.–Sat. 5 p.m.–10 p.m.

HELGELAND KOLONIAL
$$
TOROLV KVELDULVSONS GATE 41, SANDNESSJØEN
TEL 923 10 227
helgelandkolonial.no
Modern, stylish restaurant offering healthy and unique dishes, the result of experimenting with different flavors and textures. Young and friendly staff.
Mon.–Wed. 11 a.m.–5 p.m., Thurs.–Sat. 11 a.m.–11 p.m.

ARCTIC LANDS

HOTELS

CLARION HOTEL THE EDGE
$$$–4 stars
KAIGATA 6, TROMSØ
TEL 776 68 400
cl.theedge@strawberry.no
strawberryhotels.com
A new building with architecture and lighting that won't go unnoticed. The hotel serves as a venue for concerts and events, offering scenic and comfortable rooms, free Wi-Fi, a sky bar, and a 24/7 fitness center. Cashless hotel.
290

CANYON HOTELL
$$
MARKEDSGATA 6, ALTA
TEL 781 02 000
reception@canyonhotell.no
canyonhotell.no
A modern hotel with comfortable rooms. It has a fully equipped children's area, making it ideal for families. It has bars and restaurants, as well as a yoga studio and sauna. Continental breakfast included. Self check-in available.

SOMETHING SPECIAL

SVINØYA RORBUER
$$
GUNNAR BERGS VEI 2, SVOLVÆR
TEL 760 69 930
post@svinoya.no
svinoya.no
Staying in a *rorbu*, the wooden huts of the Lofoten fishermen, is an experience not to be missed. Overlooking the sea, they sleep 2 to 6 people, have a bathroom and kitchen, and a magnificent view of the island peaks. Suites and rooms in the 1828 manor house are also available. The facility offers activities and excursions on the island. There is also a restaurant and sauna.
38 cabins + manor house + suites

RESTAURANTS

RESTAURANT SMAK

$$$$
SKIPPERGATA 16B, TROMSØ
TEL 941 76 110
booking@restaurant-smak.no
restaurant-smak.no

A great opportunity to taste fresh ingredients from the fjords, mountains, and forests of northern Norway, all sourced from selected local producers. Contemporary cuisine full of color and invention.
Wed.–Fri. from 6 p.m., Sat. 1 p.m. for lunch and 7 p.m. for dinner

MAREN ANNA

$$$
GAMLE SØRVÅGEN 12, SØRVÅGEN
TEL 906 57 532
booking@marenanna.com
marenanna.com

A beautiful seaside restaurant housed in a 1914 red wooden building that was once a factory. Contemporary menu based mainly on fish and seafood, with various creative interpretations. Possible overnight stay at the Sørvågen Inn.
Wed.–Sun. 6 p.m.–9 p.m.

SOMETHING SPECIAL

RESTAURANT SAMI SIIDA

$$
ØYTUNVEIEN 4, ALTA
TEL 468 38 645
post@samisiida.no
samisiida.no

You will be greeted by Sami in traditional costume and then taken to a tent to listen to their stories. One of the few places where you can taste Sami food, especially salmon, reindeer meat, and haddock fish cake. Chance to meet the reindeer.
Tues.–Sun. 3 p.m.–9 p.m.

SVALBARD ISLANDS

HOTELS

FUNKEN LODGE

$$$$–4 stars
VEI 212-4, LONGYEARBYEN
TEL 790 26 200
info@funkenlodge.com
funkenlodge.com

Contemporary rooms and suites in a renovated historic building. A cabin is also available in the winter season to enjoy the northern lights. Facilities include restaurant, wine cellar, accessible rooms, gym, sauna, parking, and airport shuttle.
88

SVALBARD HOTELL–THE VAULT

$$$
VEI 507.01, LONGYEARBYEN
TEL 790 25 000
svalbardadventures.com

A simple yet elegant building, centrally located and inspired by the Svalbard Global Seed Vault. The rooms are very contemporary in style with sophisticated furnishings. There is a restaurant serving mainly Japanese cuisine, and breakfast is always included. Pets are not allowed.
35

COAL MINERS CABINS

$$
VEI 100, LONGYEARBYEN
TEL 940 05 833
coalminerscabins@hurtigruten svalbard.com
coalminerscabins.com

In the small satellite settlement of Nybyen, this hotel consists of a large building that once housed miners. Staying here is a way to

understand the history of the archipelago. Simple but comfortable rooms and large common areas. Please note: some rooms have shared bathrooms. Free Wi-Fi and in-house restaurant.
76

RESTAURANTS

HUSET RESTAURANT

$$$$
SJ, VEI 300, LONGYEARBYEN
TEL 480 44 545
booking@huset.com
huset.com

Contemporary cuisine with elegant and minimalist Arctic ingredients, served in an extraordinary wine cellar with thousands of bottles on display. Dishes feature game, seal, reindeer, and partridge. Also has a bistro open for lunch on Saturdays.
Tues.–Sun. 6 p.m.–10 p.m.

RESTAURANT KROA

$$
HILMAR REKSTENS VEI, LONGYEARBYEN
TEL 790 21 300
post@kroa-svalbard.no
kroa-svalbard.no

This historic building houses an old-fashioned, no-nonsense restaurant. It is an informal place, reminiscent of Svalbard's past. Meat and fish dishes are always based on seasonal ingredients.
Daily 11:30 a.m.–2 a.m.

RIJPSBURG & ICEBREAKER BAR KRASIN

$
BARENTSBURG
TEL 941 54 156
booking@goarctica.com
goarctica.com

If you visit the Russian settlement of Barentsburg, you must stop by this restaurant that serves fresh Arctic seafood in Russian, Norwegian, and English styles. It is named after the Dutch captain Jan Cornelisz Rijp, who participated in the Barents expedition. Atmospheric and unique. The bar offers 25 kinds of aquavit.
Tues.–Sun. 8 a.m.–11 p.m.

ENTERTAINMENT

Norway's terrain lends itself to all kinds of outdoor activities, especially hiking and kayaking. But there is no shortage of music festivals and indoor venues to help you unwind after a long day.

Events & Festivals

There are many important festivals and events in Norway, starting with Holmenkollen, which combines popular celebration with skiing. As everywhere, most events take place in the summer, when the midnight sun lights up the sky late into the day.

Holmenkollen Skifestival

holmenkollenskifestival.no

A series of events that have become traditional and are held every year in March on the hill near the capital. Ski jumping and cross-country skiing competitions in an atmosphere of great public celebration, with patriotic shows.

Constitution Day

May 17 is a national holiday in Norway, commemorating the signing of the constitution in 1814. Unlike in the past, when it was a military parade, today's celebration in Oslo involves children parading and waving flags along Karl Johans gate to the Royal Palace.

Oslo Jazz Festival

oslojazz.com

Jazz musicians from all over the world gather here for concerts in August. You can hear and meet the bands all over the city, in squares, parks, and cafés.

Ibsen Festival

nationaltheatret.no

Since 1990, the National Theater in Oslo and other theaters have been staging revivals of Henrik Ibsen's masterpieces, which have left their mark on Norwegian drama.

Norsk Litteraturfestival

litteraturfestival.no

Also known as the Norwegian Literary Festival, this week-long literary event featuring book presentations and cultural discussions attracts more than 30,000 visitors to Lillehammer every year between May and June. There are also activities for children of all ages.

Birkebeinerrennet

birkebeiner.no

A 33-mile (54 km) cross-country skiing marathon that takes place in March between Rena and Lillehammer, retracing the footsteps of the two Birkebeiners who carried the heir to the throne, Haakon Haakonsson, to safety in the 13th century.

Festspillene i Bergen (Bergen International Festival)

fib.no

Active since 1953, this two-week celebration of music, opera, theater, and dance features artists from around the world. The diverse program takes place indoors and outdoors from late May to mid-June.

Bergen Matfestival

matfest.no

A two-day celebration of local food in all its forms, from mountain to fjord. You can also meet many local producers at booths throughout the town center.

Strikkefestivalen

strikkefestivalen.no

An event dedicated to the world of yarn, wool, and processing techniques.

This could be a great opportunity to give yourself a warm gift.

Bergen Internasjonale Musikkfestival

bergeninternasjonalekultursenter.no

In November, Bergen becomes a meeting place for musicians from all over the world. It is a great way to get to know cultures that are different from your own and to expand your musical knowledge.

Tromsø International Film Festival

tiff.no

An important platform for Norwegian and international cinema. Held in January, it hosts seminars and events for film industry professionals.

Midnight Sun Marathon

msm.no

A unique marathon, as it takes place under the mesmerizing midnight sun that colors Tromsø in June. The start is scheduled for the afternoon in order to fully appreciate the evening finish, still bathed in light.

Trøndelag Food Festival & Trondheim Brewery Festival

oimat.no/en

In August, Trondheim becomes a must-visit culinary destination. You can sample delicacies from Trøndelag, which was named European Gastronomy Region in 2022, accompanied by frosty craft beers.

Arctic Race of Norway

arctic-race-of-norway.com

Every August, Finnmark hosts a cycling race that attracts professionals from all over the world. It is the largest cycling event on the Scandinavian Peninsula and aims to bring together athletes and fans from every continent.

Activities

Because of its landscapes, Norway is unmistakably a country of outdoor activities. The sea, fjords, mountains, islands, lakes, and inland valleys invite you to exploration and discovery. Even if you are not particularly interested in sports, you should at least try a boat trip, a hike, or a trip to the beach. And to relax, simply retreat to a nice spa and recharge your batteries.

Spas

As in other Nordic countries where the weather is predominantly cold, it is common in Norway to relax in large hot water pools or in the steam of a sauna. Many spas are set in natural surroundings, so you can enjoy the landscape with its magnificent views of fjords and forests while relaxing in the warmth.

The Well

Kongeveien 65, Sofiemyr
Tel 480 44 888
post@thewell.no
thewell.no

Considered the largest spa in all of Scandinavia, this spa boasts as many as eleven different pools and a sauna inspired by the northern lights. Rejuvenating treatments and massages are also available.

Bademaschinen

Langkaia 1, Oslo
post@oslobadstuforening.no
oslobadstuforening.no

Looking for can't-miss experiences in the capital city? Enjoy a sauna while admiring the Operahuset! The idea for this unusual combination comes from Bademaschinen, which offers a series of floating saunas right in front of the fascinating structure of the Oslo Opera House.

Farris Bad

Fritzoe Brygge 2, Larvik
Tel 331 96 000

farrisbad@farrisbad.no
farrisbad.no
Hotel with a spa center of more than 26,900 square feet (2,500 sq m). The spa is located at the source of the famous Farris spring, which has been known for its beneficial properties since the late 19th century.

Pust
Skippergata 1C, Tromsø
hello@pust.io
pust.io
Combining the wellness of sauna heat with an ice bath is a true panacea for body and mind. That's the proposition at Pust, a designer spa where you can experience the thrill of an increasingly popular activity among Norwegians: ice swimming.

Outdoor Activities

Hiking & Glaciers

From national park trails to beaches and islands, there are almost too many possibilities and options to list here. Two of the most spectacular hikes are the one to Trolltunga on Hardangerfjord and the one to Preikestolen in Lysefjord. To get to Flørlitrappene on the latter fjord, you have to climb 4,444 steps up the country's longest wooden staircase.

Also worth a try is Pilegrimsleden *(pilegrimsleden.no)*, which follows in the footsteps of pilgrims, especially along the routes dedicated to St. Olav, King of Norway in the 11th century.

For the more adventurous, a hike on one of Norway's many glaciers is highly recommended. Particularly worth seeing are the Jostedalsbreen and the Nigardsbreen branch, Folgefonna, Svartisen, and the glaciers of the Svalbard Islands.

Group excursions with guides are available through specialized tour operators such as Fyst og Fremst *(fyrstogfremst.no)*, Folgefonni Breførarlag *(folgefonni.no)*, and Svalbard Wildlife Expeditions *(wildlife.no)*.

Bike

From road cycling to mountain biking, there are so many ways to explore Norway's nature on two wheels. Fat bikes, with their wide wheels, are particularly suitable for winter excursions as they allow you to ride on the fantastic snow and ice trails.

Roads and trails are always in good condition, and there are bike rentals almost everywhere, so even if you don't want to go with a tour operator, you can rent a bike and set off on one of the many routes available, such as the Tour de Dovre, which passes through three national parks, or the Atlantic Road.

Contrast Adventure
Auragata 3, Sunndalsøra
Tel 952 31 240
post@contrastadventure.no
contrastadventure.no
Guided tours along the Aursjøveien or on the more challenging 150-mile (240 km) stretch connecting Oppdal to Åndalsnes.

Tromsø Outdoor
Fredrik Langes gate 14, Tromsø
Tel 975 75 875
post@tromsooutdoor.no
tromsooutdoor.no
This company offers snow and forest tours around the city of Tromsø to fully understand what it is like to live in the Arctic Circle. As temperatures rise in summer, e-bike city tours are also available.

Glød Explorer AS
Jordfallet 3, Alta
Tel 997 94 256
post@glodexplorer.no
glodexplorer.no

Mountain bike and fat bike tours near Alta and in Finnmarksvidda for an up-close look at the surreal landscape.

Hurtigruten Svalbard
hurtigrutensvalbard.com
Experienced guides will take you to explore the Svalbard Islands on an electric bike. A total of 27 miles (44 km) during which you can see Norway's northernmost point and its Arctic landscape.

Kayak & Rafting

When we stand in front of a fjord, we naturally want to venture out onto its waters. And what could be better than kayaking? The same goes for rivers, canyons, and lakes that offer rafting for an exhilarating experience.

Fjord Tours
Nordre Nøstekaien 1, Bergen
Tel 555 57 660
booking@fjordtours.com
fjordtours.com
Major tour operator in central Norway. Offers guided kayaking tours in Ålesund, Geirangerfjord, Nærøyfjord, and even the Lofoten Islands.

Nordic Ventures
Nærøydalen 9, Gudvangen
Tel 565 10 017
info@nordicventures.com
nordicventures.com
Kayak on Lønavatnet and Vangsvatnet lakes to get familiar with the water, then try the multiday trips in the surrounding fjords. Lakeside barbecue included in the experience.

Njord
Tel 913 26 628
post@kajakk.com
seakayaknorway.com
Three-hour kayak tours on Aurlandsfjord or three-day tours along Nærøyfjord from Flåm to Gudvangen with overnight stay in a tent.

Go Rafting Sjoa
Heidalsvegen 829, Nedre Heidal
Tel 612 35 000
post@raftingsjoa.no
raftingsjoa.no
This tour operator offers guided excursions on the Sjoa River, where calm stretches alternate with narrow gorges and cascading rapids. Full day and half day trips are available, also family-friendly packages.

Opplev Oppdal
Tel 724 04 180
post@opplevoppdal.no
opplevoppdal.no
For over 30 years they have been offering rafting and kayaking guided trips on the Driva River. Different options for both beginners and experts. Also suitable for children.

Nordland Turselskap
Tel 906 36 086
post@nordlandturselskap.no
nordlandturselskap.no
Canoe trips around Bodø to experience the wild nature of Nordland. The type of route varies according to weather conditions to ensure the best possible view of the scenery.

Via Ferratas

There are many guided routes available for mountain sports enthusiasts, allowing them to reach spectacular places with a bit of adrenaline.

Åkrafjorden Nature
Fjæravegen 138, Fjæra
Tel 908 44 918
mail@a-nature.no
akrafjordenbnb.no
The Kyrkjeveggen via ferrata, in Åkrafjorden, is perhaps the most challenging in all of Norway. It is about 2,950 feet (900 m) in length, starting at 164 feet (50 m) above sea level and finishing at 1,804 feet (550 m).

Trolltunga Active
Vasstun 1, Odda
Tel 400 04 486
mail@trolltunga-active.com
trolltunga-active.com
Guided via ferrata at Trolltunga. Lasts about 10 hours and requires good training. The view from the wall is well worth it.

Loen Active Skylift
Fjordvegen 1011, Loen
Tel 578 75 900
post@loenskylift.no
loenskylift.com
A magnificent view from the top of Innvikfjorden awaits the brave travelers who dare to walk Europe's longest via ferrata suspension bridge: Gjølmunne. Adrenaline rush guaranteed. The return trip is by skylift.

Explore Ålesund
explorealesund.no
A via ferrata of about 650 feet (200 m), from which you can enjoy a panoramic view of the entire city of Ålesund.

Ravnfloget
Sundsvoll, Vega
Tel 468 32 540
post@ravnfloget.no
ravnfloget.no
Viewing the Vegaøyan Archipelago, a UNESCO World Heritage site, from above is certainly not for everyone. The Ravnfloget via ferrata offers this unique opportunity.

Zip Lines

Gliding along a cable stretched over the landscape offers unparalleled views. And given Norway's natural landscape, zip-lining is undoubtedly an experience worth trying.

Check out the one in Flåm *(flaamzipline.com)*, which soars at 4,530 feet (1,381 m) and is the longest in northern Europe: it can reach max speeds of 62 miles an hour (100 km/h). Also worthwhile is the one in Loen, which starts at an altitude of 3,280 feet (1,000 m, *loenskylift.no*). Others include the Kollensvevet zip line in Holmenkollen *(kollensvevet.no)* and the one in Geiranger Nature Park *(exploregeiranger.no)*.

Skiing

Having snow for most of the year, Norway is a true skier's paradise. From classic downhill skiing to alpine and cross-country skiing, there is something for everyone.

Skistar Hemsedal
Skiheisvegen 110, Hemsedal
Tel 310 31 064
booking@skistar.com
hemsedal.com
The second largest ski resort in the country, full of slopes that start on three different peaks. One of them offers 3.7 miles (6 km) of continuous slopes.

Kvitfjell Alpinanlegg
Tel 612 83 600
info@kvitfjell.no
kvitfjell.no
Only 40 minutes from Lillehammer, it offers all kinds of slopes for skiing and snowboarding of all levels. Suitable for families.

Fonna Glacier Ski Resort
Tel 941 00 000
post@visitfonna.no
visitfonna.no
Situated on a glacier, the resort offers skiing in midsummer and beautiful views of Hardangerfjord.

Ute Guiden
Storgata 10, Stranda
Tel 405 54 670
travel@uteguiden.com
uteguiden.com

This tour operator offers varoius guided multiday tours of the Sunnmøre Alps, surrounded by beautiful peaks exceeding 4,900 feet (1,500 m). A must experience for alpine skiers.

Dog Sledding

If you want to live a truly Nordic experience, then ride through pristine forest trails on a sled pulled by a loyal team of huskies! Finnmark, Hardangervidda, and the Svalbard Islands are the best places for this activity. Tour operators in the area include Geilo Husky *(geilo-husky.com)*, Lyngen North *(lyngen-north.com)*, Active Tromsø *(activetromso.no)*, Snowhotel Kirkenes *(snowhotelkirkenes.com)*, and Svalbard Husky *(svalbardhusky.no)*.

LANGUAGE GUIDE

Vowels

The Norwegian alphabet contains nine vowels with unique pronunciations.

a similar to the *a* in "car"
e pronounced like the *e* in "get"
i pronounced like the *i* in "ski"
o pronounced with an *oo* sound as in "school"
u pronounced like the *u* in "flu"
y pronounced like the *y* in "syrup"
ø sounds like the *u* in the word "burn"
æ pronounced like the *a* in the word "sad"
å sounds like the *o* in "born"

Unique consonants

Sj, kj, ski, skj similar to the *sh* and *sj* sound; in the middle of a word it is pronounced *si* (as in *nasjonal*)

Names

They are often compound and have strings of consonants seemingly impossible to pronounce. Just separate the words and it will be easier to understand their structure.

Greetings

Goodbye *Til vi møtes igjen*
Good evening *God kveld*
Good morning *God morgen*
Hi *Hi*
Thanks *Takk*
Yes *Ja* / **No** *Nei*

Accommodation

Hotel *Hotell*
Apartment *Leilighet*
Room *Rom*

Travel

Bus *Buss*
Car *Bil*
Ferry *Ferje*
Gas station *Bensinstasjon*

Restaurants

Do you have a table for two?
Du har et bord for to?
Can I have a menu in English?
Kan jeg få en meny på engelsk?
Can I order?
Kan jeg bestille?
Can I get the bill?
Kan jeg få regningen?

READING A MENU

General

Bill *regningen*
Celiac *cøliaki*
Food *mat*
Food intolerance *matintoleranse*
Gluten-free *glutenfri*
Vegetarian *vegetarianer*
Vegan *vegansk*

On the Table

Bottle *flaske*
Fork *gaffel*
Glass *glass*
Knife *kniv*
Spoon *skje*

Dishes

Beans *bønner*
Bread *brød*
Cheese *ost*
Chicken *kylling*
Fish *fisk*
Meat *kjøtt*
Peas *erter*
Potatoes *poteter*
Soup *suppe*

Fruit & Desserts

Ice cream *iskrem*
Raspberries *bringebær*
Strawberries *jordbær*

INDEX

Bold page numbers indicate illustrations.

A

B

C

D

E

F

G

H

CREDITS

2–3, BublikHaus/Shutterstock; 4, Eva Hawker/Shutterstock; 9, Sergii Beck/Shutterstock; 11, robertharding/Shutterstock;12, Marius Dobilas/Shutterstock; 14, PatrickL/Shutterstock; 15, GaudiLab/Shutterstock; 16, V. Belov/Shutterstock; 17, Nanisimova/Shutterstock; 18, Nickolay Stanev/Shutterstock; 20, Bragin Alexey/Shutterstock; 21, LGieger/Shutterstock; 22, M. Pakats/Shutterstock; 23, Asmus Koefoed/Shutterstock; 24, Renata Sedmakova/Shutterstock; 25, saiko3p/Shutterstock; 27, Maylat/Shutterstock; 28, zabanski/Shutterstock; 29, BreizhAtao/Shutterstock; 30, Nightman1965/Shutterstock; 31, Arjen de Ruiter/Shutterstock; 33, Wikimedia Commons; 34, Maylat/Shutterstock; 36, El Greco 1973/Shutterstock; 38a, Pycril; 38b, Pycril; 41, Store Norske Leksikon; 43, Adellyne/Shutterstock; 44, Wikimedia Commons; 45, photovideoworld/Shutterstock; 46, Iurii Kazakov/Shutterstock; 47, Wikimedia Commons; 48, Rolf_52/Shutterstock; 49, Prachaya Roekdeethaweesab/Shutterstock; 50, Espen E/Shutterstock; 51a, kovop/Shutterstock; 51b, B. Lenoir/Shutterstock; 52–53, dibrova/Shutterstock; 54, Jane Rix/Shutterstock; 56, Stuedal/Shutterstock; 57, Stefano Zaccaria/Shutterstock; 58, Sergii Figurnyi/Shutterstock; 60, Brent Hofacker/Shutterstock; 61, Svetlana Verbitckaia/Shutterstock; 62, AS Food studio/Shutterstock; 63a, Fanfo/Shutterstock; 63b, norwegianwoods/Shutterstock; 64, Tamara Lopes/Shutterstock; 65, Kartouchken/Shutterstock; 66, William Perugini/Shutterstock; 71, saiko3p/Shutterstock; 73, EQRoy/Shutterstock; 74, Murphy1975/Shutterstock; 75, Santi Rodriguez/Shutterstock; 76, TTstudio/Shutterstock; 79, Popova Valeriya/Shutterstock; 80, JWCohen/Shutterstock; 81, Nowaczyk/Shutterstock; 82–83, Dennis Wegewijs/Shutterstock; 85, xbrchx/Shutterstock; 86–87, Morten Normann Almeland/Shutterstock; 88, Nenad Nedomacki/Shutterstock; 89, designium/Shutterstock; 91, Popova Valeriya/Shutterstock; 92, saiko3p/Shutterstock; 93, designium/Shutterstock; 98, Solodovnikova Elena/Shutterstock; 100, Tupungato/Shutterstock; 102, AR Pictures/Shutterstock; 104, Barnabas Davoti/Shutterstock; 105, fotografcic/Shutterstock; 107, Marina J/Shutterstock; 108, Wikimedia Commons; 109, Dmitry Naumov/Shutterstock; 110, Claudia Carlsen/Shutterstock; 111, Sergey Kamshylin/Shutterstock; 114, Dmitry Naumov/Shutterstock; 115, Vidar Lennart Fredheim/Shutterstock; 116, Anders Sterner/Shutterstock; 118, Trygve Finkelsen/Shutterstock; 119, BPfoto/Shutterstock; 120, Ian Peter Morton/Shutterstock; 122–123, Apostolis Giontzis/Shutterstock; 124, Rolf E. Staerk/Shutterstock; 126, Ina Meer Sommer/Shutterstock; 127, Inger Eriksen/Shutterstock; 129, Dmitry Naumov/Shutterstock; 130, Marisa Estivill/Shutterstock; 132, Nanisimova/Shutterstock; 133, by-studio/Shutterstock; 136, LGieger/Shutterstock; 137, Dmitry Naumov/Shutterstock; 139, Alex Erofeenkov/Shutterstock; 140, Andrew Mayovskyy/Shutterstock; 144, JWCohen/Shutterstock; 146, Lisa Strachan/Shutterstock; 148, Nancy Pauwels/Shutterstock; 149, mspoli/Shutterstock; 150, Dignity 100/Shutterstock; 152, Evikka/Shutterstock; 154, Maylat/Shutterstock; 155, Marius Dobilas/Shutterstock; 156, Nanisimova/Shutterstock; 158–159, Marius Dobilas/Shutterstock; 161, Kris Wiktor/Shutterstock; 163, Olga Miltsova/Shutterstock; 165, Wirestock Creators/Shutterstock; 167, Gertjan Hooijer/Shutterstock; 169, Grebner Fotografie/Shutterstock; 173, iwciagr/Shutterstock; 174, Arne JW Kolstoe/Shutterstock; 176, Peter Krejzl/Shutterstock; 178, Flash-ka/Shutterstock; 180, Francesco Bonino/Shutterstock; 182, Anetlanda/Shutterstock; 184, Mikolaj Niemczewski/Shutterstock; 187, Thorsten Schier/Shutterstock; 188, defotoberg/Shutterstock; 189, Dmitry Naumov/Shutterstock; 191, A. Aleksandravicius/Shutterstock; 193, Marisa Estivill/Shutterstock; 194–195, Victor Maschek/Shutterstock; 196, Nabil Amin/Shutterstock; 198, Ingrid Pakats/Shutterstock; 200, saiko3p/Shutterstock; 201, saiko3p/Shutterstock; 203, Joakim Sandberg/Shutterstock; 204, Jelena Safronova/Shutterstock; 207, Lasse Johansson/Shutterstock; 208, by-studio/Shutterstock; 209, Nick Fox/Shutterstock; 210, HowDee1978/Shutterstock; 212–213, Sasha Alterant/Shutterstock; 214, Ingrid Maasik/Shutterstock; 215, Sergey Bogomyako/Shutterstock; 216, Grebner Fotografie/Shutterstock; 218, Piotr Poznan/Shutterstock; 222, Strahil Dimitrov/Shutterstock; 223, Stefano Zaccaria/Shutterstock; 224, Dmitry Pistrov/Shutterstock; 225, Kersti Lindstrom/Shutterstock; 227, kajanosterud/Shutterstock; 229, Rat007/Shutterstock; 230, Photofex_AUT/Shutterstock; 232–233, Maylat/Shutterstock; 235, LouieLea/Shutterstock; 236, Steven Olsen Lopez/Shutterstock; 237, Alizada Studios/Shutterstock; 238, Harvepino/Shutterstock; 240, Rat007/Shutterstock; 241, orxy/Shutterstock; 242, HowDee1978/Shutterstock; 243, Francesco Bonino/Shutterstock; 244, evoPix.evolo/Shutterstock; 246, Chris_Hall/Shutterstock; 248, Nick Fox/Shutterstock; 249, HellyMelly/Shutterstock; 250, vtek/Shutterstock; 251, Joyce Nelson/Shutterstock; 253, Diego Fiore/Shutterstock; 254, Dynamoland/Shutterstock; 255, Alan Kean/Shutterstock; 256–257, LouieLea/Shutterstock; 258, Evgenii Mitroshin/Shutterstock; 259, V. Belov/Shutterstock; 261, Inger Eriksen/Shutterstock; 262, Pecold/Shutterstock; 263, Drima Film/Shutterstock; 267, The Arctic/Shutterstock; 269, Shandarov Arkadii/Shutterstock; 270–271, Rageziv/Shutterstock; 272, Wikimedia Commons; 273, Pecold/Shutterstock; 274, AndreAnita/Shutterstock; 275, Janus Orlov/Shutterstock; 276, rikujokinen.com/Shutterstock; 278, Yauhen_D/Shutterstock; 279, Anibal Trejo/Shutterstock; 280, Irina Kzan/Shutterstock; 281, INTREEGUE Photography/Shutterstock; 284, O.C Ritz/Shutterstock; 286, LouieLea/Shutterstock; 290, Anton_Ivanov/Shutterstock; 291, Katharine Moore/Shutterstock; 293, Per-Erik Skramstad/Shutterstock; 294, Anton_Ivanov/Shutterstock; 295, hopsalka/Shutterstock; 296–297, xamnesiacx84/Shutterstock; 298, Alexey Seafarer/Shutterstock; 299, ginger_polina_bublik/Shutterstock; 300, COULANGES/Shutterstock; 301, knelson20/Shutterstock; 302, Oskar135.

National Geographic

TRAVELER

Norway

FIRST EDITION

Since 1888, the National Geographic Society has funded more than 14,000 research, conservation, education, and storytelling projects around the world. National Geographic Partners distributes a portion of the funds it receives from your purchase to National Geographic Society to support programs including the conservation of animals and their habitats.

National Geographic Partners, LLC
1145 17th Street NW
Washington, DC 20036-4688 USA

Get closer to National Geographic Explorers and photographers, and connect with our global community. Join us today at nationalgeographic.org/joinus

Piazzale Luigi Cadorna, 6
20123 Milan, Italy
www.whitestar.it

Licensee of National Geographic Partners, LLC.

First edition: Iceigeo, Milano; - coordination: Carlo Batà; collaborators: Giulia Fiandaca, Sara Volpato, Ilaria Ghisletti; translation: Alexa Ahern; Maps: Bianco Tangerine Srl

ISBN: 978-8-8544-2063-2

Printed in China
24/JPM/1